ARMED FORCES FINANCIAL GUIDE

VIRGINIA B. MORRIS

LIGHTBULB  PRESS

D1203153

COMMON ACRONYMS

AGI	Adjusted Gross Income	HDP	Hardship Duty Pay
APR	Annual Percentage Rate	HDHP	High Deductible Health Plan
APY	Annual Percentage Yield	HDIP	Hazardous Duty Incentive Pay
BAH	Basic Allowance for Housing	HFP	Hostile Fire Pay
BAQ	Basic Allowance for Quarters	HMO	Health Maintenance Organization
BAS	Basic Allowance for Subsistence	IDP	Imminent Danger Pay
BCAC	Beneficiary Counseling and Assistance Coordinator	IHL	Institute of Higher Learning
BRS	Blended Retirement System	IRA	Individual Retirement Account
CAC	Common Access Card	ITP	Individual Transition Plan
CD	Certificate of Deposit	JKO	Joint Knowledge Online
CDC	Child Development Center	JTR	Joint Travel Regulation
CFPB	Consumer Financial Protection Bureau	JTWROS	Joint Tenants with Right of Survivorship
CHCBP	Continued Health Care Benefit Program	LES	Leave and Earnings Statement
COE	Certificate of Eligibility	MOC	Military Occupational Code
COLA	Cost of Living Adjustment	MyCAA	Military Spouse Career Advancement Account
CONUS	Continental United States	NAV	Net Asset Value
CPI	Consumer Price Index	NSF	Non-Sufficient Funds
CRDP	Concurrent Retirement and Disability Pay	OHA	Overseas Housing Allowance
CRSC	Combat Related Special Compensation	PCM	Primary Care Manager
		PCS	Permanent Change of Station
CZTE	Combat Zone Tax Exclusion	PITI	Principal, Interest, Taxes, Insurance
DEA	Survivors' and Dependents' Educational Assistance Program	PPM	Personally Procured Move
		PPO	Participating Provider Organization
		POA	Power of Attorney
DEERS	Defense Enrollment Eligibility Reporting System	POS	Point-of-Service plan
		QLE	Qualifying Life Event
DFAS	Defense Financial Accounting Service	QHEE	Qualified Higher Education Expense
		RBCO	Retirement Benefits Court Order
DIC	Dependency and Indemnity Compensation	RMD	Required Minimum Distribution
		SCRA	Servicemembers Civil Relief Act
DIEMS	Date Initially Entered Military Service	SDP	Savings Deposit Program
		SECO	Spouse Education and Career Opportunities
DSP	Disability Severance Pay		
DTI	Debt-to-Income	SGLI	Servicemembers Group Life Insurance
EFMP	Exceptional Family Member Program	SHPE	Separation History and Physical Examination
ESA	Education Savings Account	TA	Tuition Assistance
ETF	Exchange Traded Fund	TAMP	Transitional Assistance Management Program
FCC	Family Child Care		
FDIC	Federal Deposit Insurance Corporation	TAP	Transition Assistance Program
		TOE	Transfer of Entitlement
FEDVIP	Federal Employees Dental and Vision Program	TSP	Thrift Savings Plan
FICA	Federal Insurance Contribution Act (Social Security and Medicare)	USERRA	Uniformed Services Employment and Reemployment Rights Act
FRA	Full Retirement Age	USFHP	US Family Health Plan
FSA	Family Separation Allowance	USFSPA	Uniformed Services Former Spouse Protection Act
FSC	Family Support Center		
FSGLI	Family Servicemembers' Group Life Insurance	VGLI	Veterans Group Life Insurance
		VMET	Verification of Military Experience and Training

*T*he strength of our nation is found in the strength of our soldiers, sailors, marines, and airmen. The strength of these servicemembers is found in the stability of their personal affairs and in the well-being of their households. Our servicemembers must develop physical and mental resilience to succeed in an array of complex and dangerous missions. To sustain the focus required by these missions, it is critical that servicemembers are comfortable with their personal affairs and confident in their families' well-being. Financial security is at the heart of this peace of mind and reinforces our number one priority—Readiness!

The authors and contributors to the *Armed Forces Financial Guide* are experts in personal finance, but they are also seasoned military leaders who are intimately familiar with rigorous training cycles, repeated changes of station, and the challenges of overseas deployments. We have seen and experienced friction in servicemembers' lives and homes, and too often found that the cause was a financial burden or conceptual misunderstanding which could have been prevented with the right education or knowledge.

The *Armed Forces Financial Guide* is our answer to these challenges: a one-stop shop that demystifies the language of personal finance and provides appropriate resources and advice to make wise decisions. With a better understanding of personal finance and of your own goals, you can better employ the many resources and unique benefits that a military career provides. Building wealth and securing long term financial freedom while serving our country is possible. The knowledge, tools, and frameworks for success are outlined in the following pages.

The *Armed Forces Financial Guide* is also a leader's tool—we encourage you to use it as you train, mentor, and coach your units. Leaders leverage discipline and training to create tactical and technical expertise within high-performing teams; we challenge you to harness that same discipline and training to improve your subordinates' financial resilience. Do yourself and your unit a favor by creating financial well-being within your ranks. Financial well-being for our servicemembers and their families is an integral part of the readiness that leads to mission success.

Regardless of your rank, responsibilities, goals, net worth, and whether you can differentiate assets from amortization, we believe there's something here for you. You can read the guide from cover to cover, leave it in your unit's common area, use it to map a training plan, or keep it as a reference for when a subordinate seeks your help. From newly enlisted E-1 to grizzled E-9, fresh W-1 to salty W-5, brand new O-1 to crusty O-6 – there is information here for you, your family, and your unit.

SPENCER J. CLOUATRE, PhD
Colonel, US Army
USMA, Economics Program Director

Table of Contents

FINANCIAL BASICS

6	Net Worth	26	Credit Protections
8	Plan Your Spending	28	Loans
10	Financial Triage	30	Your Credit History
12	Banking Basics	32	Investing Basics
14	Checking Accounts	34	Risk and Return
16	Debit Cards	36	Asset Allocation
18	Savings Accounts	38	Diversification
20	Credit Basics	40	Tracking Performance
22	Credit Cards	42	Retirement Planning
24	Using Credit Cards	44	Retirement Accounts

PAY AND ENTITLEMENTS

46	Military Compensation	52	What You Earn
48	Leave and Earnings Statement (LES)	54	Hardship and Hazard Pay
		56	Special Benefits
50	More on LES	58	Allowances

SERVICE RELATED BENEFITS

60	Service Related Benefits	68	Education Benefits
62	Health Insurance	70	Your Retirement Plan
64	Life Insurance	72	Home Loans
66	Post-9/11 GI Bill		

FAMILY

74 When You're a Couple
76 Updating Details
78 Wills and Other Documents
80 Changing Stations
82 Deployment Readiness
84 On The Home Front
86 Tax Benefits
88 Adding Life Insurance
90 Property Insurance
92 Family Health Insurance

94 TRICARE
96 Other TRICARE Coverage
98 Childcare Benefits
100 Paying for Higher Education
102 Saving for College
104 Transferring Your GI Bill Benefit
106 Avoiding Scams
108 Ending Relationships
110 Dividing Assets

TRANSITION AND RETIREMENT

112 Leaving the Military
114 Transitioning
116 Finding a Job
118 Insuring Your Health
120 Insurance After SGLI
122 Buying a Home
124 Disability Compensation

126 Disability Claims
128 Retirement Income
130 Reserve Retirement
132 Managing TSP Investments
134 Estate Planning
136 Survivor Benefits
138 Survivor Entitlements

GLOSSARY, INDEX, AND RESOURCES

140 Glossary
154 Resources

158 Index

Net Worth

Financial security depends on having a positive net worth

When you want to check your weight, you step on a scale. To determine your running pace, you time yourself with a stopwatch. What the scale and the stopwatch give you is a snapshot of where you are at a moment in time. It's up to you to act on the information.

Suppose your concern is whether you have your personal finances under control. That's when you use a **net worth** statement. It gives you a clear picture of the financial shape you're in and a way to track the progress you're making managing your money.

FINDING NET WORTH

To figure your net worth, you use your current financial records to identify your assets, or what you have, and your liabilities, or what you owe.

Assets include the money you have in bank or credit union accounts, the current value of your investments, the balance in your Thrift Savings Plan (TSP) or other retirement accounts, plus your personal possessions and any real estate you own.

Liabilities are amounts you owe. What you include are your longer-term debts. They may be personal loans, car loans, lines of credit, mortgage loans, student loans, and any large outstanding credit card balances that you aren't able to pay off quickly. You don't include regular monthly living expenses, insurance premiums, or income taxes.

Using two columns, you list your assets and their current value on one side and your liabilities on the other. The calculation is simple. You add up each column and then subtract total liabilities from total assets. The result is your net worth.

If your assets are greater than your liabilities, you have a positive net worth. If the reverse is true, and your liabilities are greater than your assets, your net worth is negative.

ACTING ON WHAT YOU LEARN

If your net worth is positive, you're on the right track, even if, at this point in your military career, you're not on the plus side by very much. You've made the choices that have gotten you where you are. So you're prepared to build greater financial security.

If your net worth is negative, you need to turn things around, sooner rather than later. Generally the best place to start is by avoiding any new liabilities. Then you can turn your attention to paying off debt and changing the way you spend, especially on big ticket items including housing and transportation. It may not be as hard as

FAIR MARKET VALUE

The key to valuing your assets accurately—other than cash and publicly traded investments—is determining their **fair market value**. That's the price a knowledgeable buyer would pay on the open market if you were willing to sell the asset and neither of you were under any pressure to make the deal. Using fair market value is important because some assets appreciate, or grow in value, over time while others— think cars and electronic equipment—depreciate, or lose value.

IDENTIFYING GOALS

Some of your financial goals may be easy to identify, like buying a new car. Others will evolve over time as your income increases, your family grows, or your horizons broaden—or all three.

Be prepared: You'll probably have different goals, with different time frames, sometimes competing for your attention—and for your money. For example, people with small children may plan for college tuitions at the same time they're saving for retirement.

Something else to keep in mind is that your goals are certain to change. In some cases, it's because you've reached an objective, such as buying a home. In others, you may change your mind about what's important or what's achievable. That's why financial plans, like net worth statements, need to be written down, reviewed regularly, and updated.

$$\frac{\text{TOTAL ASSETS} - \text{TOTAL LIABILITIES}}{} = \text{NET WORTH}$$

you think once you start to focus on where you are financially.

Whether it's positive or negative, you'll want to update your net worth statement on a regular basis—perhaps once a year. It's a good way to stay financially responsible and to spot a potential problem before it becomes serious.

FINANCIAL PLANNING

The next step in taking control of your financial future is making a **financial plan**. Financial planning is forward looking. You identify things you want to be able to afford in the future and develop strategies for making them a reality. It's a lot like setting professional objectives as you pursue your career and following the path that will get you there.

Chances are that your financial goals will require more disposable cash than your pay alone will provide. This means creating a strategy to accumulate the money, usually by combining saving and investing, to pay for your various goals— from very short-term ones to those that are several years in the future.

DEFENSIVE PLAYS

As you plan for the future, be aware of potential obstacles that can come between you and achieving your goals.

- **Unexpected expenses**, which can strain your finances unless you have an emergency savings account
- **Inflation**, which reduces your buying power over time
- **Taxes**, which eat away at your earnings, leaving you less to save and spend

Fortunately, there are strategies for overcoming each of them.

Plan Your Spending

By managing your cash flow, you can cover current needs and still meet long-term goals.

Money doesn't spend much time in your checking account. It comes in, when you're paid, and goes out again to cover your regular living expenses as well as the unexpected costs that can—and all too often do—put a strain on your wallet.

Nobody has to tell you that it's smart to avoid spending more than you earn. But knowing what's best doesn't necessarily make it easy to do. What you want to avoid is a steady leak in your **cash flow**, or the relationship between the income coming in and the payments going out.

One way to keep your cash flow positive is to develop a **spending plan**, or budget. While following a plan doesn't guarantee you won't overspend from time to time, it does mean you're less likely to get into serious financial trouble if you stick with it.

Spending Plan

INCOME AND EXPENSES

You can create a spending plan in three steps using a spreadsheet or an app. Of course you could use pencil and paper, but there's an advantage to having a plan you can update or revise easily.

Expenses

1. List your expenses. It helps to show your expenses as monthly amounts to simplify your calculations. For example, if you pay insurance premiums quarterly, figure the total you pay for the year and then divide by 12 to get the monthly amount. Similarly, if you usually do your food shopping weekly, figure what that would come to each month.

Income

2. Add up your income, which probably comes primarily from your pay. If you're married and creating a household budget, be sure to include your spouse's income.

3. Allocate your income to your expenses, starting with your fixed essential costs.

ONLINE RESOURCES

A quick search will help you find web- and app-based resources to help you create a spending plan. If you crosscheck lists from sites such as Forbes, Consumer Reports, or NerdWallet, you can identify the apps that show up consistently as being worthwhile.

Most of the highly regarded apps are free, though some may have a small monthly fee. Some are simpler to use than others, and some may be better for singles than for couples.

One of the major differences is how spending is organized, either by category or cash flow. Another is whether you upload your information yourself or the app downloads it from your checking account. It's worth taking the time to explore several

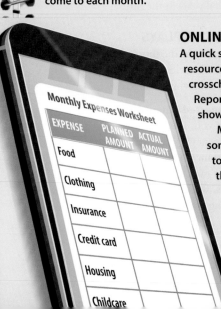

Monthly Expenses Worksheet

EXPENSE	PLANNED AMOUNT	ACTUAL AMOUNT
Food		
Clothing		
Insurance		
Credit card		
Housing		
Childcare		

If your living situation is more or less the same this year as it was last, you can use last year's expenses to project your costs for the coming year. It's a little harder to create a spending plan if you've just made a big transition—say from one duty station to the next, or from being single to life as a married couple.

As you start following your plan, you'll probably find you've underestimated some essential costs and overestimated others. But remember, a spending plan is designed to be revised and updated regularly to reflect your actual income and expenses.

FIXED AND VARIABLE COSTS

It's a good idea to separate the expenses with fixed costs, such as car payments, phone plans, and utilities, from those which vary from month to month, like food. That way, you can focus on reducing what you're spending on the costs you can control if you're running short and need to economize.

You'll do yourself and your financial future a big favor if you include savings as one of the fixed costs in your plan. Though it may be tough to put away even small amounts when money is tight, you'll never regret saving.

different apps to find one that you'll be comfortable using.

And remember, you're not making a lifetime commitment. You can always switch apps or do your tracking some other way. For example, you can create your own spreadsheet or use an interactive budget worksheet that you find online.

FOLLOWING THE FLOW

To manage money effectively, you need to keep track of where your money is actually going. It may not be where your spending plan indicates it should go.

Using an app, online tool, or a small notebook, record what you spend each day for several weeks. You may be unpleasantly surprised. But it could also be the push you need to spend differently. If what you've been doing isn't working, you'll have to make some changes. Start by taking a hard look at where you can cut back.

One approach is to create a separate checking account just for your household expenses. On payday, transfer enough money from your general account to the household account to cover these expenses. As the bills come due, pay them from the household account. If you're able to economize from time to time, and have a surplus, it's smart to leave it in the household account to help cushion potentially higher or unexpected expenses in the future.

STAYING POSITIVE

Of course, there's a direct relationship between your income and allowances and what you can afford to spend on the necessities of daily life and the extras that make living fun. One rule of thumb is 50% for needs, 30% for wants, and 20% for savings. But remember that even people earning many times more than you can find themselves in serious financial trouble if they spend more than they can afford. Mastering financial management early will serve you well throughout your career and after you retire or leave the service.

Financial Triage

A quick assessment will help you identify your fiscal priorities.

Is debt weighing you down? Are you worried that you couldn't afford an unexpected expense? Are you missing out on DoD matching funds because you're not contributing to your retirement account?

You're not alone. Just about everybody has some financial concerns. The solution is not to ignore them—they don't go away by themselves—but to zero in on those that are worrying you and act on them.

To do this effectively, you need to establish priorities. If you have serious debts, deal with them first. If debt's not a problem, build up your savings. When you have some savings, consider investing.

DEALING WITH DEBT

Consumer debt—credit card debt in particular—can create major problems even if you are making your other payments on time. That's because the interest rate you pay on credit cards is much higher than on most other forms of credit. For example, the average rate on a credit card is 18% while on mortgage loans it's 3.7%. And if you pay late or owe a lot, the rate could be closer to 25%. Substantial fees for late or missing payments only make the problem worse.

If you have significant debt, your top priority is to pay it off, starting with the debt on which you're paying the highest interest. You'll also have to stop adding new charges and pay more than just the minimum due each month. Every additional credit purchase will just compound your problem.

EMERGENCY FUND

An unexpected repair bill or a period of reduced income, perhaps because your spouse hasn't found a job at your new posting, can pose special cash flow problems even if you've been careful about managing your spending.

That's why it's so important to have a financial safety net—usually from two to six months of living expenses—on deposit in an emergency fund. The money can be in a bank or credit union savings account, or in short-term certificates of deposit (CDs). Those accounts are liquid, which means you can access the money easily when you need it with little or no loss of value.

You build the emergency fund by including it as a regular expense in your spending plan and allocating income to deposit in the fund, just as you allocate income to pay your car loan or your electric bill.

In addition, you should have a cash reserve in a secure place in your home. If a natural disaster cut off power or if there were a national emergency, banks could be closed and ATMs and credit card readers inoperable. Without money for food, gasoline, and other necessities you could face serious problems. As a start, you could save $50 a pay period, accumulating $1,000 within a year's time.

TAX-ADVANTAGED INVESTING

Savings are essential for meeting short-term objectives and surviving unwelcome financial surprises. The money you keep in a bank or credit union is insured, so it won't disappear on you. But it's not going to grow very much in value either. That's why you should also be thinking about investing once your debt is under control and your emergency fund is set. Investments have the potential to increase in value over time. That can make the difference between meeting your long-term financial goals and having to settle for what you can afford.

One place to start investing is in accounts that give you tax advantages. When you put money into a tax-deferred account, any interest or dividends you earn, and, in some cases, the amount you invest, are not reported as income and no taxes are withheld, as they are from your pay. (You pay any taxes that may be due only when you take the money out.)

As a member of the military, you can benefit from tax-deferred investing by contributing a percentage of your pay to your US government Thrift Savings Plan (TSP) retirement account. If you've joined since 2018, the DoD matches what you put in up to 5% of your base pay. Just think of it as a gift that can double the size of your contribution.

Granted, retiring seems light years away and is probably the last thing on your mind. But having a steady source of income later in life is essential to your financial independence and being able to do what's important to you.

TAKING RISKS

Unlike savings, which are insured, investments fluctuate in value. There may be times when an investment is worth less than you paid for it. So you have to be willing to take a certain amount of risk. While there's no guarantee that the future will repeat the past, there's strong historical evidence that investments like stocks, and the mutual funds and exchange traded funds (ETFs) that invest in stocks, have gained value over the long term.

If you need money that's readily available to cover financial emergencies or make a large purchase in the short term, you'll be more interested in the liquidity that savings can provide. But when you invest for long-term goals, liquidity is less important than the potential for growth and income that stocks and bonds can provide. However, caution is advised. Investing is a skill that you can learn successfully. But it's a bit like flying: You don't want to take off before you know how to land.

Banking Basics

Choose a financial institution whose cost, convenience, and services are right for you.

If you make a quick list of life's necessities, banks and credit unions probably won't make your top ten. But having a relationship with one is essential if you have bills to pay and savings to protect. Credit unions and banks are also the primary source of consumer credit, including providing credit cards and a variety of loans.

Large banks and credit unions operate either nationwide or within an extended region, offering multiple branches in various locations and online access to your accounts. Smaller local, or community, institutions offer many of the same services within a limited area. There are also virtual institutions, which operate entirely online, with access to customer service by telephone. What you're looking for is the best combination of cost, convenience, and personal service that you can find.

SAFETY FIRST

Money in a bank or credit union account is in the safest place it can be.

Your deposits in savings and checking accounts are automatically insured for up to $250,000 in each eligible account category, including individual, joint, retirement, trust, and business accounts. For example, if you have an individual checking account, an individual savings account, and a joint checking account in a credit union, each of the three is insured up to $250,000.

The insurance guarantees you'll recover the full insured value of your accounts if the bank or credit union fails.

If you have identically owned accounts in different branches of the same institution, it's considered one account. But accounts in different institutions are insured separately—which can help if you keep a substantial amount in cash.

FDIC

The Federal Deposit Insurance Corporation (FDIC) insures banks and the National Credit Union Share Insurance Fund (NCUSIF) insures credit unions.

NCUSIF

KEY CONSIDERATIONS

Convenience. You evaluate convenience, in the age of online banking, by being able to:

- Have 24-7 access to review current balances as well as recent deposits, debits, and payments
- Pay your bills online or with a mobile app that you can also use to make deposits
- Withdraw cash from a locally available ATM
- Easily contact customer service

Because the physical location of the bank or credit union isn't as important as its online services, you won't have to open a local account each time you move to a new duty station or close it when you leave.

There are major military credit unions and banks that have multiple branches around the country and robust online services. Or you might look into some of the large national banks with multiple locations that offer specialized programs to active duty service members and veterans.

However, that's
not usually the wisest long-term choice.

MORE THAN ONE?

Sometimes it makes financial sense to
use two credit unions and banks, or even
three, rather than just one.

For example, if you choose a large
bank or credit union as your primary
institution, you might still keep some
money in one that's local to provide easier
access to a nearby network of ATMs. That
could help if your primary bank puts a
limit on free withdrawals or has a limited
ATM network.

In addition, if you are applying for a
loan or credit card, you might find that

the rates offered by
the local institution are more competitive than your primary credit unions
and banks. In that case, it would usually
make sense to use a loan or credit card
that costs you less.

On the other hand, you'll find that
banks and credit unions often offer their
existing clients lower loan rates and
easier access to credit than you may be
able to negotiate with an institution
where you have no other relationship.
That may be true as well if you needed a
small loan to see you though a difficult
period. Many credit unions and banks
make these loans available at more
reasonable cost than non-bank lenders.

Convenience, cost, and customer service are the criteria that
matter when you're choosing a bank or credit union.

Cost. Cost is a major
consideration in
choosing where to bank
because the more you
pay, the less you have
to spend on everything
else. Each bank and credit union is free
to set its own fees for maintaining an
account, writing checks, using ATMs,
and making online bill payments.

It can also set the rates it pays on
interest-bearing accounts and what it
charges on loans. By comparing the
fees and rates of different institutions,
you'll be able to identify the one that's
least expensive overall.

You'll just want to be sure the institution meets all of your requirements.
You won't save anything if there is no
monthly fee but instead a restrictive
ATM policy or a charge for each online
bill payment.

Services. If you know
how you plan to use
your account, the more
likely you'll be to find
one that's right for you.
You might want to think about:

- How frequently you use an ATM,
  since withdrawing from out-of-
  network ATMs, especially ATMs
  in non-bank settings, can be
  extremely expensive
- Whether you pay most bills electronically, because an institution that
  charges for online payments could
  increase your costs significantly
- The bank or credit union's reputation
  for customer service, which you can
  find out from others you know who
  use the institution and from websites
  that rate these institutions

Checking Accounts

Checking accounts are a central feature of your financial life.

The account you use to pay your bills and access cash—called a **checking account** at a bank and a **share draft account** at a credit union—is also known as a **transaction** or **demand deposit** account.

Transaction means you can tell your bank or credit union to transfer money from your account to a **payee's** account. That's the person or institution—for example, a utility company—who's owed the money.

Demand deposit means you can move money from your account at any time without having to notify anyone first.

NONSUFFICIENT FUNDS

There has to be enough money available in your account to make the payments you authorize. If there isn't, you'll face a problem that may be called **nonsufficient funds (NSF)**, insufficient funds, unavailable funds, or overdraft.

When there's not enough to cover the payment, the credit union or bank can refuse to pay what you owe. You'll be charged an overdraft fee—often between $29 and $36—and the payee's bank almost always charges a similar fee that the payee passes on to you. The payee may also tack on a late-payment fee and charge interest on your unpaid balance.

Clearly, this is something you want to avoid. The first line of defense is keeping careful track of your checking account balance, which you should be able to do online. As backup, you can often arrange

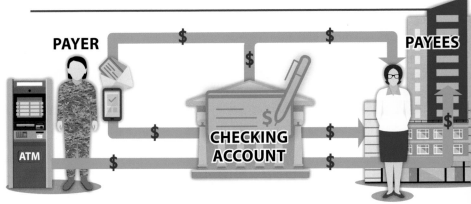

PAYER $ $ PAYEES

ATM

$ CHECKING ACCOUNT $

MAKING PAYMENTS

You, as the **payer**, can authorize payments by check, on your computer, tablet, or mobile app. And you can use a bank or credit union's ATM to move money between accounts, such as transferring a loan payment from your checking account. You can also arrange to have amounts you owe debited from your account by the payee.

Be sure payments you make arrive by the date they're due to avoid late fees or other charges. Electronic payments from your account to the payee's are made directly, on the date you authorize them to be paid. The same is true with debits withdrawn directly by the payee.

Checks, of course, have to be mailed in enough time to reach their destination by the deadline. So do payments you authorize electronically but that the bank has to mail because the payee doesn't accept electronic payments.

Some payees may encourage you to authorize automatic recurring payments. While your payments will never be late, if those bills vary significantly from month to month and your account balance is low, you may not have sufficient funds to cover the payment. You have the right to refuse that request. Or you might consider using a credit card for these recurring payments.

FUNDS

for **overdraft protection**. That's a line of credit linked to your account. If you overdraw, the bank or credit union automatically transfers money from the line of credit to your account to cover the payment or payments.

You'll have to repay the amount that's transferred, plus interest. Sometimes the bank or credit union also charges the overdraft fee. But while this protection may not be cheap, it's cheaper and less worrisome than bouncing a check.

Your bank or credit union may not offer overdraft protection unless you ask. But being able to arrange this protection may help you decide where to open an account or the type of account you choose. Unfortunately, overdraft service may not be available with basic accounts, which are typically those that don't charge a monthly fee.

STOPPING PAYMENTS

If you authorize an electronic payment for a future date, you can usually cancel or modify it until the payment date. And if you have set up a recurring debit from your account—to pay a utility bill or gym membership, for example, or to repay a loan—you can usually end the arrangement by sending a written request to the credit union or bank three days before the next debit is scheduled.

If a debit continues to be paid after you've ended, or revoked, it, you should notify the bank or credit union in writing within 60 days from the date the debit is reported on your statement. The institution must investigate within ten days.

If the problem continues, you should file a complaint with the Consumer Financial Protection Bureau (www.consumerfinance.gov) or with the state banking department in the state where you are currently living.

HOW MONEY MOVES

Electronic payments, including **direct deposit** of your paychecks, move through an automated clearinghouse (ACH) network operated by the Federal Reserve Banks.

ACH deposits are usually available on the day that they're paid to your account or the next business day. Similarly, ACH payments and debits are taken from your account on the date you've authorized and are available to the payee either the same day or the next. In that sense, they work a lot like cash.

Checks you deposit into your account may not be available as promptly, especially if they're non-local checks. That lag, which can be up to five days, may mean you end up with a nonsufficient or unavailable funds situation, even if you thought your account had enough money to cover your payments.

CHECKING YOUR BALANCE

You should regularly review your online account statement to be sure all the payments and debits are ones that you made and that all the deposits you were expecting have been made. Generally you have 60 days to report problems with electronic fund transfers (EFTs) but only 14 days for other types of errors. Always follow up a verbal report with a written one as soon as you discover the problem.

Debit Cards

ATM withdrawals are only the tip of the iceberg.

A **debit card** looks like a credit card. But that resemblance is superficial. A debit card, which your bank or credit union provides when you open a checking account, is linked directly to that account.

When you use the card and your personal identification number (PIN) to withdraw cash at an ATM, the amount is subtracted immediately from your account balance. The same thing happens when you use the card to make an online or in-person purchase.

Sometimes, when you swipe, insert, or wave the card at a point-of-sale (POS) reader, the debit is almost instantaneous. In cases when you sign your name, as you also do with a credit card, it may take longer for the amount to be debited from your account.

USING YOUR CARD

You might prefer using a debit rather than a credit card to help keep your spending under control. But there's a catch. Your credit union or bank will offer you overdraft protection on your debit card. So if you spend more than your account balance—say to pick up pizza for your team—the purchase will be covered and you avoid the embarrassment of having your card rejected.

If the overdraft kicks in, however, it works the same way as it does with your checking account. The bank or credit union transfers money to your account and charges interest on the loan. Often there's also a fee for each overdraft, which can be more expensive than the purchase you made. The real danger, though, is how easy it is to overspend and rack up unwanted, expensive debt.

So it's smart to decline **overdraft protection** on your debit card when your institution asks your agreement to provide it, which they must do by law. All you have to do is say no. Declining this protection will not affect the coverage you have for your checking account.

PREVENTING PROBLEMS

One of the risks of using a debit card is unauthorized use. True, to make ATM withdrawals, someone would need to know your PIN, which you can protect by not sharing it with anyone but your spouse. You can also be careful not to write it on the card or on a piece of paper in your wallet.

But there are lots of ways someone could make unauthorized charges if they had your card or just its number. Signatures are rarely checked, and when you use a debit card on the phone nobody asks you to prove your identity.

The law does protect you in case of misuse. If you notify your bank or credit union that your card is missing or has been used without your permission within two business days of discovering the loss or fraudulent use, then the most you can lose is $50. And most credit unions and banks limit your loss to $0. But if you wait more than 60 days to report the problem, your possible loss jumps to

$500, plus everything that's withdrawn on the 61st day and after.

On top of that, if a substantial amount of money is gone from your account, you may find yourself in an overdraft situation while you wait for the money to be restored. If you've filed a written report, your bank or credit union has ten days to investigate your loss and refund your money. But if you haven't, it may extend the investigation for up to 45 days. If your account has been open for less than 30 days, however, the credit union or bank may extend the investigation even longer, leaving you without the money.

transfer or direct deposit. When the balance is gone, you reload.

The advantages of prepaid cards are that you can use them to make purchases but it's harder to overspend since there's no overdraft option. A potential downside is that the fees on some—but not all—prepaid cards consume much of the amount loaded to them. Others may not refund your balance if the card is lost or stolen. You'll want to compare card terms before you choose one.

PREPAID DEBIT CARDS

A **prepaid debit** card isn't linked to a bank account. Instead, you load money to the card at the retail or financial institution that provided the card or arrange a

WHEN NOT TO USE A DEBIT CARD

Using a debit card may pose other risks, where your losses are not protected. For example, if you use a card to make an online purchase and the product is defective or never shows up, you're plain out of luck. If you'd used a credit card instead, you'd have the right to dispute the charge rather than fighting the seller yourself.

If you use your debit card to reserve a hotel room or a rental car, that amount is frozen and no longer available in your account. When you settle your bill, the actual amount is debited too. So you're out double the amount until the original charge is lifted, which could take days.

You should also think twice before making online purchases with a debit card. If anything goes wrong with the transaction, especially with regard to security, your entire account could be vulnerable. The same applies to authorizing recurring payments with a debit card. Once the money has been debited, it's almost impossible to recover. Here, too, a credit card is a better choice.

Savings Accounts

Saving now means you'll have money to spend later.

Good money management requires you to save regularly, ideally by having a small part of every paycheck—maybe 5% to start—deposited directly into a savings account. You can do that by signing up for an allotment at **mypay.dfas.mil** and designating the account. It can be at the same bank or credit union as your checking account or at one that pays higher interest.

True, upfront saving reduces the amount you have to meet your living expenses. But there's a tradeoff: When you need extra cash to pay for an unexpected cost you'll have it. It's a situation you can count on facing from time to time.

As an added benefit, savings can be essential for achieving short-term financial goals that are important to you.

TYPES OF ACCOUNTS

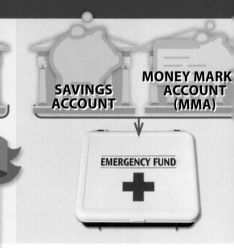

CHECKING ACCOUNT

CERTIFICATE OF DEPOSIT (CD)

SAVINGS ACCOUNT

MONEY MARKET ACCOUNT (MMA)

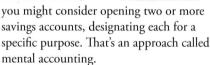

SEPARATE ACCOUNTS

Savings accounts, also called deposit accounts, do more than serve as a buffer against an occasional cash shortfall. In fact, you might consider opening two or more savings accounts, designating each for a specific purpose. That's an approach called mental accounting.

You might set aside one of your savings accounts for short-term goals, such as an account strictly for funding your next vacation. Being able to afford something you really want can take some of the sting out of self-imposed financial discipline.

A savings account is also the perfect place to build your **emergency fund** that can help see you through a serious financial emergency.

WAYS TO SAVE

Credit unions and banks generally offer several types of savings accounts—regular savings, money market accounts (MMAs), and certificates of deposit (CDs). CDs may be called share certificates at some credit unions and money market certificates at others.

Regular savings typically earn the lowest rate of **interest** the institution pays, require the smallest minimum balance, and offer the greatest flexibility on withdrawals. Sometimes larger balances qualify for higher interest rates in what's called a prime savings account.

MMAs are hybrids. They share some features with checking accounts and some with savings accounts. You can make up to three transfers to a third-party payee each statement period, which is usually a month. MMAs typically pay somewhat higher interest, but there's a catch. You must maintain the required minimum on deposit, often $2,500 or more. If your balance dips, you may lose interest, be charged a fee, or both.

BUILDING A LADDER

If you're using CDs for your emergency fund, you can use a strategy known as laddering. Instead of opening just one CD, you split your principal into three CDs that mature in a stepped pattern. To start, you choose terms of six months, a year, and 18 months. Each time a CD matures, you roll it over into a new 18-month CD to extend the ladder. That way one-third of the total is available every six months if you need to use it. If not, you just roll it into the next CD for the same term.

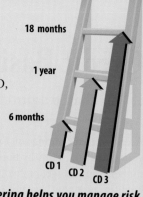

CD laddering helps you manage risk

18 months
1 year
6 months
CD 1 CD 2 CD 3

CDs are **time deposits**. They last for a fixed term, from as short as six months to five years. The amount you deposit to open a CD must stay in the account until the term is up or you may forfeit the interest you would have earned.

The interest is usually higher than on other deposit accounts, and the longer the term, the higher the rate tends to be. The rate is **fixed** with most CDs, as it is on other savings accounts. But sometimes it's **adjustable**, or could change up or down. In that case, there's usually a floor limiting how low it can go. Floating rates are pegged, or linked, to a published interest rate, such as the rate on US Treasury notes, and go up or down as that rate changes.

RATES AND YIELDS

Banks and credit unions are free to set the interest rates they pay, but they must disclose the **annual percentage yield (APY)** you earn and the fees you'll pay. That means you can make an informed comparison among accounts.

BANK'S % — **Nominal Interest Rate**

% YOU EARN — **Annual Percentage Yield**

The difference between the rate that's paid—or what's called the **nominal rate**—and the APY is that the APY tells you what you actually earn as a percentage of your principal. You'll find the nominal rates being offered at the same time are typically very similar because they reflect the current cost of borrowing. When borrowing is expensive, savings accounts pay higher rates, and when borrowing is cheap, they pay lower rates.

The APY depends on the **compounding** method the credit union or bank uses. The higher the rate and the more frequent the compounding, the greater the **yield**, or what you earn.

You'll want to think twice about institutions offering CDs with APYs substantially higher than the competition. Often, they're not insured by the FDIC or NCUSIF, so your money could be at risk. Risks apply as well for CDs whose terms are longer than five years.

ALL ABOUT COMPOUNDING

When you save, and when you invest, compounding is your greatest ally. When savings compound, the interest you earn is added to your **principal**, or the amount you deposit, to form the new base on which future interest is paid. The next time interest is calculated—often on a daily basis—the amount you earn is incrementally larger because you're earning interest on your interest as well as on your principal.

PRINCIPAL
+ % APY (INTEREST EARNED) = NEW BASE PRINCIPAL — 1 year
+ % APY (INTEREST EARNED) = NEW BASE PRINCIPAL — 2 years
+ % APY (INTEREST EARNED) = TOTAL EARNINGS OVER TIME — 10 years

Credit Basics

If you charge a purchase or take a loan, you're using credit.

Access to credit means you can pay for your needs and wants by borrowing the money. You arrange for credit with a **creditor**, or **lender**, usually a credit union or a bank. The creditor agrees to advance an amount called the **principal**, and you agree to repay that amount plus a **finance charge** for using the money.

TYPES OF CREDIT

Loans and **lines of credit** are the most common types of credit. With a loan, you borrow a specific amount and repay it in regular installments over a specific **term**, or period of time. Terms vary by type of loan and lender. A car loan might be four or five years and a home mortgage as long as 30. So you should always do a careful review of a loan's details before you sign.

With a line of credit, you have access to a fixed sum, called your **credit limit**, which you can borrow against at any time over an extended period. When you repay what you've borrowed, it's available to borrow again. Credit cards are the most common line of credit. But if you have overdraft protection on your bank account, that's a line of credit, too.

HOW BORROWING WORKS

Creditors are happy to lend because they make money on the **interest** you pay for borrowing. The rate the creditor uses to determine the interest depends on:

- The type of credit you're using, with credit cards normally having higher rates than loans
- The amount you owe to other creditors figured as a debt-to-income ratio, or what you owe divided by your income
- Your reputation as a borrower, derived from your **credit report**
- The current **benchmark rate**, which banks and credit unions are charging their most creditworthy borrowers

FEES APPLY

Creditors typically charge an application fee to arrange a loan plus other upfront fees based on the type of loan it is. There's no application fee with a credit card, but there may be an annual fee.

If your loan payment is late or you don't pay the full amount that's due on time, you'll owe a fee. And you may face substantial penalty fees on credit cards as well. For example, late fees are capped at

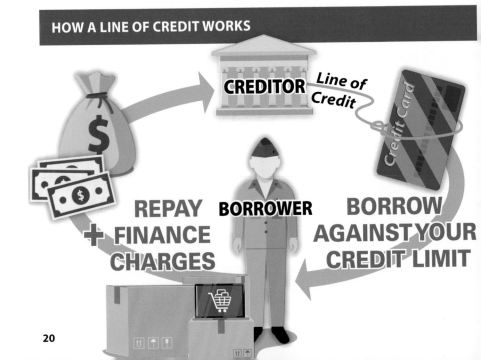

HOW A LINE OF CREDIT WORKS

CREDITOR · Line of Credit · Credit Card

REPAY + FINANCE CHARGES · BORROWER · BORROW AGAINST YOUR CREDIT LIMIT

RED FLAG ON CASH ADVANCES

You can use your credit card to take a **cash advance** from an ATM if you've chosen a PIN for the card. But it's almost always a bad idea, except perhaps in a real emergency. You'll pay an access fee plus a finance charge on the amount you withdraw calculated at an APR that's higher than the rate you pay on purchases.

$27 for a first missed payment but may be $37 or more each time you're late again.

Creditors must tell you in writing the cost of borrowing for a year, expressed as an **annual percentage rate (APR)**. With a loan, the APR includes all the fixed fees and the interest rate that applies but not late fees or other penalty fees. With a credit card, the APR includes the interest rate on purchases but not penalty fees or the card's annual fee if you pay one.

If your payments are late, the card issuer may also increase the APR it charges on your outstanding balance as well as on future purchases.

A MILITARY SAFETY NET

If you're called to active duty, the Servicemembers Civil Relief Act (SCRA) provides vital protection for you and your family if your service affects your ability to meet your financial obligations. If you took a loan or had credit card debt *before you joined the military*, and you notify your lender in writing, your interest rate should be capped at 6% for the entire time you're on active duty. For help, you can contact an office of the Armed Forces Legal Assistance Program.

CREDIT PROS AND CONS

Credit can work for you. But it's way too easy to pay with credit without thinking about how much you're actually spending.

Pros

You can use your credit card to:

- Take advantage of sales and shop conveniently online or by app

- Pay recurring bills, such as car installments or insurance premiums, so you don't risk paying late

- Reserve hotel rooms and rental cars

And you can use a credit card to simplify bill paying. By charging most purchases to the card, you can make a single payment for the month. If your card has a rewards program or provides money back on purchases, extended warranties, or purchase protections, you can take advantage of those offers as well.

Through longer-term arrangements like car and mortgage loans, credit makes it possible for you to pay for things you need but couldn't otherwise afford.

Cons

Using credit does have a downside. If your monthly credit card bill is regularly more than you can afford to pay off in full, the finance charges will increase the cost of your purchases. That's a major problem if you're paying interest on items that no longer have value, like tools you never use or food you ate weeks ago.

If you use credit to live beyond your means or you're unrealistic about what you can afford, like an expensive car, or tempted by things that aren't worth the price, you may find yourself in serious debt. Worse, if you **default** on a loan because you can't make your payments, you could lose your property and jeopardize your access to future credit. It might also hurt your career.

Credit Cards

The cycle of borrowing, repaying, and borrowing again is described as **revolving credit**.

All credit cards work the same way. You make an agreement with the card issuer—typically a bank or credit union—that establishes your credit limit, your nominal APR, potential penalty charges, various benefits, and your rights as a card user.

As you use your card, the issuer tracks your purchases and payments and creates 12 billing statements each year, each covering about 30 days. The statement shows the amount of your **outstanding** **balance** (what you owe), the day payment is due, and the required **minimum payment**. That's the smallest amount you can pay to meet your obligation.

The payment date must be the same every month and at least 21 days after the statement is posted online or mailed to you. It's a good idea, though, to check your account online from time to time to verify the purchases you've made and check on your spending.

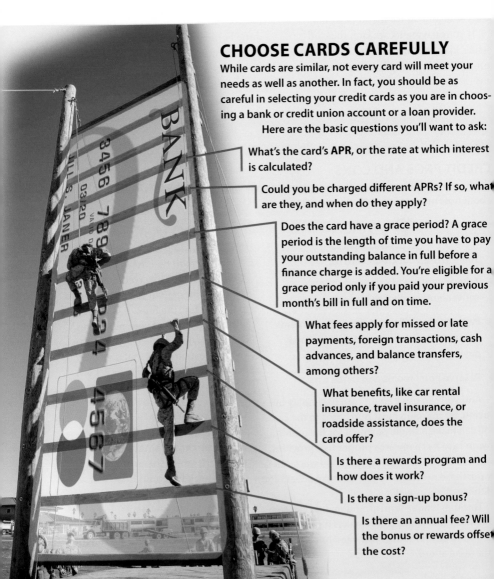

CHOOSE CARDS CAREFULLY

While cards are similar, not every card will meet your needs as well as another. In fact, you should be as careful in selecting your credit cards as you are in choosing a bank or credit union account or a loan provider.
Here are the basic questions you'll want to ask:

What's the card's **APR**, or the rate at which interest is calculated?

Could you be charged different APRs? If so, what are they, and when do they apply?

Does the card have a grace period? A grace period is the length of time you have to pay your outstanding balance in full before a finance charge is added. You're eligible for a grace period only if you paid your previous month's bill in full and on time.

What fees apply for missed or late payments, foreign transactions, cash advances, and balance transfers, among others?

What benefits, like car rental insurance, travel insurance, or roadside assistance, does the card offer?

Is there a rewards program and how does it work?

Is there a sign-up bonus?

Is there an annual fee? Will the bonus or rewards offset the cost?

THE COST OF CREDIT

There may be times when using credit costs you more than paying cash, such as when you're buying gas, for example. But mostly the cost of using revolving credit depends on how you pay your bill.

If you always pay in full and on time, and your card has a **grace period**, there's no cost for using the credit. But if you pay only part of what you owe, here's the rub: you'll owe a **finance charge** on the unpaid balance as well as on every purchase you make in the next billing cycle, starting on the day you buy it.

Your billing statement includes a chart that alerts you to the cost of paying off your bill over three years and of paying only the required minimum each month. This information is a wake-up call about rising debt. Worse, the calculation assumes that you'll stop spending with the card. If you continue to use it, you'll rack up more interest and your repayment cost will go even higher.

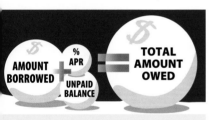

For example, assume you owed $5,400, paid only the minimum due, and had an APR of 18%. You'd pay $14,063 in interest over 36 years—almost three times the amount you borrowed.

To calculate the cost of repaying your outstanding balances by making minimum payments, you can use the credit card calculator at www.federalreserve.gov.

WATCHING THE CLOCK

Your statement will tell you what time your payment must be made to be timely, which means *on time*. You must have until at least 1700 on the due date to pay, though it could be 1900. If the due date is a weekend or holiday, you have until the next business day.

MULTIPLE CARDS?

You may find that you manage just fine with a single credit card. But often using two might make more financial sense.

For example, suppose you normally pay your credit card bill in full and on time every month. If your card has a grace period, it doesn't really matter what the APR is. But what if you need to make a major purchase, such as a refrigerator or furniture, that costs more than you could pay for in a single month?

In a situation like this, which is pretty common, you'd make out better with two cards from different issuers. You could use the first for most purchases and the second, with the lowest possible APR you can find, for major purchases that you pay over time. That way you don't take a hit on the card you use regularly, and you're paying off the second at a lower rate.

Another approach is to apply for credit from the retailer for your one-time purchase. You may be offered credit-free terms for making scheduled payments over time. But if you do, be careful. If you're late even once, you'll probably face stiff interest charges and perhaps a demand for payment in full.

FLOATING ALONG

One benefit of paying by credit card is the **float**—the time between when you buy something and when you have to pay for it. If you time a major purchase for just after the account closes for the current cycle and before your new statement has been issued, you'll have about seven weeks before payment is due. The float works, however, only if you always pay your bill in full and on time.

Using Credit Cards

With credit cards, the devil is in the details.

If you're applying for a credit card, the challenge is deciding which one to choose. So here are some of the things to consider as you sort through what's available to you or decide whether to keep a card you already have.

ANNUAL FEES

It's easy to find credit cards with no annual fees. So should you just rule out any card that has one? The argument in favor of cards with fees is that they may offer benefits you could really use. These are often **affinity cards**, or cards co-issued by an organization and a credit union or bank. For example, cards jointly sponsored by an airline and a financial institution may offer priority boarding even if you're not in uniform, free checked bags, travel insurance, frequent flier miles, upgrades, or some combination. Those sponsored by nonprofits may mean you're making a regular contribution to a place or a cause that's important to you.

The argument against choosing a card with an annual fee is that it increases the cost of using credit. If you do, you'll want to be sure that you'll actually take advantage of the benefits it offers, and that those benefits will offset any added cost.

WHAT ABOUT REWARDS?

The credit card business is very competitive, something that works to your benefit if you're careful about choosing a card with a rewards program that makes sense for you. The trick is that while many of these programs resemble each other, there are important differences.

For example, some cards offer a cash bonus or bonus points for signing up, provided you spend a specific amount on purchases in a specific time period. But if the amount you must spend to qualify is high—say $3,000 or $4,000 in three months—there may be no way to spend this much while sticking to your budget. In that case, you probably want to continue your search.

Other cards offer cash back on purchases, though the purchases eligible for the highest benefit vary from card to card. Sometimes it's food, but it could be gas, or hotels. Some cards even let you choose the category for which you want to receive the highest cash-back rate. But if you have to use the cash-back dollars on products available from the card issuer, you'll want to be sure they are products that you'll use.

BALANCE TRANSFERS

If you have an outstanding credit card balance, you may consider moving the balance to a new card with a lower interest rate. In fact, to encourage balance transfers, some cards offer a period of 0% interest on your debt or waive the fee that usually applies. You'll want to check the details, however, including how long the promotion lasts and what the interest rate will be when it ends.

A CARD TOO MANY

While one or two credit cards are probably essential, the more cards you have, the harder it is to keep track of what you're spending and the easier it is to overspend or pay late.

As a general rule, except where you use a retail store's credit card to make a major purchase, it's probably best to avoid retail cards altogether. Stores offer all kinds of discounts and rewards to encourage you to sign up. But the APRs on these cards tend to be higher than on most other cards, and the cards can be used only with that retailer.

CALCULATING APR

The APR on your credit card may be **fixed** or **variable**. With a fixed rate, the APR remains the same unless the card issuer notifies you it is being raised. If that's the case, you must have a 45-day warning of any rate increase, though you don't have to be given a reason.

In contrast, a variable rate is tied to an index that the issuer selects and must identify. If the index increases, your rate will increase. The change could occur monthly, quarterly, or annually, depending on your card's terms.

To calculate the interest you owe each month, the issuer converts the annual rate to a daily rate (DPR) by dividing the APR by 365 or 360. Most issuers multiply the DPR by your **average daily balance** over the billing cycle to find the interest you owe.

CHARGE CARDS

Another approach is to combine a credit card with a **charge card**. You use the two the same way, but with a charge card your outstanding balance is due, in full, at the end of each billing period.

Charge cards generally have an annual fee but they have some major selling points. Some offer veterans attractive benefits, including waiving the fee. Others have a feature that allows you to withdraw cash directly from your bank account at an ATM rather than taking a cash advance. The fee is often $5 or 3% of the amount, but no interest is due.

That can be especially useful if your bank or credit union has a limited ATM network or if you travel frequently, including out of the United States.

CREDIT INTERMEDIARIES

If you're uneasy using a credit card to make online purchases because you fear its security could be compromised, you may want to investigate an online payment system or payment app. These systems use encryption and tokenization—a series of randomly generated numbers— to mask or replace your card details.

Credit Protections

Your rights as a card user are established in the law.

Chances are that at some point you'll run into a problem with your credit card. You may discover it's missing, and you won't remember where you used it last. Your statement might include two or three purchases you never made. Or something you've bought with your card may have a major defect.

The good news is that you're protected against the potential downside of any of these situations, and more, thanks to a series of federal and state credit protection laws dating back to the **Truth in Lending Act of 1968**. All you have to do is take advantage of them.

BE PROACTIVE

The most effective way to avoid credit card problems is to be careful. Something as routine as keeping your receipts and checking them against your statement will alert you to charges you never made. It's a little harder with online purchases, since there may be no receipt, though you can keep a list of the sites where you buy and the amounts you spend there.

If you don't recognize a charge, you can always contact the card's customer service number and ask them for more details. The response will either refresh your memory or confirm that there's a problem.

CARD SECURITY

You can protect yourself against certain credit card risks by the way you use your cards.

Never respond to anyone who asks you to verify your credit card number over the phone or online. Legitimate organizations never make this request.

Never use your credit card on public wifi networks, including those that say they are password protected.

Never email your credit card number or tell someone what it is in a public space where you could be overheard.

Don't allow online retailers to store your credit card information even if you shop with them frequently.

Be sure to logout from any website as soon as you finish your transaction.

CREDIT PROBLEMS

Despite the legal protections that take some of the worry out of using credit, it's still possible to find yourself in credit trouble. The most effective way to handle evolving credit problems is to recognize the danger signals. Then you need to take corrective measures.

Here are some things to monitor:

! If your monthly payments are more than 38% to 40% of your monthly income, your debt-to-income ratio is dangerously high.

! If you regularly make only the required minimum payment on one or more credit cards, you risk finding yourself in serious debt.

! If you skip some payments every month, you're not only paying late fees and more interest, but you may risk losing the ability to use the card.

! If you're maxed out on the credit limit of one or more of your credit cards or you're using savings to pay your monthly bills, you have no financial cushion to see you through an emergency.

Most card issuers are alert to potential fraud. If they suspect a problem, often based on an uptick in activity or the places your card is being used, they will contact you and may replace your current card with a new one. That's why it makes good sense for you to alert your issuer if you'll be travelling away from your regular post, especially if it's overseas.

LOST OR STOLEN CARDS

If your credit card is lost or stolen, the law limits your liability for unauthorized charges to $50. In fact, most card issuers won't hold you responsible for any amount. But you are responsible for notifying the issuer as soon as you realize the card is gone. The card will be cancelled, and no further charges will be approved.

A similar $50 liability rule applies to lost or stolen debit cards. A major difference, however, is that misuse of debit cards means that the money has been withdrawn from your account, and there may be a delay before the bank or credit union restores the missing amount. With a credit card, you're not out anything.

BILLING ERRORS

Billing errors can take many forms, though they're unlikely to be mathemat-

ical. There may be purchases you didn't make or ones you made that were never delivered, orders that were fulfilled incorrectly, or services you paid for that were unacceptable. There may be recurring charges that you had cancelled in writing but that continue to appear, or other problems, including defective merchandise, that you haven't been able to resolve with the seller.

You have 60 days to notify the card issuer after the charge you want to dispute appears on your statement, though the time limit may be extended in some cases. The card company then has 30 days to respond and up to 90 days to investigate and resolve the problem. If the issuer doesn't get back to you, it can't collect the amount you dispute or impose finance charges.

If you pay the other charges on the statement by the due date, the issuer can't restrict your use of the card, file a bad credit report, or charge a finance charge on the unpaid amount while they're investigating. They may suggest, though, that you pay and promise a refund if your complaint turns out to be valid. The good news is that, more often than not, consumers are successful in their claims.

Loans

You can borrow and repay the money you need for specific expenses.

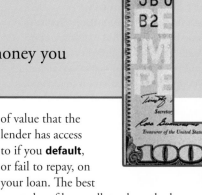

All loans are alike in one important way. They provide a cash infusion for an expense that you can't pay for out of pocket or put on a credit card. But there are different types of loans, each with distinctive features. The more you understand about how they work, the easier it will be to choose the most suitable one for your particular need.

HOW LOANS WORK

With a loan, you borrow an amount called the **principal** and agree to repay it, plus **interest** figured as a percentage of the principal, over a specific **term**. These factors determine what the loan costs you. Generally, the larger the principal, the higher the interest rate, and the longer the term, the more expensive the loan.

You repay an **installment loan** on a regular schedule, usually once a month, over a fixed term until the outstanding balance is $0. They differ from **lines of credit** that provide access to money as you need it, up to a certain limit, over an extended period.

A loan's interest rate can be **fixed** or **adjustable**. A fixed rate remains in place from the day you take the loan. With an installment loan, it means that each payment you make over the term is for the same amount. With a variable rate, the rate is linked to a public index, such as the rate on a ten-year US Treasury note. It can change monthly, quarterly, annually, or sometimes less frequently, based on the provisions of the loan agreement.

Some loans are **secured** and others are **unsecured**. With a secured loan, you provide collateral. That's something of value that the lender has access to if you **default**, or fail to repay, on your loan. The best examples of loan collateral are the homes that secure mortgage loans and the cars that secure automobile loans. Unsecured loans, granted on your promise to repay, don't require collateral and generally have higher interest rates than secured loans. Some unsecured loans require a cosigner who promises to repay if you default.

CHOOSING A TERM

A loan's term has a major impact on the cost of borrowing. Assuming the principal and the interest rate are the same, a loan with a shorter term will cost you less over the loan's term because you'll pay less interest. With the important exception of high-cost emergency loans, shorter-term loans typically offer lower rates. For example, if you were applying for a mortgage loan, the rate on a 15-year fixed-rate loan would be lower than the rate on a fixed-rate 30-year loan.

So why does anyone take a longer loan? The answer is affordability. If the principal is the same, payments on the longer-term loan will always be smaller than those on a shorter-term loan. If you're concerned about being able to fit the monthly payments on a mortgage into your budget, taking the longer-term loan makes financial sense even if it costs you more over time. Remember, too, that real estate has the potential to appreciate in

SECURED   UNSECURED

FIXED OR ADJUSTABLE

If you have a choice between a fixed-rate loan and an adjustable-rate loan, it pays to compare the benefits and potential drawbacks of each type. (In some cases, especially with shorter-term loans or lines of credit, you may not have a choice.)

	ADVANTAGE	DISADVANTAGE
FIXED-RATE	One advantage of a fixed-rate loan is that the installments stay the same, so you always know what the loan will cost every month. That makes it easy to budget.	One disadvantage is that if rates go down, the rate on your loan will not. But you can usually refinance.
ADJUSTABLE-RATE	The advantage of an adjustable-rate loan is that the initial rate you pay is often lower than if the rate were fixed. That means it may be easier to qualify for the loan. It's also possible that your payments will drop in the future if rates go down, which would save you money. And, if rates do go up, there's often a cap limiting how much the rate could increase.	There are some obvious disadvantages, though. It's harder to budget for potential increases. Rates could rise rather than fall. So despite its lower initial cost, an adjustable-rate loan could end up costing more overall.

value, which isn't true of other things, such as vehicles, you may buy with a loan.

The other factor you'll want to consider when deciding on the term is the useful life of the thing you're buying. For example, is a 60- or 84-month car loan with lower payments a better deal than a 36- or 48-month loan with its higher payments? Consider what the car will be worth and how well it will be running at the end of the loan.

RISKY LOANS

Payday loans, vehicle title loans, and refund anticipation loans promise to solve your short-term needs. But these loans always mean long-term financial problems. Lenders charge upfront fees

for very short-term loans—with a payday loan it's typically 14 days—that translate into exorbitant interest rates, trapping you in an endless cycle of ever more expensive borrowing.

The Federal Military Lending Act caps APRs on all loans at 36%, but, thanks to unscrupulous lenders that bend the rules, the average APR may be between 391% and 521% based on upfront charges of $15 or $20 for each $100 you borrow.

A wiser solution is to contact the Family Support Center at your installation or the financial institution where you have a checking account for legitimate loan programs that will meet your needs.

Your Credit History
Past credit use affects your ability to borrow again.

When you need a loan, you want to know how much you can borrow, how long you'll have to repay, and what borrowing will cost.

What the lender wants to know is if you'll repay. To decide, the credit union or bank investigates your **creditworthiness**, or how responsible you are with the credit you already have. Lenders aren't the only ones who want to know. Landlords check before renting to you. Employers investigate before offering you a job. And, for service members, credit reputation plays a major role in gaining and maintaining security clearances and the ability to continue to serve.

CREDIT HISTORY

A **credit report** and the credit score derived from it are the primary sources of information about your creditworthiness. The credit report is a constantly updated record of all your outstanding credit accounts and the way you repay them. The three-digit credit score is calculated using this data and a proprietary algorithm that considers these details:

- Your payment history, or if you regularly pay on time
- How much credit you're using
- How long you've been using credit
- The types of credit you use
- How much new credit you've applied for recently

The most common credit scoring models range between 300 and 850. Generally, scores above 700 are considered good, making you eligible to borrow at a competitive rate. Lower scores may mean you're turned down or that the interest rate you're offered is **subprime**, or higher than the current average. That makes borrowing more expensive.

A NEW TAKE ON SCORING

Recognizing that the way you manage your money in checking, savings, and money market accounts is also an important indicator of financial responsibility, FICO is introducing a new approach to creating credit scores.

It looks at accounts you, as the applicant, designate that have been open for several years, show frequent transactions, and haven't been overdrawn. The goal is to increase the number of loan approvals for people who might not qualify because they don't have a credit score or have a low one that might normally limit their ability to borrow.

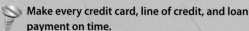

MAKE IT STRONGER

If you'd like your credit report to be stronger, you can make that happen. It may take time, but it's worth it.

- Make every credit card, line of credit, and loan payment on time.
- Keep your outstanding balances below 30% of your credit limit. Below 10% is best.
- Don't apply for new credit.
- Be diligent about paying off expensive credit card debt as quickly as you can.
- Continue to use some credit, and remember you don't need to carry a balance to have a good score.

TRACK YOUR REPORT

If you're thinking about applying for a loan, it's smart to check your credit report with one of the three national credit-reporting agencies—Experian, Equifax, and TransUnion—to see what's there and confirm there's no negative or incorrect information you should be prepared to explain. The reports aren't identical, but they're similar enough so major issues appear on all three.

You can access each report for free once every 12 months at www.annualcreditreport.com or by calling 877-322-8228. In fact, it's a good idea to check your credit standing regularly by looking at a different report every four months so you see all of them during a year.

If you spot a problem, you might decide to postpone your application until you're in a stronger position. But if you do apply, and your loan or credit card application is rejected, you should find out why. The lender must tell you the major reasons you were turned down, the credit score it used, and the name and contact information of the credit agency on whose report the score was based. You can request a free copy of that report from the credit agency within 60 days of being turned down. That's in addition to the reports you can access for free.

DON'T SWEAT THE SCORE

Credit scores get a lot of hype. If your score is available for free, which it may be from your bank, credit union, or credit card issuer, by all means pay attention. But while checking your credit report is essential, paying for your credit score is not.

That's because the score you'll see is almost certainly not the same one a potential lender, insurance company, or landlord sees. Score providers create different versions of your score for different users by weighting the factors in their formula in different ways. In addition, each score provider uses its own algorithm, which produces different results from the same information.

NO MAGIC SPELL

Anyone who claims to be able to make your credit report stronger or your credit problems disappear with no effort on your part is at best misinformed and more often a fraud. There are legitimate ways to get help solving credit problems, such as Military OneSource (www.militaryonesource.mil). But instant fixes aren't among them.

CORRECTING ERRORS

If you find errors in your credit report, which you may, you can follow the instructions on the credit reporting agency's site to correct them. The agency must investigate and report back to you, but it doesn't have to change anything it believes is accurate. If the harmful information remains after 90 days, you have the right to attach an explanation of up to 100 words to the report stating your position. You should also alert any potential new lenders about the problem and provide an explanation, with written evidence if you have it.

TO SHIFT YOUR FINANCIAL PLAN INTO ACTION, CONSIDER INVESTING.

INFLATION

When you **invest**, your goal is to increase your **net worth** by buying financial assets you expect to grow in value, pay dividends or interest, or provide both growth and income.

But investing means you have to be prepared for **risk**. You might gain less than you expected or even lose some of your **principal**, or the amount you've invested, at times.

That doesn't happen when you save.

With saving, the primary risk is **inflation**, or the gradual increase in the cost of goods and services. If you earn less than the rate of inflation on your savings, your buying power is reduced.

In contrast, taking some investment risk means that over time your investment gains have the potential to outpace inflation, sometimes by a wide margin.

INVESTMENT CATEGORIES

As you begin investing, you'll want to concentrate on three types of investments, called **asset classes**:

- **Equity investments,** primarily **stocks** and the **mutual funds** and **exchange traded funds (ETFs)** that invest in stocks

- **Fixed income investments**, primarily **bonds** and the mutual funds and ETFs that invest in bonds

- **Cash equivalents**, including certificates of deposit (CDs) and US Treasury bills (T-bills)

When you own stock, you have **partial ownership** in the corporation that issued, or sold, it. Ownership means you have a right to your share of any **dividends** the corporation pays out, the right to vote for corporate officers, and the right to sell at any time.

Stock prices aren't fixed and may increase in response to positive investor demand. Then you can sell at a profit if you wish or keep the stock, increasing your net worth. But you have to be prepared for the possibility that stock prices can fall for a variety of reasons including problems in the economy or a decrease in investor demand.

Bonds are actually **debt investments**. When you buy a bond you're loaning money to the issuer—a corporation, government, or government agency. In return, the issuer promises to pay you interest over the bond's term, which can range from a year to 30 years or more, and return your principal when the term ends.

Bond prices can move up or down from the value at which they're issued—$100 for US Treasury issues and $1,000 for most others—but they tend to vary less than stock prices. Among the reasons bond prices may change are changes in market interest rates.

CDs and T-bills are considered cash equivalents because they can be converted to cash at any time with little or no loss of value. That's described as **liquidity**.

CHOOSING INVESTMENTS

Before you invest, you need a strategy to guide your decisions about what to buy based on your goals, when you want to achieve them, and the types of investments that can help you reach them.

This means zeroing in on the **potential return** that an asset class, though not every investment in that class, may provide.

Potential return is what you can reasonably expect to gain from an investment. The average return each asset class has provided in the past doesn't guarantee how it will do in the future. But it does provide guidance about the return it's reasonable to expect over time.

For example, the average annual return on large company US stocks since 1926 has been about 10%, while the return on long-term US corporate bonds has been 5.3%. The average annual return on cash equivalents, in contrast, has been about 3%. Those returns, however, are before accounting for taxes and inflation.

INVESTMENT ACCOUNTS

To invest, you need an investment account. There are three major types, defined by the tax treatment of the earnings in the account: taxable, tax-deferred, and tax-exempt. You can invest through just one type or use all three, based on your goals and the amount you have to invest.

You can open a **taxable** investment account with a **brokerage firm**, the brokerage arm of your credit union or bank, or with an investment company that sells mutual funds directly to individual investors. You invest after-tax income and owe tax on your investment earnings and on any capital gains, or profit you make from selling an investment for more than you paid for it. But the tax rate that applies to most long-term capital gains is lower than the rate on your regular income.

TAX-ADVANTAGED INVESTMENTS

If you're investing for retirement or to pay for your children's education, you can use accounts that provide tax advantages.

A traditional **tax-deferred retirement account** is opened in your name in an employer-sponsored plan, such as the DoD Thrift Savings Plan (TSP). You contribute pretax income each pay period. Taxes on any investment earnings and on your contributions are postponed, or deferred, until you withdraw.

You may also open a tax-deferred **individual retirement account (IRA)** with a credit union, bank, or brokerage firm to invest additional amounts to help build your long-term financial security. Taxes on IRA earnings are deferred just as they are in the TSP account, and, in some cases, contributions may be tax-deductible.

You can also use **tax-exempt accounts** to invest for retirement and education. You contribute after-tax income as you do with a taxable account. But investment earnings aren't taxed as they accumulate and no tax at all is due when you withdraw from the account provided you follow rules that apply to the account. Examples are tax-exempt Roth IRAs, Roth TSP accounts, and 529 College Savings Plans.

Risk and Return

An investment's risk is linked to its potential return.

You measure investment success by **total return**. To find return, you add the income the investment provides as interest or dividends to the change in its market price over a specific period, such as a year.

For example, suppose you invest $4,000 to buy 100 shares of a stock for $40 a share on June 1. Over the year you collect $80 in dividends. On June 1 of the following year, the market price is $43. So there's a **positive return** of $380 (100 x $3 = $300 + $80). You could sell your shares for a $300 profit before taxes and fees or keep the stock for its growth potential.

In contrast, a **negative return** can stall your progress, at least in the short term. Suppose you collected the same $80 dividend but the market price of your stock dropped to $38 a year after purchase. In that case, your return would be a loss of $120 (100 x -$2 = -$200 + $80). You might sell. But if you think the price could go back up, you might keep the stock in hopes of recovering your loss.

What makes some people uneasy is that there's no way to predict whether an individual security or the market as a whole will gain or lose value in any given year.

MAKING RISK DECISIONS

The most dramatic consequence of risk is losing money. But the more probable risk is that you won't accumulate as much as you need to meet your goals.

AMOUNT YOU INVEST	X	100 shares
		$40 per share
	=	$4,000

If market price increases to $43 per share:

		100 shares
	X	$43 per share
	=	$4,300
	+	$80 dividends
	=	$4,380

POSITIVE RETURN OF $380

If market price drops to $38 per share:

		100 shares
	X	$38 per share
	=	$3,800
	+	$80 dividends
	=	$3,880

NEGATIVE RETURN OF -$120

PERCENT RETURN

Total return is typically reported as a percentage to make it easier to compare returns on different investments. You find percent return by dividing the gain or loss in value by the amount you invested. In the examples here, you would have had a 0.095, or 9.5% gain or a – 0.03, or -3% loss.

The two risks are interrelated. If you focus primarily on safety, or reducing the risk of loss, you usually reduce your potential return. But if you can tolerate some fluctuation in your investments' value, the most productive path is often a middle ground. That means that you choose some investments with limited risk, a few with considerable risk, and the

LEVEL RISK

HIGH MEDIUM LOW

RETURN

majority that pose some risk but have the potential to provide a strong return.

By looking at the way an asset class has performed in the past, you can get a sense of the level of return it's reasonable to expect. For example, if the annual return on large company US stocks—the stocks tracked in the benchmark S&P 500 Index—has averaged around 10% since 1926, it's reasonable to expect future returns will be in the 10% range but not 20% or more, even if they hit that level from time to time.

UNDERSTANDING RISK

Risk has many faces. The more you understand about what these risks are and how they could affect your investments, the more effectively you can manage their impact.

The risk that the financial markets could lose value is known as **market risk**, sometimes called **systemic risk**. When investors are selling but not buying, demand dries up, and prices drop.

Investment risk, sometimes called **nonsystemic risk**, is the possibility that a specific investment won't produce the return you were expecting. For example, suppose two new technologies are competing for market share. If only one of those technologies ends up being widely adopted, the other is unlikely to survive. If you had invested in the one that didn't make it, you probably lost money. But if you had chosen the other, you may have made out really well.

Management risk is the possibility that a company's managers make serious errors in running the business. Investors could suffer if they sold after its price declined. The other perspective, though, is that superior management is often the reason a company succeeds, even under difficult market conditions.

Credit risk refers to the potential that a bond issuer won't meet its obligation to pay interest or return principal to bondholders.

VALUE = PRICE
When you talk about an investment's value, you're talking about its **market price**. That's what you would pay to buy or receive for selling a share before transaction costs.

DEALING WITH VOLATILITY

Volatility is a fact of life when you invest. It's the fairly quick and potentially dramatic change in an investment's value or in the value of a market as a whole.

Volatility is more typical of certain investments than of others. The stock price of a small new company, for example, can rise quickly based on investor enthusiasm for a new product or service. But it can drop equally fast if the company faces a new competitor, a legal challenge, or negative news coverage.

While volatile investments offer the potential for a big profit, there's also the very real possibility of a major loss. So you'll want to invest only disposable income, or money you won't need in the next several years.

Remember, though, it can be a good idea to hold on to your investments during periods when markets as a whole are more volatile than usual. That volatility is generally the result of economic and political uncertainty and is likely to stabilize eventually, although it is difficult to predict the timing.

RISKS TO AVOID
You should be skeptical of any investment that claims to be risk free or promises an unusually high yield. It's highly unlikely to deliver on its promise.

Asset Allocation

Asset allocation is a strategy for managing market risk.

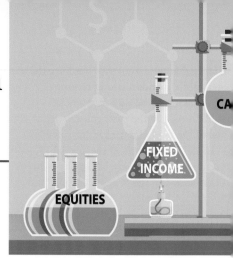

When you allocate your financial assets, you divide your investment portfolio among **asset classes** on a percentage basis. That is, you assign a portion of your investment principal to **equities**, such as stocks and stock funds, a portion to **fixed income**, including bonds and bond funds, and a portion to cash equivalents.

A LOGICAL CHOICE

Allocation is not simply a matter of investing equally in each asset class. You don't do yourself or your investment goals any favors by putting 33% in stock funds, 33% in bond funds, and 33% in cash equivalents and forgetting about it.

That's because your allocation typically has a major impact on your investment **return**. Here's why:

1. Each asset class puts your money to work in a different way. You choose stocks for growth or a combination of growth and income, bonds primarily for income, and cash equivalents for security. So it makes sense to emphasize the class that's most likely to help you meet your goals.
2. Each asset class provides strong returns in some years and weaker returns in others. You never know which class will be strong, or how strong it will be, in any given year. Typically when one class is booming another is faltering. So, if you always have a portion of your portfolio in each asset class, you're always positioned to benefit from whichever one is gaining.

ALLOCATION PERCENTAGES

Deciding what percentage of your investment dollars to allocate to different asset classes depends on several factors, including your financial goals, your willingness to take a certain amount of investment risk, and the investments you already own. Your age is important too.

If you have a long time to meet your goals, the unpredictability of investment return is less of a problem. When you're in your 20s or 30s, you might invest close to 100% of your retirement portfolio in stock funds to maximize your potential for long-term growth, with the rest in bonds or cash equivalents. By your 60s or 70s, you might gradually move toward a portfolio closer to 50% stocks to reduce your exposure to volatility at a time when you may be depending on investment income for living expenses. But if you have the security of regular retired pay, you might continue to invest more of your portfolio for growth.

There is an interesting range of potential allocations you may want to review at https://personal.vanguard.com/us/insights/saving-investing/model-portfolio-allocations.

MANAGING SYSTEMIC RISK

Each asset class, though not each individual investment within the class, responds in relatively predictable ways to specific, and often recurring, market conditions. For example, if corporate earnings are strong and interest rates are low, stocks tend to gain value.

Under the same conditions, the return on cash equivalents can be low or non-existent. But when interest rates are going up, the prices of existing bonds tend to drop while returns on cash equivalents, such as CDs, increase.

By creating a portfolio that's attuned to these systemic risks—which tend to occur in recurring cyclical patterns—you increase your chances of weathering losses without significantly reducing the

ALLOCATION MODELS

Asset allocation models suggest different ways you might divide your investments among asset classes. But remember, these models are just a starting point. The best allocation for you depends on your goals, your age and family situation, the amount you have to invest, and other sources of income you may have.

AGGRESSIVE

MODERATE

CONSERVATIVE

An aggressive allocation is focused on growth potential and typically assigns 80% to 90% to stock, stock mutual funds, and stock ETFs.

A moderate allocation strikes a balance by assigning 50% to 70% of a portfolio to stock and stock funds, most of the rest to bonds and bond funds, and the balance to cash equivalents.

A conservative allocation emphasizes safety and income, putting 60% or more in cash equivalents, bonds, and bond funds, and perhaps 40% or less in equities for more stability.

potential for long-term growth. That's because the gains in one class have the potential to offset losses in another.

ALLOCATION AT WORK

Once you've chosen an appropriate allocation, you can put it to work. One example is what you might do with the money you contribute to your TSP account when you begin to participate. The plan offers a choice between five individual funds—three stock funds, a fixed income fund, and a cash equivalent fund. There is also a lifecycle fund that is allocated among the five individual funds.

Suppose you decide to allocate 80% to stock funds and 20% to the fixed income fund. For every $100 you contribute to your account, $80 will be divided among the stock funds and $20 will go into the fixed income fund.

The way you decide to allocate is important, but not permanent. You can **reallocate**, or change the mix of assets in your portfolio when your goals, financial situation, or risk tolerance changes. You can also **rebalance** if one investment's return is strong enough to throw the allocation you intended off track.

MUTUAL FUNDS AND ETFS

Mutual funds are investment products that pool the money they raise from investors to buy a portfolio of individual stocks or bonds. The purchase or sale price of a mutual fund share is determined by the net asset value (NAV) of its holdings, and a fund will buy back at NAV any shares an investor wants to sell.

Exchange traded funds (ETFs) resemble mutual funds in holding a portfolio of individual investments, but they're traded like stocks. The price at which an investor buys or sells shares is determined by supply and demand, and may be higher or lower than the ETF's NAV.

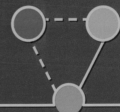

Diversification

Diversification is a strategy for managing security-specific risk.

One of the challenges you face in choosing investments is determining which ones will live up to your expectations and which won't, or why that happens.

You can help manage this risk when you diversify, or buy a number of investments within the same asset class instead of concentrating on just a few. It's an important strategy, as it helps protect you against losses if some of your investments do less well than their class as a whole.

One way to diversify is to focus on mutual funds or ETFs rather than individual stocks or bonds. The return these funds provide is driven by the combined return of all their holdings, called their **underlying investments**. This means that disappointing returns from a few investments in the fund will have a limited impact on its overall return.

In fact, expectation of a higher return at lower risk is one of the reasons that most retirement savings plans, including the DoD's TSP, feature mutual funds as the primary investment alternatives.

micro—is measured by **market capitalization**, which is calculated by multiplying the number of shares a company has in the market by the current market price.

Stocks and the funds that invest in them are also differentiated by the **sector** and **industry** of which they're a part. As one illustration, stocks in a sector whose products and services—like electricity and water—are in demand whatever shape the economy is in tend to be less volatile than those in a sector where demand for its products and services—like household appliances and new automobiles—rises when the economy is strong and falls off when it's weak.

Another important distinction is whether the stock is issued by US or

CLASS DISTINCTIONS

Whatever route to diversification you choose—whether focusing on individual securities, on funds, or on a combination of individual securities and funds—the key is to create a portfolio that reflects the variety of investments within each asset class. The two major classes, **equities** and **fixed income**, are made up of many smaller **subclasses**, or groups, that differ from each other in important ways.

TYPES OF EQUITIES

With equities, company size has a major impact on growth potential, price volatility, and ability to survive an economic downturn. Size—large, medium, small, or

overseas corporations and whether an overseas corporation operates in a mature or developing economy.

As an example, a stock fund investing in small US companies working in artificial intelligence is likely to provide a different return and carry a different level of risk than a stock fund investing in large German automobile firms or mid-sized Mexican banks.

TYPES OF FIXED INCOME

In the fixed income space, there are notable differences in yield, or what the bond pays, among issues from governments rather than corporations. Other factors that affect yield are whether the bond income is taxable or tax-exempt,

DIVERSIFYING WITH FUNDS

In addition to their built-in diversification, mutual funds and ETFs simplify the task of narrowing down your investment choices. Each fund tells you the kind of investments it makes, the number of investments it holds, the risks it carries, its past performance history, the minimum investment, and what it costs to own.

Some broad-based funds hold a hundred or more securities drawn from a specific asset subclass. Examples include large-company US stock funds, short-term tax-free municipal bond funds, and international stock funds. Narrow-based funds may hold only a few

securities or may concentrate their holdings in a single industry, like defense and aerospace or wireless technology.

A diversified portfolio of funds would probably include both equity and fixed income funds in whatever asset allocation you have chosen, with a focus on broad-based funds, and a few of the more narrowly focused funds.

This approach is likely to make your portfolio more price stable overall than a diversified portfolio of individual securities. But there is a major caution. If the stock or bond market—or both markets—drop in value, the value of most funds invested in those markets will drop as well.

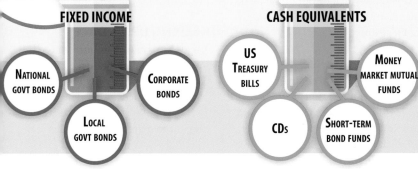

and what the bond's term is, which could be anywhere from a year to 30 years or more. Credit rating matters too. Highly rated bonds pay interest at a lower rate than high-yield—or junk—bonds, but pose much less risk.

There's less variety in cash equivalents, where the goal is to provide safety by avoiding investment risk. The primary choices are CDs with various terms and US Treasury bills, with terms from 4 to 52 weeks. Money market mutual funds and short-term bond funds with terms of less than a year are also part of this class.

ACTIVE VS. PASSIVE INVESTING
Many mutual funds and a few ETFs are **actively managed**. A fund's professional

manager chooses its portfolio of underlying investments to meet its investment objective. The manager's choices, and the timing of his or her buy and sell decisions, determine the fund's return.

Other mutual funds and most ETFs are **passively managed** index funds. Each index fund's portfolio holds the same securities as the market index to which it's linked. For example, funds linked to the S&P 500 Index hold the 500 large-cap US stocks included in that index. An index fund's objective is to replicate the performance of its index.

Actively managed funds have higher administrative and investment costs than index funds do. These costs can be a drag on a fund's return.

Tracking Performance

Choosing investments is only the beginning. Then you have to watch how they're doing.

Building the investment accounts that will help you meet your financial goals requires more than asset allocation and diversification. You also have to monitor your portfolio's **performance**, and the performance of each of your holdings, to see if they're adding value or acting as a drag.

At the same time, you have to be realistic. If the investment markets are struggling to stay positive—as they do from time to time—you're not likely to improve performance by replacing your current investments with new ones from the same asset class.

Another thing that rarely works is selling off your investment assets and putting the cash in a savings account or CD. If you do, you'll be out of the market as the tide turns and the markets begin to move up again.

USING BENCHMARKS

While you may want to compare the returns on several investments to each other, it's probably more relevant to compare their returns to the performance of their **benchmark index**. That's the public index that reflects the changing value of a particular financial market or market segment and serves as the standard or yardstick for measuring performance of the securities in that market or segment.

Suppose you own a mutual fund that invests in large company US stocks that gained 8% in value last year. That might seem okay, but if the S&P 500 Index, which is the benchmark index for that market segment, gained 15%, your fund underperformed to a significant degree. So you'll want to investigate what's holding your fund back.

But if the Russell 2000, the benchmark for small company stocks, loses 10% of its value, and your small company fund loses 8%, you've actually done better than the market, even though you had a loss for the year on that part of your portfolio.

It's essential, though, when you're using benchmark indexes to evaluate return, that you use the index that's appropriate for the investment you're evaluating. For example, you don't want to evaluate a small company stock using a large company index. Mutual funds make it easy by telling you what the benchmark is.

KEEPING UP TO DATE

You don't have to wait until you sell an investment to determine the kind of return you're getting. If an investment's market price increases while you still own it, you have what's known as an **unrealized gain**. But that higher value still increases your net worth.

If you sell an investment for more than you paid to buy it, you would have a **realized gain**. If you owned the investment in a taxable account, you might owe tax on the increased value, and on any dividends you received, reducing your actual return. But if you owned the investment in a tax-deferred or tax-exempt account, the gain would be reinvested to increase your account value and no tax would be due.

FINDING THE RANGE

One of the core principles of evaluating performance is that an investment's return tends to move in a statistically predictable way above and below its **mean**, or average value. This variation, called standard deviation, is generally seen as a measure of an investment's level of risk. It lets you anticipate the probable range of future returns over a full market cycle. The cycle runs from a market high through a drop of at least 20% and back to a new high.

MEASURING YIELD AND RETURN

The key to performance testing is **return on investment**, or **ROI**. That's what you get back in relation to your investment principal, or the amount you invest.

Yield is what you earn, expressed as a percentage of the amount you invested. **Annual percentage yield (APY)** is what you earn on an investment paying compound interest. It's determined by the interest rate and the frequency with which the interest is compounded.

The formula used to calculate APY:

$$(1+r/n)^n-1 \ = \ APY$$

r = Annual interest rate

n = Number of compounding periods per year

Fortunately, you don't have to calculate APY yourself, as the credit union or bank will tell you both the nominal rate and the APY.

With cash equivalents, you look at APY. For example, if you deposit $1,000 in a 12-month CD with a rate of 2.5%, compounded daily, the APY is 2.53%, paying $25.31. Different compounding frequency would produce slightly different yields.

It's a little harder with bonds, because there are several ways to figure yield. That's because the price of the bond may fluctuate over time.

If you keep the bonds you buy until they mature, as you may do for the stability they add to your portfolio, then the current or coupon yield depends on the interest rate the bond is paying.

For example, a $2,500 10-year US Treasury bond paying $75 in interest will provide an annual yield of 3%.

$$\frac{\text{Annual Interest}}{\text{Price}} \ = \ \text{YIELD}$$

For Example

$$\frac{\$75}{\$2,500} \ = \ 3\%$$

Total return is the change in value plus any earnings divided by the amount you invested.

$$\frac{\text{Change in Value + Earnings}}{\text{Amount You Invested}} \ = \ \frac{\text{Total}}{\text{Return}}$$

With stocks, mutual funds, and ETFs, you'll want to evaluate comparative **percent return**. To find percent return, you divide each investment's total return by the amount you paid to buy it. You'll also want to find an investment's **annual percent return (APR)** to make comparisons among investments on a yearly basis. To do that, you divide the investment's percent return since the date of purchase by the number of years you've owned it.

For example, if you buy 100 shares of a small company mutual fund for $15 and sell it a year later for $20, your return is $5 a share or $500. That's an impressive return of 33% ($500 ÷ $1,500 = 0.333 or 33%).

$$\frac{\text{Total Return}}{\text{Initial Amount Paid}} \ = \ \frac{\text{Percent}}{\text{Return}}$$

For Example

$$\frac{\$500}{(100 \times \$15) \text{ or } \$1,500} \ = \ 33\%$$

But if you hold the shares for five years before selling for $30 a share, your return is a more modest 6.7% ($500 ÷ $1,500 = 0.33 ÷ 5 = 0.0666 or 6.7%).

$$\frac{\text{\% Return}}{\text{Years Investment Owned}} \ = \ \text{APR}$$

For Example

$$\frac{.33}{5} \ = \ 6.7\%$$

FINANCIAL BASICS

Retirement Planning

An early start is the best prescription for long-term financial security.

You probably aren't thinking about retiring. But that's actually a bigger problem than you might think. If you wait until you're ready to retire to start thinking about whether you can afford to live without a regular paycheck, you'll have missed the boat. The time to start retirement planning is right now.

That explains why many employers, including the DoD, want you to participate in their retirement savings plans. It's also why the federal tax code provides tax incentives for contributing to one of these plans, opening an **individual retirement account (IRA)**, or—even better—doing both.

HOW EMPLOYER PLANS WORK

There are two basic types of employer-sponsored retirement plans. In most cases, an employer offers one or the other, but some employers, including the DoD with its Blended Retirement System (BRS), offer both.

In a **defined benefit (DB) plan**, often called a pension plan, the employer promises regular income after you retire. The plan document specifies how you qualify and includes a formula for determining the amount you'll receive. Typically, the factors are how long you were employed and what you were earning at the time you retired or left the job. The employer contributes to a general pension fund and is responsible for managing its assets to meet plan obligations.

In a **defined contribution (DC) plan**, you, your employer, and sometimes both contribute to an individual account that's set up in your name. You defer a percentage of your salary, called your contribution, to your account each pay period and choose the way the money is invested from among the alternatives

PLAN INVESTMENTS

In most defined contribution plans, the investment choices include a number of mutual funds and a fund of funds known as a **lifecycle fund** or target date fund (TDF). Plans that offer a lifecycle fund actually offer several similar funds, each linked to a specific date, such as 2040,

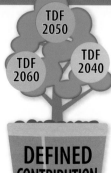

2050, or 2060. You choose, or, in the case of automatic enrollment, are assigned to the fund whose date is closest to the approximate date you'll reach retirement age.

A lifecycle fund allocates assets using a formula that stresses growth in the early

BLENDED
RETIREMENT
SYSTEM

offered in the plan. The employer may **match** a percentage of your contribution, up to a cap.

Unlike a pension, no specific amount of income is guaranteed after you retire. The amount you receive will depend on how much was contributed, the way the contributions were invested, the return the investments provided, and how long the account was open.

ARE YOU IN?

Employers who offer pension plans enroll you as soon as you're eligible to participate. Increasingly, that's true in defined contribution plans as well, including in the DoD's BRS plan. You're enrolled automatically, and the percentage of pay you contribute is set initially by the plan. So is the way your contributions are invested.

But you're not locked in to these defaults. You can choose to contribute a different percentage, but there's an upper limit and often a lower one. Similarly, you may want to make your own choices from the investment menu. In most cases, the way you allocate your contributions governs the way the employer's matching contributions are invested.

years of the fund and gradually shifts to an emphasis on income and safety as the target date approaches. If you invest in individual funds rather than the lifecycle fund, you choose your own allocation. That means if you're comfortable taking more or less risk than the lifecycle fund linked to your prospective retirement age does, you can invest to seek higher return or greater safety.

While you can elect not to participate in the plan, you're working against your own self-interest.

COMPOUNDING IS KEY

When you're investing for retirement, starting as soon as you can is important because of the power of **compounding**. It's the same process that works in your savings account when the interest you earn is added to the amount already on deposit, increasing the base on which the next round of interest is figured.

Compounding works a little differently in a defined contribution plan than it does in a savings account. All your earnings are automatically reinvested to buy additional shares in the mutual funds you've selected. As that happens, and as you continue to make contributions, the number of shares you own increases. The more shares you accumulate, the more any increase in the fund's **net asset value (NAV)**, or share price, boosts the total value of your account.

Of course the NAV could decrease rather than increase in any given period, based on whether the fund's holdings lose or gain value. But your earnings still continue to buy shares. So when the NAV goes back up, the value of your investment may be even higher.

When you contribute the same amount to an investment account every month, you're using a strategy called **dollar cost averaging**. When the NAV goes down, you buy more shares, and when it goes up, you buy fewer. But you never pay more than the average price per share.

ADDING AN IRA

Whether or not you're participating in an employer plan, you can contribute to an IRA. You open an IRA with a credit union, bank, brokerage firm, or mutual fund company—called your IRA **custodian**—and choose the investments you want from among those offered by the provider. That lets you diversify more broadly than you may be able to do in your employer plan.

43

Retirement Accounts

If you know your choices, you can make smart decisions.

All retirement savings accounts are effective in helping you
reach your long-term goals for three reasons.

The account gets regular cash
infusions from your contributions and your employer's
matching contributions,
increasing the base on which
earnings are calculated.

The assets in the account
compound faster because
all earnings are automat-
ically reinvested, also
increasing the base.

Taxes on increases in
the account's value are
deferred for the entire
period in which you
contribute.

Traditional tax-deferred plan	Tax-exempt Roth plan
Contributions with pretax dollars	Contributions with post-tax dollars
Required minimum distributions at 72	Required minimum distributions at 72
Tax due on distributions	No tax due on distributions

DETAILS OF TAX DEFERRAL

While all retirement savings accounts offer
tax deferral, there are differences in the
way it works in different accounts.

In a **traditional tax-deferred plan**,
you make pretax contributions to your
account. Pretax means no tax is deducted
from the portion of your pay that goes
into your account, and that amount is not
reported to the IRS as income. As a result,
your current income tax bill is reduced.

The trade-off is that you typically can't
withdraw before 59½ without owing a
10% tax penalty plus the tax due. Starting
at 72 you must begin taking **required
minimum distributions (RMDs)**, paying
the income tax that's due on each withdrawal. If your income is lower when
you withdraw than it was when you contributed to the account, you may pay less
tax overall. But if your income is higher,
you could pay more tax at withdrawal
than you saved when you contributed.

In addition to the traditional tax-
deferred account, a number of employers
offer a **tax-exempt Roth alternative**. That's
true of the DoD's TSP and in many
civilian 401(k), 403(b), and 457 plans.

The contribution amounts, investment
choices, and tax-deferral of earnings are
identical in traditional and tax-exempt
plans. But instead of contributing pretax
income to your account, you contribute
after-tax income to a Roth account. That
is, the amount you contribute is included
in the income reported to the IRS, so
your current taxes aren't reduced by
your contribution.

The upside comes down the road,
and it can be significant. After you turn
59½, you can begin taking tax-exempt
withdrawals, provided your account has
been open at least five years. And while
you must take RMDs after 72, no tax is
due on these amounts. You also have the
option of rolling over a Roth account to a
Roth IRA. That way, your full account can
continue to compound.

ALL ABOUT VESTING

Any amounts you contribute to a retirement savings account and the earnings they provide are always yours to keep. But the right to keep the contributions your employer has made to your account are set by the plan's **vesting rules**. Civilian plans, which are governed by the federal government's ERISA rules, cap the vesting period at six years for defined contribution plans and seven years for pension plans.

Civilian 6 Years | DoD 20 Years

In contrast, you are fully vested in the automatic contributions of 1% of base pay the DoD makes to your TSP account after you complete two years of service. At the same time, you're eligible for, and immediately vested in, matching DoD contributions, which are linked to the amounts you contribute to your account.

Vesting for a DoD pension takes longer, normally requiring 20 years of qualifying service.

TSP INVESTMENT CHOICES

With a TSP account, you have a choice of investments, including five individual investment funds and five Lifecycle, or L, Funds.

G overnment

- The Government, or G, Fund invests in a portfolio of short-term US Treasury securities. The other four funds are index mutual funds.

C Common Stock

- The C Fund invests in large company US common stocks and tracks the Standard and Poor's (S&P 500) Stock index.

S Small-Cap Stock

- The S Fund invests in stocks of small and medium US companies and tracks the Dow Jones US Completion Total Stock Market Index.

I International Stock

- The I Fund invests in international stocks from 21 developed countries and tracks the MSCI Europe, Australasia, Far East (EAFE) Index.

F Fixed Income

- The F Fund invests in US investment-grade bonds and tracks the Barclays Capital Aggregate Bond Index.

CHOOSING AN IRA

In addition to contributing to a TSP account, you can open an IRA. The only requirement is having earned income, which you do as a member of the armed forces. You can choose a **traditional tax-deferred IRA** or a **Roth IRA**, provided your modified adjusted gross income (MAGI) is less than the annual cap.

When you withdraw from a Roth, no tax is ever due if you're at least 59½ and your account has been open at least five years. And since your marginal tax rate while you're in uniform is likely to be lower than it will be when you separate or retire, you're likely to pay a lower rate on the after-tax amount you contribute than you would on withdrawals you had to take from a tax-deferred IRA.

- Each L Fund invests in a portfolio of the plan's five individual funds. Over time the balance among those funds in an L Fund changes, from an emphasis on equity funds in the early years to an emphasis on more conservative funds as the date when its participants expect to retire grows closer. So investing in an L Fund reduces the stress of choosing investments to achieve your retirement income goal.

L Fund

ACCOUNT INFORMATION
Download *Managing Your Account for Members of the Uniformed Services* at www.tsp.gov/forms/index.html

Military Compensation

Your income as a service member is far more than just basic pay.

In addition to your **base pay**, you may qualify for additional compensation and specific **allowances** that can increase your income, sometimes in small increments and sometimes in larger amounts.

For example, you may earn added pay based on specific skills, participation in special or unusual assignments, or by taking on dangerous jobs. And, you may sometimes qualify for substantial incentive payments, including retention or reenlistment bonuses or career continuation pay if you're part of the BRS.

ABOUT myPAY

myPay is a mobile-friendly DFAS website that allows you to access your LES, manage your allotments and tax withholdings, and see and print your tax documents. You can also use the website to update your banking information, review and print travel vouchers, and handle other financial matters electronically.

To learn more about this service, visit www.dfas.mil and click on the myPay link. To open a myPay account, you'll need to choose an ID and password. To complete enrollment, you'll need your DoD Common Access Card (CAC) and Smart Card reader to complete the enrollment. If you don't have the reader, you'll get a temporary password by email or regular mail.

Since documents that are delivered electronically arrive more quickly and are more secure than those that are mailed, you can opt in for that service—or opt out of it—at any time. But as with everything you do online, you should take precautions to safeguard access to your account and protect it from scams and identity theft.

You are also entitled to tax-exempt allowances for food, for housing if you don't live in government quarters, and for separation from your family if your assignment takes you away from home.

Taking full advantage of these opportunities for extra pay, incentives, bonuses, and allowances can increase your overall compensation while you're on active duty. And they can improve your long-term financial situation, even after you leave the military.

To keep up to date on your income, you should review your **Leave and Earnings Statement (LES)** each month. It shows your current wages, special pays, and the allowances you are receiving as well as amounts that have been deducted. You can find a sample LES in the following pages.

COMPENSATION STATEMENTS

As a service member, you'll also receive a **Personal Statement of Military Compensation** that provides monthly and annual totals for the value of your:

- Base pay plus special pay and bonuses
- Basic allowances, such as for housing and food
- Expense allowances, such as cost of living (COLA) and family separation allowance
- Service-estimated indirect compensation, such as health insurance coverage and tax benefits

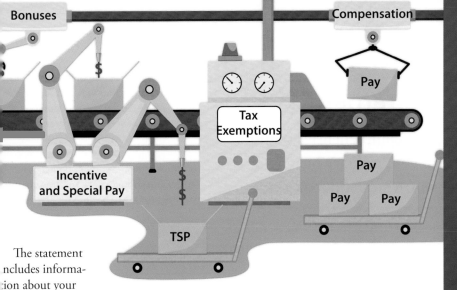

The statement includes information about your retired pay and eligibility to collect it, the formula used to calculate what you'll receive, and the associated COLAs.

In addition, the statement provides an extensive list of other benefits that are available. Some, including access to the commissary and PX, you may use regularly, while others you may or may not choose to take advantage of, such as education programs, legal counseling, spouse employment counseling, and space-available travel.

You can use the summary to help determine how much you'd have to earn in a civilian job to maintain a standard of living comparable to what you have in the military.

TAX IMPLICATIONS
A significant feature of military compensation is that substantial percentages of your income are **tax-exempt**, reducing the tax you owe and increasing what you have available to spend and save.

When you're in a combat zone or receive hostile fire or imminent danger pay, you qualify for the **Combat Zone Tax Exclusion (CZTE)**. This means that some or all the pay you receive during this period, including a bonus if you re-enlist while you're there, is fully tax-exempt.

Tax-exempt allowances, including the Basic Allowance for Housing (BAH), the Overseas Housing Allowance (OHA), and the Basic Allowance for Subsistence (BAS), can account for between 25% and 35% of your annual compensation. These amounts may also be exempt from state income taxes, depending on the state where you file.

PAY THAT KEEPS PAYING
The tax-exempt incentive pay you receive when you're deployed in a combat zone or other designated area offers significant investing and saving opportunities—provided you can resist the impulse to spend it. You can use at least a portion of this pay to increase your contributions to your **Thrift Savings Plan (TSP)** account or achieve your other long-term goals, such as accumulating a down payment that will make it easier to buy a home.

What's more, the incentive income you earn while you're deployed in a designated combat zone for at least 30 days can be deposited in a **Savings Deposit Program (SDP)** account. It pays an impressive 10% interest on deposits up to $10,000 for each deployment, though your monthly contributions can be no more than your base pay, or, in the case of officers, an amount equal to the highest enlisted pay rate.

That super-sized interest rate ends 90 days after you return to your permanent duty station and the balance is paid to you after 120 days. However, you can deposit the amount into an account designated for retirement or education savings, such as an individual retirement account (IRA), a 529 college savings plan, or an education savings account (ESA). That way, the account value can continue to compound to help you achieve these specific goals.

Leave and Earnings Statement (LES)

This comprehensive snapshot of your military benefits is worth a careful look.

Keeping track of your allowances, entitlements, deductions, leave, incentive pay, TSP contributions, and a host of other financial details, can be a major challenge. Fortunately, all this information is readily available and updated monthly on your **Leave and Earnings Statement (LES)**, issued by the Defense Finance and Accounting Service (DFAS).

CHECKING YOUR LES

You can access your LES through your myPay account as soon as it's issued, on the fourth Friday of each month. Making sense of what it's telling you may seem a bit daunting at first—it has 78 specific fields or boxes, several of which have multiple entries. But on closer inspection, you'll find that the statement is divided into six sections, each addressing a specific type of information. There are also three additional fields (76 to 78) for remarks and other timely information.

Once you're familiar with the format, you'll be able to zero in on the specific information you want to check.

Some elements won't change from month to month while others may vary, sometimes significantly. If you're not sure why there's been a change, or if you have questions about the amount or timing of your allowances, entitlements, or other details, you should contact your disbursing or finance officer.

IDENTIFICATION (FIELDS 1-9)

The first section of the LES (Fields 1-9) identifies you, including your name, Social Security number, years of service, and branch. If you have just enlisted, or you have recently had a career change, such as a promotion or reenlistment, you should check this information carefully to be sure it's accurate.

DEFENSE FINANCE AND ACCOUNT					
ID NAME (LAST, FIRST, MI) 1				SOC. SE	

ENTITLEMENTS		D
TYPE	AMOUNT	TYPE
A B C D E F G H I J K L M N O	10	
TOTAL	20	

LEAVE	BF BAL 25	ERND 26	USED 27	CR BAL 28	ETS BAL 29	LV LOST 30
FICA TAXES	WAGE PERIOD 39		SOC WAGE YTD 40		SOC TAX YTD 41	
PAY DATA	BAQ TYPE 50	BAQ DEPN 51		VHA ZIP 52	RENT AMT 53	
Thrift Savings Plan (TSP)	BASE PAY RATE 63		BASE PAY CURRENT 64		SPEC PAY RAT 65	
	CURRENTLY NOT USED 71				TSP YTD DED 72	

REMARKS	YTD ENTITLE _____
76	77

ENTITLEMENTS (FIELD 10)

This field lists all the wages, bonuses, incentive and combat pay, special skills pay, and allowances that you earned during the pay period. If there are more than 15 entries, the overflow is shown under Remarks (Field 76). Any retroactive amounts you are owed will be included in the appropriate listing.

You should review this portion of your LES very carefully each month to be sure that the information is accurate.

BRANCH DETAILS

The LES format and the information it provides is essentially the same for all service branches, though there are some minor differences in format, depending on your branch. You can review the one for your branch at https://www.dfas.mil/militarymembers/pay-entitlements/aboutpay.html.

ALLOTMENTS (FIELD 12)

This field lists discretionary and non-discretionary allotments. This is money that has been direct deposited to non-primary checking or savings accounts, used to purchase US savings bonds, or allocated to charitable organizations, insurance, or other accounts that you have designated. For example, you could use an allotment to contribute money to an individual retirement account (IRA) or build an emergency fund in a savings account at your credit union or bank. That information would appear here.

If you have two or more allotments of the same type, the dollar amount will reflect the total allotment for that type, and they won't be listed separately. You can initiate and cancel allotments through your myPay account.

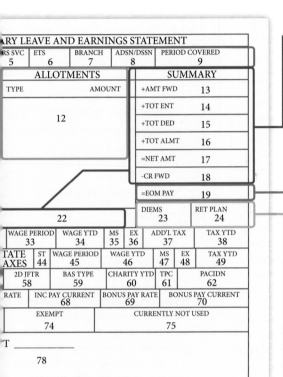

TOTALS AND SUMMARY OF OTHER CALCULATIONS (FIELDS 13 TO 18, FIELDS 20 TO 22)

These fields show the totals for entitlements, allowances, deductions, and allotments as well as unpaid amounts for these categories.

TAKE-HOME PAY (FIELD 19)

In some ways, this is the bottom line—the actual amount you are paid on the End-of-Month (EOM) payday.

RETIREMENT PLAN (FIELDS 23 AND 24)

Field 23 shows the date you initially entered military service (DIEMS). It's a fixed date that is used only to determine the retirement plan of which you're a part. Field 24 names your retirement plan—for example, High-3 or BRS, which went into effect for everyone who joined the armed forces on or after January 1, 2018, as well as for existing members who opted-in to the plan.

DEDUCTIONS (FIELD 11)

This field lists the amounts that were deducted from your pay, including federal income tax withholding, FICA tax withholding, and, Servicemembers Group Life Insurance (SGLI) premiums.

Typically, you're paid twice a month. So this field includes a deduction for mid-month pay to account for the paycheck you received earlier in the month. If there are more than 15 deductions, the overflow is shown under Remarks (Field 76).

You should review these entries carefully to be sure they're correct. Since most deductions tend to be the same from month to month, you can usually spot a line item that varies from the norm.

More on LES

Your LES provides vital information about your leave, taxes, and retirement account.

Every month your LES provides detailed information about benefits that have been credited to your account and amounts that have been deducted from your base pay. The benefits include updated information on the leave you have accrued and allowances you receive for housing, food, and travel. The deductions include amounts the DoD is required to withhold.

LEAVE INFORMATION (FIELDS 25-32)

As a service member, you receive 30 days of paid leave each year by accruing 2.5 days leave for each month of active service. If you're deployed in support of contingency operations, Special Leave Accrual may apply. See your local finance officer for details.

You can carry over leave from one year to the next so you can use it in larger increments if you choose. But a "Use/Lose" provision applies. You must use any days you accrue beyond 60 in a year by October 1—the first day of the new fiscal year—or you will lose them.

If you have accrued leave left at the time you're discharged or retire, you may be able to sell back a maximum of 60 days. The dollar value of those leave days is determined by your base pay.

Fields 25 through 28 show the days of leave that you carried over from previous years, the days you've accrued in the current fiscal year, the leave days you've already used, and the number available for the period covered by the LES.

Field 29 shows the number of leave days you'll earn until your Expiration of Term of Service (ETS).

ETS is important for new members, especially those arriving at a unit at holiday time or during block leave periods, who may want to take leave though they

FICA WITHHOLDING (FIELDS 39-43)

A fixed percentage of your earnings—7.65% for most people—must be withheld to comply with The Federal Insurance Contribution Act (FICA). It's the money that you pay into Social Security and Medicare.

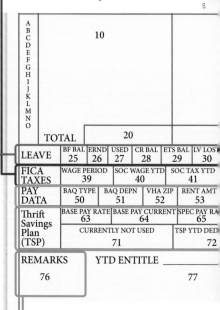

REMARKS (FIELD 76)

It's important to check the Remarks section each month and confirm its accuracy because it includes timely and sometimes actionable information. For example, it lists deadlines that apply to your pay and benefits, the start and stop dates for certain entitlements, and leave dates you have been charged. It also lists entitlements, deductions, and allotments that did not fit in Fields 10 to 12.

have low leave balances. At the commander's discretion, these members may be authorized to use leave they haven't yet earned but are projected to earn.

Leaders should ensure that members of their unit know the leave rules and deadlines and should monitor leave days so that no one loses leave days unknowingly.

Field 30 shows leave days you have lost because they have expired, Field 31, the number of leave days that have been paid to date, and Field 32 the projected number of leave days you must use in the remaining fiscal year to avoid losing them.

FEDERAL TAX WITHHOLDING (FIELDS 33-38)

This section shows the federally taxable income you've earned this period, the income taxes that have been withheld from your paycheck, and the information that has been used to compute the withholding.

Withholding is mandatory to ensure you have prepaid most of the money that will be due when you file your tax returns, typically each April 15.

The amount that's withheld is determined by the number of allowances you claim on IRS Form W-4. Claiming the correct number of allowances can help prevent having too much or too little deducted from each paycheck.

You can use the IRS calculator at www.irs.gov/individuals/irs-withholding-calculator to figure the appropriate number of **allowances** and make any adjustments to your W-4 through myPay.

		-CR FWD	18				
		=EOM PAY	19				
22		DIEMS 23		RET PLAN 24			

WAGE PERIOD 33	WAGE YTD 34	MS 35	EX 36	ADD'L TAX 37		TAX YTD 38

TATE TAXES	ST 44	WAGE PERIOD 45	WAGE YTD 46	MS 47	EX 48	TAX YTD 49

2D JFTR 58	BAS TYPE 59	CHARITY YTD 60	TPC 61	PACIDN 62

RATE 7	INC PAY CURRENT 68	BONUS PAY RATE 69	BONUS PAY CURRENT 70
EXEMPT 74		CURRENTLY NOT USED 75	

CT _____
78

STATE TAXES (FIELDS 44 TO 49)

Your State of Legal Residence (SLR) may or may not have a state income tax. If it doesn't, nothing will be withheld. If it does, the information that's reported includes your wages, marital status, number of exemptions, and the total withheld so far during the year.

While you're in the military, you can choose your SLR, which can be your home state of record, the state where you're stationed, or the one where your current duty station is located—whichever offers the greatest tax advantage. You can change your SLR by submitting form DD2058 to your local pay office.

THRIFT SAVINGS PLAN (FIELDS 63 TO 75)

This section shows your contributions to your Thrift Savings Plan (TSP) retirement savings account. Specifically, it reports the percentage of your base pay, special and incentive pay, and bonus pay that you've contributed to the account, as well as the dollar amount of those contributions that have been deducted for the year. It also shows the total contributions that have been deferred and the dollar amount of the tax-exempt contributions, if any, reported to the IRS.

ADDITIONAL PAY INFORMATION (FIELDS 50 TO 62)

This section reports allowances and information about the number and type of dependents that impact those allowances. For example, it shows the Basic Allowance for Quarters (BAQ), the Variable Housing Allowance (VHA), the Joint Travel Regulation (JTR), and the Basic Allowance for Subsistence (BAS). This data is also used in calculating your BAH and Overseas Housing Allowance (OHA).

What You Earn

Military pay has two components, **base pay** and many types of **special pays**.

Your base pay, which is direct-deposited twice a month into the bank account or accounts you've designated, is the core of what you earn while serving on active duty.

Base pay, along with length of service, determines the allowances you receive and the amount the DoD automatically contributes to your TSP account if you're part of the BRS.

All service members with the same pay grade and years of service earn the same base pay across all service branches. What does vary by branch are the titles linked to the pay grades.

In addition to progressive increases in your base pay, you can qualify for incentive pay to increase your income. There are more than 60 categories of special pays for which you may qualify. Some are based on special skills, like language fluency or professional expertise. Others are based on what your job is and where you serve.

Some special pays apply across service branches, but individual branches offer their own special pays and incentives and set the qualifications for them.

BASE PAY

You can find your current monthly base pay, as well as what others with the same pay grade but with a different number of years of service are earning, by checking the pay tables.

Pay grades—28 of them—are shown in the left column and years of service in the top row. In the example here, an E5 with more than six but less than eight years of service would have a base monthly pay of $3,001.50

The table is updated every year on January 1, increasing the pay across the board for each pay grade and each year of service. The goal is to have annual pay raises linked to increases in private sector wages to help ensure that the DoD pay scale keeps pace with inflation.

> You can find the pay tables at https://dfas.mil/militarymembers/payentitlements/Pay-Tables.html.

MONTHLY BASIC PAY TABL

EFFECTIVE 1 JANUARY 2019
YEARS OF SERVICE

4	6	8	10	12
0.00	0.00	0.00	0.00	0.00
0.00	0.00	0.00	0.00	0.00
11315.40	11604.90	12088.20	12200.70	12659.70
9619.20	9893.40	10164.60	10477.80	10790.10
7870.50	7900.50	8239.20	8283.90	8283.90
6832.50	7105.50	7268.40	7627.20	7890.90
6054.00	6400.80	6772.80	7236.00	7596.30
5671.50	5943.60	6241.50	6434.40	6751.20
4981.20	5083.80	5083.80	5083.80	5083.80
4011.90	4011.90	4011.90	4011.90	4011.90

COMM

4	6	8	10	12
5671.50	5943.60	6241.50	6434.40	6751.20
4981.20	5083.80	5245.50	5518.80	5730.00
4011.90	4284.00	4442.40	4604.40	4763.40
0.00	0.00	0.00	0.00	0.00
4995.30	5225.10	5452.80	5683.20	6029.10
4407.60	4586.70	4940.40	5308.50	5482.20
4060.50	4290.90	4648.80	4826.10	5000.40
3732.60	3957.90	4290.30	4445.10	4662.00

Pay Grade				4	6	8	10	12
E-9	0.00	0.00	0.00	0.00	0.00	0.00	5308.20	5428.50
E-8	0.00	0.00	0.00	0.00	0.00	4345.50	4537.50	4656.60
E-7	3020.70	3296.70	3423.30	3590.10	3720.90	3945.00	4071.60	4295.70
E-6	2612.70	2875.20	3002.10	3125.40	3254.10	3543.30	3656.40	3874.80
E-5	2393.40	2554.80	2678.10	2804.40	**3001.50**	3207.00	3376.20	3396.60
E-4	2194.50	2307.00	2431.80	2555.40	2664.00	2664.00	2664.00	2664.00
E-3	1981.20	2105.70	2233.50	2233.50	2233.50	2233.50	2233.50	2233.50
E-2	1884.00	1884.00	1884.00	1884.00	1884.00	1884.00	1884.00	1884.00
E-1 >4 Mon	1680.00	1680.90	1680.90	1680.90	1680.90	1680.90	1680.90	1680.90
E-1 <4 Mon	1554.00	0.00	0.00	0.00	0.00	0.00	0.00	0.00

ASSIGNMENT INCENTIVE PAY (AIP)

If you are on a special or unusual assignment, which may be determined by your location or skill set, you may receive Assignment Incentive Pay (AIP) to extend the time of this assignment. The amount of this pay ranges from $300 to $1,000 per month, depending on the skill set and the length of the extension. AIP has been paid to members serving in Iraq, Afghanistan, Kuwait, and South Korea, among other locations.

OVERSEAS TOUR EXTENSION

If you have certain critical skills and are authorized to extend your tour of service overseas, you are qualified to receive Overseas Tour Extension Incentive Pay (OTEIP) of up to $80 a month, with a cap of $2,000 a year.

RETENTION AND PROFICIENCY

You may receive extra pay for retention or re-enlistment, especially if you have certain critical skills or proficiencies that the DoD or branch Secretary deems vital or to be in short supply. For example, the Selective Reenlistment Bonus (SRB) is an incentive for members with critical military specialties who agree to continue to serve. It can pay up to $90,000 for a three-year commitment.

There are also a variety of pay inducements and bonuses, including ones for especially difficult assignments and those with high priority units or that require designated critical skills. There are also incentives for converting to a military occupation to ease a personnel shortage and for continuing service for Naval warfare officers and those in the nuclear power community.

LANGUAGE PROFICIENCY BONUS

If you're proficient in certain foreign languages, you may qualify for the Foreign Language Proficiency Bonus (FLPB). To be eligible, you must have at least two skills—listening, reading, or speaking—in an Immediate or Emerging Language, such as Arabic, Hindi, Swahili, or Vietnamese.

You can see the full list of eligible languages on the DoD's Strategic Language List (DoD SLL) at https://dlnseo.org/content/flpb.

The bonus can be up to $500 a month, depending on the language and your proficiency score, which must be recertified annually. If you're certified in multiple qualifying languages, your total FLPB can be up to $1,000 a month.

The FLPB may also apply to Enduring languages shown on the Strategic Language List. That may occur if your branch Secretary determines that language-proficient personnel are needed to accomplish DoD-specific missions or to ensure such personnel are available should the need arise. However, the Secretary may decide not to pay the FLPB for an Enduring language if there is an oversupply of members with that proficiency.

CAREER CONTINUATION PAY

The DoD offers a bonus, officially known as career continuation pay, to everyone enrolled in the BRS who stays in the military for at least eight years. As a condition of receiving the bonus at some point between your eight and twelfth year of service, you must agree to serve a minimum of three additional years.

If you're on active duty, the Secretary of your branch sets the timing of your bonus and determines the amount, which is calculated by multiplying your base pay by a minimum of 2.5 and a maximum of 13. Typically, members with the skills the Secretary is most interested in retaining tend to be offered the higher amounts.

INCENTIVE CHECKLIST
You can check the full list of special and incentive pays, how much you can earn, and how you qualify at https://militarypay.defense.gov/Pay/Special-and-Incentive-Pays/Index/

Hardship and Hazard Pay

The challenges of hardship and hazardous duty are rewarded with extra pay.

At some point you may be deployed to a combat zone or designated location where you perform duties or undertake missions that put you at special risk or pose hardships not ordinarily encountered at your permanent duty station. To recognize these hazards and hardships, your branch authorizes special pay and incentives.

HARDSHIP DUTY PAY

If your assignment is particularly arduous or stressful, you may be eligible for **Hardship Duty Pay (HDP)**. The hardship may recognize your location, mission, or extensive time away from your permanent duty station. In most cases, the Secretary of your service branch determines eligibility for hardship duty.

The chart on this page shows the three categories of HDP you may receive and under what conditions.

By statute, the maximum you can receive for HDP-L, HDP-M, and HDP-T in any one month is $1,500.

Special rules apply to short absences, temporary duty, flight duty, hospitalization, and service in more than one designated area.

HDP TYPE	ELIGIBILITY AND AMOUNT
HDP-L (Location)	• Applies to duty in locations with living conditions substantially below those found within the continental United States (CONUS) • To qualify, you must be permanently assigned, serving in temporary additional duty or temporary duty, be deployed, or have attached status for over 30 consecutive dates in a designated location • Monthly amount is limited to $100 maximum if concurrently receiving $225 per month for IDP or HFP
HDP-M (Mission)	• Applies to permanent or temporary assignment under especially arduous conditions and for required duties outside of normal military operations • Eligibility criteria established by the Assistant Secretary of Defense for Manpower and Reserve Affairs and may include missions involving missing personnel or their identification • $150 for each month or partial month
HDP-T (Excessive Time)	• Applies to extended or excessive time outside of your permanent duty station • Eligibility based on service-specific needs, including retention, quality of life, family separation, and other factors causing dissatisfaction • Up to $500 per month, based on number of days that HDP-T applies

HOSTILE FIRE, IMMINENT DANGER

If you are deployed to a combat zone or other designated area and assigned to duty where there is danger from hostile fire or mine explosion, or death resulting from hostile action, you may be eligible for **Hostile Fire Pay (HFP)** for each month or partial month you serve.

If you are serving in an area listed in Figure 10-1 of the DoD Financial Management Regulation, you may be entitled to **Imminent Danger Pay (IDP)**.

HFP and IDP also apply if you are captured or missing, hospitalized as a result of hostile action, or entitled to receive either because you are missing from your duty location for a full calendar month.

Both HFP and IDP payments are made on a monthly basis until you are redeployed from the zone. You cannot receive both of these entitlements in the same month.

ON THE HOME FRONT
The ways deployment impacts your financial life at home depends to a significant extent on whether you're single or have dependents. Without dependents, the issues are ensuring that continuing bills are paid and reducing costs. With dependents, the primary concern is maintaining a financially and emotionally stable home life in your absence—something that requires collaboration and preplanning.

HDIP PAY OR INCENTIVE	PAYMENT AMOUNT
Hostile Fire Pay (HFP)	• $225 for each month or partial month
Imminent Danger Pay (IDP)	• $7.50 a day, up to $225 per month
Hazardous Duty Incentive Pay (HDIP)	• Non-Air Crewmembers: $150 per month or $225 per month for HALO jumps and diving • Air Crewmembers: Flight pay from $150 to $250 per month, depending on pay grade

HAZARDOUS DUTY INCENTIVE PAY

If you perform certain tasks considered to be especially dangerous, you may be entitled to Hazardous Duty Incentive Pay (HDIP).

Non-Air Crewmembers. Hazardous duty includes demolition of explosives, handling toxic fuels and pesticides, chemical munitions duty, flying and flight deck duty, pressure chamber duty, thermal duty, and experimental stress duty, among others. You also receive HDIP for parachute jumping with additional pay for HALO (High Altitude Low Opening) jumps and for diving.

You are eligible to receive up to two types of hazardous duty pay during the same period provided your unit's mission involves the performance of these duties.

Air Crewmembers. If you perform flight duties as part of operational requirements, you are eligible for HDIP, also known as flight pay.

For a full list of hazardous duties see https://militarypay.defense.gov/Pay/Special-and-Incentive-Pays/Index/

Submarine Duty Incentive Pay (SUBPAY). You receive SUBPAY if you're a qualified sailor with the requisite number of hours and are:

• Attached to a submarine crew
• Serving on an operational submersible (including undersea exploration and research vehicles)
• Undergoing training for nuclear or advanced design submarine
• Undergoing rehabilitation after serving on a nuclear-powered submarine

SUBPAY ranges from $75 to $835 per month, depending on pay grade and years of service. You can find duty time requirements and pay tables at www.military.com/benefits/military-pay/special-pay/submarine-duty-incentive-pay.html

The Navy and the Air Force provide special pay for active flight duty through the Career Enlisted Flyer Incentive Pay (CEFIP) and substantial bonuses through the Navy's Aviator Career Continuation Pay (ACC) and the Air Force's Aviation Continuation Pay (ACP) programs. The amounts depend on the service's needs and the length of time the pilot agrees to serve. Navy and Air Force Reserve pilots may be eligible for CEFIP at one-third the rate for active duty members.

Special Benefits

Earning more in a combat zone is just the beginning of what deployment means for you.

If you serve in a designated combat area and receive Hostile Fire Pay (HFP) or Imminent Danger Pay (IDP), you're entitled to a **Combat Zone Tax Exclusion (CZTE)**. This tax exclusion applies to commissioned officers, who can exclude part, and enlisted personnel, who can exclude all, of their pay, bonuses, and incentive pay for this period.

If you reenlist in a combat zone, the incentive pay you receive is also tax-exempt. So is annual leave you accrue during deployment, at the same rate of 2.5 days per month. But you must use that leave within three years, and before other leave you already have.

BUILDING RETIREMENT SAVINGS

When you're deployed to a combat zone, not only are your earnings tax-exempt, but the annual cap on contributions to a defined contribution retirement plan that normally applies is waived if you contribute to a tax-deferred account. This gives you an extraordinary opportunity to increase your contribution to your TSP or civilian account in the years you're eligible.

If you're part of the BRS and aren't already contributing 5% of your pay to qualify for the full DoD match, consider adding enough to meet that threshold. Another benefit is that the amount you contribute from this pay remains tax-exempt even when you withdraw it from your account any time after you turn 59½. That will increase the amount of retirement income you'll have to spend.

If you make your combat zone contribution to a traditional tax-deferred TSP account, the earnings portion of your withdrawal will be taxed. But you can avoid the tax on earnings by contributing your tax-exempt pay to a TSP Roth account up to the annual cap. Then anything you withdraw from the account in the future will be nontaxable, provided you're at least 59½ and the account has been open at least five years.

You can also deposit tax-free income in a Roth IRA in addition to amounts you add to your TSP account. Contributions and earnings are always nontaxable, including at withdrawal. Another benefit of a Roth IRA is that there are no mandatory withdrawals, allowing the account balance to continue to compound.

SAVINGS DEPOSIT PROGRAM

If you are serving in a designated combat zone, the Savings Deposit Program (SDP) offers a major financial benefit you don't want to overlook. Money deposited in an SDP account pays an impressive 10% interest annually on deposits of up to $10,000. The deposits are federally insured, and the $10,000 cap applies separately to each deployment.

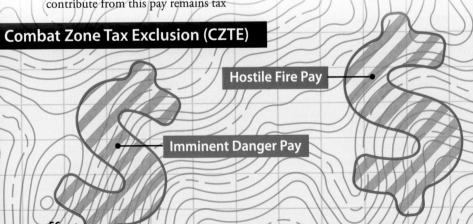

Combat Zone Tax Exclusion (CZTE)

Hostile Fire Pay

Imminent Danger Pay

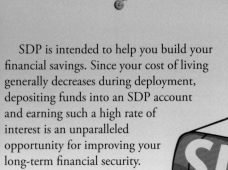

SDP is intended to help you build your financial savings. Since your cost of living generally decreases during deployment, depositing funds into an SDP account and earning such a high rate of interest is an unparalleled opportunity for improving your long-term financial security.

To be eligible for the SDP, you must be deployed in a designated combat zone for at least 30 consecutive days, or one day in three consecutive months, and be receiving Hostile Fire Pay or one of the following: Hardship Duty Pay, Imminent Danger Pay, Assignment Incentive Pay, or Hazardous Duty Pay.

account balance will continue to earn 10% interest for 90 days after you've returned to your permanent duty station. After 120 days, the account will be closed, and your account funds will be transferred electronically to the direct deposit account on record or to another account that you designate. You can also access your funds earlier through your myPay account, but the longer you can let your money collect the 10% interest, the more you'll earn.

MANAGING YOUR SDP ACCOUNT

A military finance officer in your operating theatre can help you set up your SDP account. You can make deposits at the local pay office as cash or a check, or through payroll allotments, which may vary as your financial situation changes.

You can withdraw money from your SDP account through myPay. Once your account exceeds $10,000, you can withdraw any funds over that amount on a quarterly basis, since they won't be eligible to earn 10% interest. You can also make emergency withdrawals with the approval of your commanding officer.

You cannot close the account until you have left the combat zone, and the

TAX ALERT

Unlike the CZTE-qualified money you earn while you're in a combat zone, the earnings in your SDP account are taxable. Since no federal or state taxes will have been withheld, you'll need to be prepared to pay tax on the full amount of these earnings when you file your return for the year. That's true whether or not you have withdrawn the earnings or they continue to compound.

ADVICE? IT'S ESSENTIAL

If you don't customarily use a tax adviser experienced in military policy to prepare your income tax returns, it may be smart to do so when you have substantial incentive pay, a large bonus, or CZTE income. He or she should be able to advise you on how to take best advantage of provisions of the tax code. You can find free or low-cost advice through Military OneSource at www. militaryonesource.mil/financial-legal/ tax-resource-center/tax-services-benefits. One caution: seek the advice before you make investment decisions, since some are difficult or expensive to undo.

IT IS GOOD *AND* TRUE

To illustrate the true value of the SDP account and the guaranteed 10% interest it pays consider the following: most civilian savings accounts may pay less than 1% interest, with CDs paying somewhere between 2% and 2.5% interest. Since there's no risk of losing money, opening a SDP account is an opportunity you don't want to miss.

Allowances

The DoD compensates you for the impact that military life has on you and your family.

In addition to your pay, you may be entitled to allowances for food, housing, and being separated from your family. Allowances are designed to standardize your living costs, regardless of your duty location. They're also intended to compensate you for certain expenses, such as relocation, that you normally incur in the course of your military career.

In most cases, allowances are nontaxable, so nothing is deducted from the benefit to prepay taxes, making the full amount available to you. The exception is the cost of living allowance (COLA) you may receive if you're stationed in the continental United States (CONUS).

BAS

The Basic Allowance for Subsistence (BAS) is designed to help cover what you pay for meals, including those provided by the military. The fixed amount you're granted each month, which is higher for enlisted personnel than for officers, is adjusted each year based on increases in the cost of food as measured by the United States Department of Agriculture (USDA) food cost index.

Your BAS is the same whether you're single or married and isn't intended to pay the cost of providing food for your dependents.

BAH

If you are stationed in CONUS and the military is not providing your living quarters, you'll receive a Basic Allowance for Housing (BAH). The allowance is intended to offset what you'll need to spend for private housing on base or in the civilian market. That figure is calculated using the median rental cost by ZIP code, and includes money for utility bills based on average consumption for similar homes.

The total amount of your BAH is determined by several factors in addition to duty location, including your pay grade, whether or not you have dependents, and the current BAH rate, which is reset annually.

BAH also offers rate protection. If the current BAH rate for your location is lower this year than last, you still receive at least the same BAH as you did the previous year. If the BAH rate goes up, you'll receive the higher BAH rate.

The BAH is based only on local rental properties, and not on homeowners' costs, such as mortgages and property taxes. The allowance is not intended to cover all housing costs, so you may have to pay some expenses out-of-pocket.

MARRIED MILITARY COUPLES

If two service members are married to each other, both members qualify for a BAH. If they don't have children, they each receive the BAH that would apply if they were single. If they have children, the partner with the higher rank qualifies for the BAH with dependents rate and the other partner qualifies for the BAH without dependents rate.

Specific BAH rules apply if the couple is not stationed together, if there are dependents at one or both locations, if one partner lives in military housing and the other doesn't, or if the couple lives in military housing.

OHA

If you are stationed outside CONUS, including in US territories and possessions, and military housing isn't provided, you're eligible for the Overseas Housing Allowance (OHA). The OHA is determined by:

- The maximum rental allowance for the particular region
- The utility or recurring maintenance allowance
- The Move-In Housing Allowance (MIHA)

In some cases your OHA may be reduced to reflect your actual rental payments.

WHERE TO LEARN MORE

To find out more about BAH, OHA, and COLAs, and see the rates that apply to your duty location, visit https://www.defensetravel.dod.mil/site/allowances.cfm.

COLA

The Cost of Living Allowance (COLA) compensates you for non-housing costs that you incur while serving in uniform in parts of CONUS where those costs are at least 8% above the national average. If those costs are at least 10% above the national average, your COLA is larger.

Transportation, goods and services, and sales taxes are among the costs that the COLA is designed to cover. Unlike other allowances, however, the CONUS COLA is taxable income.

If you are stationed outside the United States, you are normally eligible for an Overseas COLA, which is nontaxable. This allowance is intended to equalize the purchasing power you would have at a CONUS location by offsetting the higher prices of non-housing goods and services when serving abroad.

FSA

If military duty, such as operational or training requirements, takes you away from dependent family members for more than 30 consecutive days, and you incur additional living costs as a result, you may be eligible for the Family Separation Allowance (FSA).

To qualify, you must submit a certified Form DD1561. If you are approved, the FSA will pay you $250 a month during the period of separation.

The FSA normally applies if:

- Your dependents do not live in the vicinity of your permanent duty station, and the DoD is not paying their transportation expenses.
- You have chosen an unaccompanied tour of duty because your dependent cannot accompany you due to a certified medical reason. This applies even if the DoD would pay dependent transportation expenses.
- You are on duty aboard a ship that is away from the homeport continuously for more than 30 days.
- You are on temporary duty or temporary additional duty away from your permanent station continuously for more than 30 days.

Service Related Benefits

You're entitled to much more than just your pay when you're part of the military.

To supplement your regular income, the DoD, the VA, and the service branches provide a range of valuable benefits while you're on active duty, in the Reserve component, or a veteran.

Some, including free or low-cost access to health and life insurance, can last through your military career and beyond. This insurance protects you and your dependents against potentially devastating financial consequences of illness, accidents, and early death.

A modernized retirement plan, the **Blended Retirement System (BRS)**, combines the opportunity for lifetime retired pay with a retirement savings plan that addresses the long-term needs of all service members, whether or not you make the military your career.

You may want to take advantage of other popular benefits, including

the **Post-9/11 GI Bill**, which helps you cover the costs of advancing your education and the VA home loan program, which makes it easier and more affordable to buy a home.

THE HEART ACT

In 2008, Congress passed the **Heroes Earnings Assistance and Relief Tax Act—the HEART Act—**to benefit service members who are called to active duty from civilian employment but cannot return to their jobs because they died or were disabled after having served for more than 30 days. The Act extends the provisions of the **Uniformed Services Employment and Reemployment Rights Act (USERRA),** which gives service members the right to return to their civilian employment when their service ends. It also protects them from discrimination in hiring, promotion, and retention on the

DEPLOYMENT PROTECTION

The Servicemembers Civil Relief Act (SCRA) provides financial protections to deployed active duty members and members of the Reserves and National Guard called to active duty for 30 days or more.

Some of the most important SCRA provisions allow you to:

- Cap the interest rate on loans, including mortgage loans, and credit cards *you had before entering the military* at 6% a year if your service materially affects your ability to repay

- Terminate real estate or automobile leases or phone service under specific conditions. A typical example is receiving a new permanent change of station

(PCS) or deployment order of 90+ days that forces you to leave before a real estate lease ends

- Postpone a court or administrative hearing

- Vote in your home state

In addition, a court order is required before foreclosure on a property you bought before being called to active duty. This requirement also applies to eviction from a rental property where rent doesn't exceed the annual limit. Your life insurance can't be ended and you can't be charged higher premiums.

You should check with your legal assistance office to determine if you qualify for these protections and how to obtain them.

basis of their having been a member of the uniformed services.

The specific benefits of the HEART Act depend on the terms of the civilian employer's qualified retirement plan. They may include compensation the employee would have received while on active duty, faster vesting in the plan, and additional life insurance benefits, among others. Any paid compensation must be classified as wages rather than self-employment income so the earnings can be contributed to the retirement plan.

Another provision of the Act allows service members on active duty for more than 180 days to withdraw from their employer-sponsored retirement plan without owing the 10% tax penalty that would otherwise apply. Service members have two years from the day after the end of active duty to re-contribute some or all of the withdrawal to an IRA where it can resume growing tax-deferred.

OTHER BENEFITS

You'll also want to check out other benefits.

You and your family may use space-available military flights to travel domestically and abroad at little or no cost. While they're unpredictable, they're ideal if your timing is flexible. Alternately, if you use your DoD ID as your known traveller number, you qualify for TSA PreCheck on commercial flights.

ID.me (www.id.me) and similar websites provide links to a wide range of military discounts. ID.me simplifies how service members prove their identity online, making it easier to qualify for savings.

Additionally, a number of retail stores, rental agencies, and airlines offer discounts of between 5% and 25% off regular prices to service members, veterans, and sometimes their spouses and other dependents. It always pays to ask.

MILITARY AID SOCIETIES

Four military aid societies provide free financial planning and counseling services and offer education scholarships to service members and their families.

The societies also offer grants for necessary but expensive equipment, such as children's car seats, and make interest free loans to cover emergency situations, including food, rent, utilities, and travel. Service members can use these loans as a more economical alternative to pay day loans and overextended credit cards. If the loan would cause undue financial hardship, it may be turned into a grant, which wouldn't have to be repaid, or a combination of a grant and a loan.

Each society provides somewhat different services but they share the common goal of helping their members, providing financial assistance when the alternative might be a high-cost payday loan or overextending credit card use.

If you are away from your home base but near another military installation, military aid societies have reciprocal agreements that allow you to receive assistance through any agency, regardless of your military service branch or affiliation. If you aren't near a military installation, you may contact the American Red Cross for assistance at 877-272-7337. **You can find contact information for your branch in the Resources pages.**

Health Insurance

Insurance helps pay the costs of routine healthcare, serious illnesses, and accidents that may occur.

You might not spend much time thinking about health insurance. That's hardly surprising when you're young and healthy. Your visits to doctors or hospitals are probably few and far between. But you do need health insurance to protect against the risks of serious illnesses and major accidents that may require extended and expensive care.

Fortunately, your health insurance is provided automatically at no cost as a benefit of being employed by the DoD.

TRICARE

As a service member on active duty, you must enroll in **TRICARE Prime,** a health insurance plan that's available through the Military Health System. It's a managed care plan with a network of doctors, specialists, and other professionals to provide the services you need.

With TRICARE, there are actually two CONUS regional networks—East and West—that supplement the care provided directly by the military. Each of the networks is aligned with military hospitals, major civilian medical centers, and a number of regional hospitals.

As part of TRICARE, you'll have a **primary care manager (PCM)**—either a military or network doctor—who provides most of your care. He or she keeps your health records, files your claims, and, when necessary, refers you to specialists within the TRICARE network for their expertise in specific areas. If you don't have a PCM referral, consultations with specialists or other medical providers aren't covered by the plan.

Dental care is available from military dental clinics. But if you need to see a civilian dentist, the TRICARE Active Duty Dental Program is available in the United States and its territories.

There's no charge for medical or dental TRICARE coverage and no out-of-pocket costs while you're on active duty. That typically represents a savings of many thousands of dollars over civilian plans. To learn more about how this insurance works, check www.tricare.mil, the website of the Defense Health Agency (DHA).

TYPES OF INSURANCE

For most people younger than 65, heath insurance in the United States is available in three types of plans: managed care, point-of-service, and high deductible.

Managed care plans, which include both participating provider organizations (PPOs) and health maintenance organizations (HMOs), are networks of hospitals, doctors, and other health professionals who agree to accept the fees that the plan provider, usually an insurance company, will pay for specific services.

In addition to a monthly **premium**, there's an annual **deductible**, which you must pay out-of-pocket. Once you've paid the full deductible, the insurer will begin to pay for your care.

MANAGED CARE PLANS

- Monthly Premium
- Annual Deductible
- Copayments

INSURING YOUR FAMILY
You can get health insurance for your dependents at a much lower cost than you'd pay for civilian coverage. See Page 92.

PREGNANCY COVERAGE

If you're expecting a baby while you're on active duty, TRICARE provides all your medically necessary care. That includes:

- Regular prenatal visits to your doctor during pregnancy

- Tests and ultrasounds to check the baby's health and development

- Labor and delivery

- Check-ups following the birth, or what's called post-partum care

- Treatment for complications that may occur at any stage of your pregnancy

Your PCM or the doctor or midwife to whom you're referred will be able to answer your questions. You can also check the maternity section of the TRICARE website at https://tricare.mil/CoveredServices/IsItCovered/MaternityCare.

WHAT'S A FORMULARY?

A formulary is a list of drugs available through your insurance plan. In the case of TRICARE, it's the Basic Core Formulary.

PRESCRIPTIONS

Your TRICARE health insurance also provides **prescription drug coverage**. To get your medications, you need a written or electronically transmitted prescription from your healthcare provider plus a valid uniformed services identification card.

Prescriptions you fill at a military pharmacy, a network pharmacy, or through the system's home delivery program are free while you are on active duty. If you use a non-network pharmacy, which you should consider only if it can't be avoided, you'll have to pay full price for the drugs and file a claim to be reimbursed. You may not get the full amount.

You may also be charged a small **copayment**, such as $25, for each doctor's visit, with higher amounts to see a specialist. The deductible and copayments don't apply, though, when you receive preventative services, such as vaccinations, or what are described as essential benefits.

Using a doctor or hospital outside the network means either that your care may not be covered or that you'll have to pay a potentially large percentage of the cost.

Point-of-service (POS) plans allow you to go to any provider you choose. The provider may submit the bills to your insurance company or you may have to submit them yourself. In addition to the monthly premium, there's an annual deductible, which you pay out-of-pocket, before the insurer begins to pay a percentage of the cost—often 80%—it has determined is reasonable for each service. You pay the balance, or what's called **coinsurance** or **cost share**.

If the health provider charges more than the insurer considers allowable or provides a service the insurer doesn't cover, you're responsible for amounts not paid.

High deductible health plans (HDHPs) are managed care plans with lower premiums and substantially higher deductibles than standard plans. Higher deductibles mean more out-of-pocket costs before the insurer begins to pay. But HDHPs do limit your annual costs if you spend up to the cap the federal government sets. You can find the out-of-pocket caps at www.healthcare.gov/glossary/high-deductible-health-plan/.

If you have an HDHP, you're eligible to open a tax-free **health savings account (HSA)** to help you accumulate money to cover healthcare costs.

POINT-OF-SERVICE

- Monthly Premium
- Annual Deductible
- Coinsurance

HIGH DEDUCTIBLE

- Monthly Premium
- Higher Annual Deductible
- Eligible for HSA

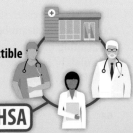

Life Insurance

Life insurance is an essential part of your financial plan.

If anyone depends on you for financial support, you need life insurance to fill the income gap that would be created by your death. Of course dying is something nobody wants to think about, especially when you're young, healthy, and actively pursuing your military career. But it's essential to be prepared for this possibility.

Life insurance can cover immediate bills, pay off debts, and help your survivors meet the long-term goals you and they shared.

COMMERCIAL LIFE INSURANCE

There are two basic types of life insurance, **term** and **permanent**, or **whole-life**. Each has several varieties. Term insurance covers you for a specific period of time, often between five and 20 years, and may be renewable when the term ends. Permanent insurance covers you for your lifetime, or at least until you turn 100 or 120.

When you buy life insurance, you sign a contract, called a **policy**, with an insurance company. If you own the policy, you're the policyholder and you're also usually the insured. To keep your coverage **in force**, or active, you must pay **premiums**, or what the insurance costs, on schedule. If you don't pay, the policy **lapses** and provides no benefits.

Every policy has a **face value**, sometimes called the **death benefit**, which is the amount the **beneficiary** or beneficiaries you name in the policy receive at your death. In most cases, there's no income tax due on the death benefit that's paid.

Naming the right beneficiary is essential. In most cases, if you're married, it should be your spouse. And if you

weren't married when you bought your policy but you are now, one of the first things you should do is update the policy's beneficiary designation.

If you're not married, you can name anyone you like. Remember, though, that if you name a minor, you

COMMERCIAL INSURANCE POLICY

Death Benefit

TERM	OR	PERMANENT
Premiums go up with renewal		Fixed or Flexible Premiums

BENEFICIARY

should also name a guardian to manage the money. That responsibility usually falls to the child's surviving parent, but you may name someone else if you wish.

INSURANCE AS A BENEFIT

Servicemembers' Group Life Insurance (SGLI), which is offered through the VA, is **level term life insurance** available to members of the armed forces. Level term means that your premium remains the same each time you renew—though with SGLI you don't actually have to renew, you simply continue to participate.

SGLI is also very low cost, especially when compared to commercial civilian policies. Premiums are $0.06 for each $1,000 of coverage, a cost that grows even more reasonable as you advance in your career. By contrast, commercial term insurance typically gets more expensive with each renewal. After age 40, increases of 10% to 15% a year are fairly typical. As a rule, too, life insurance is more expensive for men than for women, which is not the case with SGLI.

The current maximum face value of a SGLI policy is $400,000, with a premium of $25 a month, or $300 a year. That includes $1 a month for **traumatic injury protection (TSGLI)**, which provides up to $100,000 coverage in case you're seriously injured while on active duty.

SGLI PROTECTED

You're automatically insured with SGLI if you're on active duty, a cadet or mid-

SGLI

LEVEL TERM
Premiums never go up

shipman at a US service academy, or a member of the Reserve Officers Training Corps (ROTC). You're also insured if you're in the Ready Reserve or National Guard and scheduled to perform at least 12 periods of inactive training a year, or a mobilization volunteer of the Individual Ready Reserve (IRR).

You're automatically issued the maximum $400,000 coverage, but you can decline the insurance or choose a smaller face value. It's available in $50,000 increments.

You identify your beneficiary or beneficiaries through the SGLI Online Enrollment System (SOES). You can change that designation or make any other adjustments to your coverage through that system as well.

If you change the face value, perhaps as you take on additional financial obligations or you have children, you'll want to be sure that the new SGLI premium

is reflected in your LES statement. It appears in Field 11 along with other deductions from your pay.

OTHER DEATH BENEFITS

In addition to SGLI, your beneficiary or beneficiaries are entitled to tax-free compensation, known as a **Death Gratuity**, of $100,000 from the DoD if you should die while on active duty or in Reserve component training.

The gratuity is also paid if you die within 120 days of release or discharge from active duty provided the VA determines your death was the result of a service-related illness or injury.

The VA provides eligible surviving spouses with other death benefits, too, including Dependency and Indemnity Compensation (DIC) if you die on active duty or duty training and the Survivors' and Dependents' Educational Assistance Program (DEA).

BUY WISELY

Before you buy additional life insurance, you'll want to evaluate your choices with a financial counselor at your Military and Family Support Center or Military OneSource. For example, you never want to buy a policy with a war-risk clause. The policy will not pay the death benefit if you're killed in combat.

BENEFICIARIES

You can go to www.benefits.va.gov to find more detailed information about SGLI and download the handbook *VA Life Insurance Programs for Veterans and Servicemembers.*

INSURING YOUR FAMILY
If you're interested in life insurance for your spouse or want to learn about types of permanent insurance, check page 88.

Post-9/11 GI Bill

Your access to higher education gets better and better.

The Post-9/11 GI Bill pays tuition and fees for up to 36 months—or the equivalent of four academic years—when you enroll for post-secondary education in:

POST ☆ 9/11 GI BILL

- A degree-granting undergraduate or graduate program at an accredited college or university, or what the VA refers to as Institutions of Higher Learning (IHLs)

- Accredited private or state-approved technical, vocational, or training programs

- Certification or licensing programs

- Flight training

- Apprenticeships

A STEM BENEFIT

An additional nine months of benefits, up to $30,000, may be available if you're pursuing a degree in a science, technology, engineering, and math (STEM) program that requires more than the standard 128 semester credit hours or 192 quarter credit hours to complete. You apply separately for this extended benefit near the end of your first 36 months of study.

% OF MAXIMUM BENEFIT PAYABLE	LENGTH OF SERVICE
100%	At least 36 months
100%	At least 30 continuous days on active duty and discharged for service-related disability or having received a Purple Heart
90%	At least 30 months, but less than 36 months
80%	At least 24 months but less than 30 months
70%	At least 18 months but less than 24 months
60%	At least 6 months but less than 18 months (effective August 2020)
50%	At least 90 days but less than 6 months (effective August 2020)

WHO QUALIFIES?

To qualify for the full benefit, you must serve at least 36 months on active duty, excluding training or initial commitment, after 9/11/2001. You're also fully qualified if you are discharged because of a service-related disability or have been awarded the Purple Heart.

Once you've qualified, your right to this education benefit never expires. That's a change from the past, when you had a 15-year window after your last discharge or release from service to use it or lose it. This time limit still applies if you left the service before January 1, 2013.

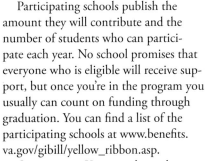

TUITION PAYMENTS

Tuition and fee payments are made directly to the school in which you enroll. If you qualify for the maximum benefit, the GI Bill covers the full cost of in-state tuition and fees at a public college or university.

To be approved to receive payments under the GI Bill, public institutions are required to charge in-state tuition and fees if you are accepted by the school and qualified to use the program's benefits regardless of your legal residence, which could be in another state. You must remain continuously enrolled at the same school, but you don't lose eligibility if you leave the state for breaks between courses, semesters, or terms.

However, veterans enrolling for the first time or transferring credits must do so within three years of discharge from a period of active duty lasting at least 90 days to qualify for in-state tuition.

Alternatively, the GI Bill pays a fixed amount, adjusted each year, toward the cost of tuition and fees at a private US college or university or a qualifying institution located outside the United States. That amount is equal to the maximum being paid to public colleges in the year.

Up to the same amount is available for non-degree granting programs, though specific programs, including flight school and correspondence courses, are eligible for a smaller dollar amount.

YELLOW RIBBON PROGRAM

The Yellow Ribbon program, created at the same time as the Post-9/11 GI Bill, allows approved colleges and universities to cover some or all the tuition and fees that the GI Bill doesn't cover. In addition, the VA matches the amount the institution provides. For example, if a college provides $10,000, the VA will add $10,000. That $20,000 is in addition to the standard GI Bill benefit.

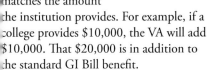

Participating schools publish the amount they will contribute and the number of students who can participate each year. No school promises that everyone who is eligible will receive support, but once you're in the program you usually can count on funding through graduation. You can find a list of the participating schools at www.benefits.va.gov/gibill/yellow_ribbon.asp.

One caution: You must be at the 100% benefit level to take advantage of the Yellow Ribbon program and no longer on active duty. But an eligible dependent child to whom you transferred your benefit may qualify.

HOUSING AND BOOKS

You may be eligible for a **monthly housing allowance (MHA)** when you take advantage of the GI Bill, provided you're not on active duty. This amount, which is paid directly to you, is based on the Basic Allowance for Housing (BAH) for an E-5 with dependents and the ZIP code for the campus where you take the majority of your classes. Rates change each year on August 1 and vary from location to location. If you're enrolled in an online or distance learning program, though, the MHA is a smaller fixed amount.

You'll also receive an annual stipend of up to $1,000 to pay for books and supplies. And, if a national entrance exam, such as the SAT, ACT, GMAT, or LSAT, is required for your program, the cost of the fee is generally reimbursed. So is the cost of meeting licensing or certification requirements.

READY TO APPLY?

To apply for Post-9/11 GI Bill benefits, you complete VA Form 22-1990, "Application for VA Education Benefits," at www.benefits.va.gov/gibill/apply.asp or call 888-442-4551.

SHARING GI BILL BENEFITS
If you want to learn more about how you can transfer your Post-9/11 GI Bill benefit to your spouse or children, check pages 104-105.

Education Benefits

You can pursue your education while you're on active duty.

If advancing your education is important to you, you can pursue this goal while you're on active duty by enrolling in off-duty classroom, independent study, or remote learning courses at accredited institutions.

Military installations have local education centers with trained staff to help you navigate the range of available programs, evaluate their quality, and optimize the benefits for which you're eligible.

TUITION ASSISTANCE

The cost of **tuition**, which is the amount an educational institution charges you to enroll in one or more of its courses, could slow down or even derail your quest for more education. That doesn't have to happen, though, thanks to the **Tuition Assistance (TA) educational financial aid programs** sponsored by the individual service branches.

TA pays $250 per semester hour, $166.67 per quarter hour, or $16.67 per clock hour, up to a cap of $4,500 in a fiscal year, for eligible active duty service members who enroll in off-duty courses or programs. That's generally enough to cover courses offered on military installations, though it's less than the average credit cost at off-base schools.

There are conditions, though. Enlisted personnel must be on active duty for the full period during which the course meets. Officers must agree to remain on active duty at least two years after the course ends, though those years run concurrently with an existing obligation rather than extending it. If they resign without completing their obligation, they must repay, on a pro-rated basis, TA funds paid on their behalf during their last two years of active duty.

WHAT'S COVERED?

You can use tuition assistance to pursue:

- A high school diploma
- A vocational or technical certificate
- An undergraduate degree (associate's or bachelor's)
- A master's degree

What you can't do is study for a lower or lateral degree. For example, if you have a bachelor's degree, you can pursue a master's degree, but not another bachelor's or associate's degree.

Books and other required materials aren't covered, and there's no housing allowance.

In most cases, you're encouraged to take no more than one or two courses each semester. An over-ambitious schedule could make it hard, or perhaps impossible, to complete the coursework successfully. If you fail a course or drop out, you must repay amounts paid on your behalf.

THINGS TO KEEP IN MIND

To make the most of advancing your education, there are some things to keep in mind.

If TA covers only part of your tuition, and you're qualified for Post-9/11 GI Bill benefits, you can use them to make up the difference. But plan ahead. Any benefits you use to pay tuition while you're on active duty won't be available after you separate from service. You can find more information at www.benefits.va.gov/gibill/tuition_assistance.asp.

Online courses, while less expensive, provide little or no interaction with the instructor or other students. Staying

Tuition help
TA + Post-9/11 GI Bill

ADVANCED DEGREE PROGRAMS

Many officer positions require a graduate degree as a prerequisite for a specific assignment or to enable candidates to assume responsibility for essential research, strategic planning, and other critical tasks.

The Army's Advanced Civil Schooling (ACS) program identifies officers for these positions and fully funds their full-time study at a participating civilian university. ACS is available to Regular Army officers with fewer than 17 years of service. By taking advantage of this opportunity to acquire an advanced degree, officers agree to the follow-on assignment, typically a two to three year tour.

The Naval Postgraduate School (NPS) offers fully funded programs in a variety of disciplines at the master's and doctoral levels to qualified Navy and Marine officers. NPS has four primary graduate schools: Business and Public Policy, Engineering and Applied Sciences,

Operational and Information Sciences, and International Studies. The Navy also funds graduate work for qualified officers at civilian institutions.

The Air Force Institute of Technology has three continuing education schools—Civil Engineer, Strategic Force Studies, Systems and Logistics—and a Graduate School of Engineering and Management. There is also a Civilian Institution Program for officers enrolled in civilian universities, research centers, hospitals, and industrial organizations.

In addition, all branches fully support candidates for medical, dental, and legal degrees, with the understanding that the support carries a seven-year service obligation.

focused and up-to-date with the material requires significant self-discipline and self-direction.

You'll want to be sure that course credits you accumulate using TA will be accepted by institutions to which you may transfer to complete your degree. In fact, you'll want to research any school you're considering for its accreditation, veteran graduation rates, typical employment outcomes, and total cost.

HOW TO APPLY

While all TA programs provide the same core benefits, the application process can vary from branch to branch. You can find the information you need by going to the appropriate website.

- Airmen: www.my.af.mil
- Army: www.goarmyed.com/
- Navy, Marines, and Coast Guard: www.navycollege.navy.mil/ tuition-assistance/index.htm

CIVILIAN CREDENTIALING

Military skills can lead directly to civilian careers, but you need the necessary licenses or certifications to show that you meet the standards for a specific job. In some cases, that may require additional education or experience that may be paid for by TA or the GI Bill.

Each branch has a credentialing website to help you understand the steps to take:

Army: www.cool.army.mil/index.htm
Navy: www.cool.navy.mil/usn/
Marines: www.cool.navy.mil/usmc
AirForce: www.afvec.us.mil/afvec/Public/ COOL

You can find additional credentialing information online at www.careeronestop. org/Toolkit or www.dantes.doded.mil.

Your Retirement Plan

Employer-based plans are the basis of long-term financial security.

BRS

Planning for retirement may not seem as critical as making the right career choices and staying on top of your finances. But you may want to rethink that view. Because you're part of the DoD's retirement plan, you'll have income in the future that's likely to prove essential to your long-term financial security.

A TWO-PART PACKAGE

The **Blended Retirement System (BRS)**, which became operational in 2018, has two parts. One is a **pension** that guarantees lifetime income after you retire provided you complete 20 years of active duty or the equivalent of 20 years of service as a member of the Reserve component.

If you receive this retired pay, you're also entitled to an annual **cost of living adjustment (COLA)**. That's a percentage increase in your retired pay, with the amount determined by rising inflation as reflected in the Consumer Price Index (CPI). The COLA helps prevent erosion of your buying power.

The second part of BRS is a **retirement savings plan** through the federal government's Thrift Savings Plan (TSP). If you joined the armed forces after January 1, 2018, you're automatically enrolled in the plan. After 60 days, the DoD begins to contribute 1% of your base pay every pay period to an account that's been opened in your name. At the same time, a percentage of your base pay is deferred to your account as your contribution to your account. The rate that's used initially is 3%, and is known as the **default rate**.

After you've completed two years of service, the DoD begins matching your contributions. For example, if you're contributing 3%, the DoD adds another 3% to your account in addition to the automatic 1% contribution it's already making. That's a total of 7% of base pay going into your account each pay period.

If you increase your contribution to 4%, the DoD adds 3.5% plus the 1% for a total of 8.5%. If you contribute 5%, the DoD adds 4% plus the 1% for a total of 10%. Contributions above the 5% rate aren't matched. But if you contribute less, you'll miss out on the full match.

CHOOSING INVESTMENTS

When you're automatically enrolled, your contributions go into the TSP Lifecycle (L) Fund that's appropriate for your age. But if you prefer, you can redirect the contributions into any combination of the five other funds that TSP offers. You can benefit from talking with a financial counselor at your installation about what may be best for you.

YOUR RETIREMENT INCOME

Your retired pay depends on your **retirement pay base** and the number of years you serve. Retirement pay base is a dollar amount determined by your average base pay during the 36 continuous months it was the highest—usually in the final three years you serve, or **High-3**.

LEGACY SYSTEM   **BEFORE 2018**

EXTENDED OPT-IN PERIOD

Cadets and midshipmen who were enrolled in a service academy by December 31, 2017, and ROTC cadets and midshipmen who signed their contract before that date, are grandfathered into the Legacy system. They may elect to opt into BRS within 30 days of their first day of duty following commissioning or remain in the older plan.

SERVICE RELATED BENEFITS

If you're in the Reserve component and meet your 20-year requirement, you can learn how your retired pay is calculated at https://militarypay.defense.gov/Pay/Retirement/Reserve.aspx.

In contrast, a retirement savings plan like TSP doesn't promise how much retirement income you'll receive. Instead, it depends on how much is contributed to your account, how you invest your contributions, and how long your account is open before you begin to withdraw.

To estimate your income based on your current and future TSP contributions, you can use the BRS retirement calculator at https://militarypay.defense.gov/Calculators/Blended-Retirement-System-Standalone-Calculator/.

UNDERSTANDING VESTING

When you're vested, you have a right to the retired pay you have been promised or to the matching funds an employer adds to your retirement savings account. In the BRS, vesting rules that apply to the two types of accounts differ.

Unlike the 20 years required for a retired pay, your contributions to your TSP account, plus any of the earnings these accounts generate, are always yours, regardless of how long you serve. After two years of service, you're fully vested in the 1% contributions the DoD has been making, plus any earnings on those contributions.

At the two-year mark, you qualify for matching contributions. You're immediately vested in these amounts as they go into your account and in the earnings they produce.

All your vested assets are **portable**, which means you can take them with you to a new job or move them to an IRA when you leave the military. Or you might leave them in your TSP account where they would continue to grow tax-deferred.

LEGACY SYSTEM

Your retired pay is calculated differently if you were on active duty before January 1, 2018, and you remain in the **Legacy High-3 system**.

The larger multiplier means you receive more retired pay than someone in BRS with the same pay base and years of service. For example, if your pay base is $9,000 and you have 25 years of service, your retired pay would be $5,625 a month under the Legacy system but $4,500 a month under the BRS.

However, while you're encouraged to defer income to a TSP account, the DoD doesn't make automatic or matching contributions. If you were to leave the military before completing 20 years of service, your retirement income could be limited.

You can find more information on the TSP funds on page 45.

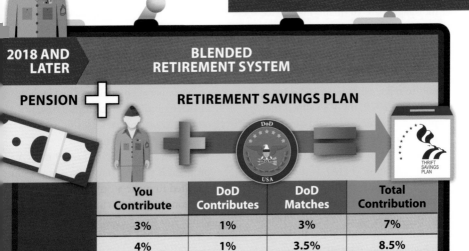

2018 AND LATER — **BLENDED RETIREMENT SYSTEM**

PENSION + **RETIREMENT SAVINGS PLAN**

You Contribute	DoD Contributes	DoD Matches	Total Contribution
3%	1%	3%	7%
4%	1%	3.5%	8.5%
5%	1%	4%	10%

Home Loans

The VA guarantees mortgage loans, reducing the cost of buying a home.

The **VA home loan program** is one of the most popular—and valuable—benefits of military service. The program helps eligible active duty, Reserve, and National Guard service members who have served a minimum of at least 90 consecutive days qualify for low-cost mortgage loans. Veterans and certain surviving spouses are also eligible. Without this program, it would be significantly more difficult, and sometimes impossible, to purchase a home.

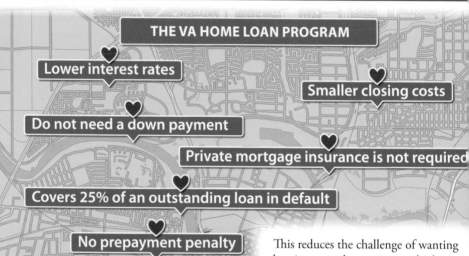

THE VA HOME LOAN PROGRAM

- Lower interest rates
- Smaller closing costs
- Do not need a down payment
- Private mortgage insurance is not required
- Covers 25% of an outstanding loan in default
- No prepayment penalty
- Loans may be assumable

HOW THE GUARANTY WORKS

The VA makes borrowing easier by protecting private lenders who provide mortgage loans to qualifying service members. Specifically, the protection is a guaranty that the VA will cover a minimum of 25% of the outstanding loan balance if the borrower **defaults**, or fails to repay what he or she owes.

Before 2020, the VA capped the price of a home you could buy using its loan guaranty to the maximum amount set annually by the Federal Housing Administration (FHA). If the purchase price was higher, a down payment of 25% of the difference between the purchase price and the FHA limit was usually required. But that cap has been eliminated, and the VA will guarantee 25% of any loan a lender is willing to make.

This reduces the challenge of wanting to buy in areas where prices are higher than the national average.

THE GUARANTY ADVANTAGE

In addition to the guaranty against default, there are several other advantages to the VA home loan program. Most notably, you often qualify for lower interest rates and smaller **closing costs** than you would pay with a conventional loan to buy the same property. Closing costs are the amounts paid to finalize transfer of property between owners. They include, but aren't limited to, transfer taxes, real estate taxes, attorney fees, title search costs, and title insurance.

Another appealing feature of the VA program is that, in most cases, you aren't required to make a cash down payment as a condition of buying. With civilian loans, you may be required to pay up to 20% of the purchase price in cash. But in the VA program, you can borrow 100% o the price plus the customary VA funding ee of 2.35% of the purchase price that applies if you're a first-time borrower.

That funding fee is reduced if you do make a down payment—a smart move for several reasons if you can afford it—and is waived for veterans receiving VA disability pay and for Purple Heart recipients.

Another advantage of a VA guaranty is that you aren't required to have private mortgage insurance (PMI), which increases your monthly payment. And, you can pay off a loan early with a VA guaranty without owing a prepayment penalty.

QUALIFYING FOR A GUARANTY

To qualify for a VA loan guaranty under the home loan program, you need a Certificate of Eligibility (COE). That requires an application and an accompanying statement that provides identifying information about you and your service and is signed or authorized by the adjutant, personnel office, or commander of your unit or higher headquarters.

You can complete the application at www.ebenefits.va.gov or call 877-827-3702. You may apply by mail using VA Form 26-1880. You may also be able to apply through your lender.

You must certify that you'll occupy the property as your primary residence and have evidence to show that:

- You have an acceptable **credit history** and enough income to make your mortgage payments, maintain the property, and cover your living costs. That requirement typically translates to a credit score of 620 or higher and a **debt-to-income ratio (DTI)** of no more than 41%.

- The purchase price of the property isn't more than the value the VA appraiser assigns to it.

While buying a home may be tempting, you'll want to consider the impact on your budget. While you can use BAH to make mortgage payments, the costs of owning are likely to be higher than renting and may be more than your allotment will cover. And since you have to anticipate frequent moves, you have to consider how you'll manage not only the payments but the property when you're not in residence.

REUSING YOUR LOANS

If you pay off one mortgage loan, often because you have sold the property, your right, or entitlement, to a VA loan guaranty is restored and you can use the benefit again to buy another primary residence. You submit VA Form 29-1880 along with evidence from your lender that the previous loan has been paid in full. You may also be eligible to use the guaranty again while you still own a home you purchased previously with a VA loan or to have more than one VA loan at a time.

What's more, once you are eligible for this benefit, you can take advantage of it at any time by obtaining a COE.

REPAYMENT PROBLEMS

The VA loan guarantee doesn't protect you from foreclosure if you fall behind on your loan payments. But you can ask a VA Regional Loan Center counselor for advice by calling 877-827-3702 or click on the "Trouble Making Payments" tab on the VA Home Loans website at www.benefits.va.gov/homeloans/index.asp.

AVOIDING SCAMS

Unscrupulous lenders profit by offering to refinance VA mortgage loans with misleading offers that sound attractive but will actually increase your costs and may even result in your losing your home. These lenders may be extremely aggressive, refusing to take "no" for an answer. So be prepared to hold your ground and report the incident to the VA at 877-827-3702 or the Consumer Financial Protection Bureau at www.consumerfinance.gov or 855-411-2372.

When You're a Couple

It's smart to be ready for the financial challenges married couples and committed partners face.

When you're a couple, you and your partner or spouse are likely to face a period of adjustment when you live together for the first time. One of the major challenges is resolving how to handle your finances compatibly.

While you've probably made lots of plans, from whether or when to get married to what your career goals should be, you may not have talked much about the part that money will play in your new life together.

You could start the conversation by exploring topics like these:

- Do you agree on what your major financial goals should be, how much they will cost, and the steps you should take to reach them?
- Do you know how much debt or other financial obligations, if any, each of you brings to the relationship and how they will be paid?
- Do you agree on financial priorities? Is building an emergency fund to cover unexpected expenses more important than buying a new car?
- Do you share expectations for the future, such as having children and managing two careers?

You shouldn't feel pressure to resolve differing points of view in a single conversation. In fact, you should plan on a continuing dialogue.

TALK IT OUT

Not being candid about what you think about managing money can be a big mistake. Unspoken feelings about unpaid bills, overdrawn accounts, or other financial missteps often result in anger and mistrust that can undermine even a solid relationship.

MARRIAGE IN THE MILITARY

What's inescapable is that the realities of military life can add a level of complexity to a relationship that most civilian couples don't experience.

From a benefits perspective—and benefits have a major impact on your cash flow—being married makes a major difference in the military. The DoD doesn't provide the ID cards, health insurance, commissary access, or a host of other benefits to a significant other that it provides for a spouse.

Initially, at least, you're likely to have limited income, especially if being together means a non-military partner has left his or her job and hasn't found a new one, or one that pays as well. If you're also paying off wedding and honeymoon expenses—or that new car—you may find yourselves uncomfortably short of cash.

You have to expect frequent moves, which can be stressful in the best of circumstances, and the potential for deployments and other, sometimes extended, separations that can test you both. In addition to being alone, the one who remains at home must assume responsibilities, including financial ones, that you might otherwise share.

Military marriages can be especially hard on spouses who find their own careers interrupted or stalled. Exploring the options together can be an important part of finding a good solution.

BUDGET

REVIEWING YOUR BUDGET

Part of managing your money together is knowing how much income you have and how much you're spending. As a reality check, you might have a conversation that answers the following questions:

- How much money do you have coming in every month?
- What are the fixed expenses, like rent or car payments, that are due?
- What do other necessities, like food and transportation, cost you each month?
- Where else is your money going?
- Where (and how quickly) can you cut back if necessary to keep your cash flow positive?

If you regularly find yourself short of cash or falling behind on credit card payments, you might want to talk through these harder questions:

- What are the things that tempt you into spending more than you know you should?
- How can you prevent overspending the next time you're tempted?
- What if one of you is overspending but the other isn't?

Check out the help that's available through your branch family support center or financial management program. There's a list in the Resources section.

PAYING THE BILLS

One of the first big decisions of your married life is how you'll manage your day-to-day finances. Basically that means paying the bills and spending less than you earn.

You might adopt one of the standard approaches to family money management or devise a variation of your own. For example, you could pool income in a joint account and pay all bills from that account, or you could keep separate accounts and add a joint account to which you both contribute to cover certain expenses.

You'll also want to agree on who will make the payments and keep track of the account balances. But both of you should have the user names and passwords to all joint financial accounts. It's also important to share access information to separately held accounts in case something happens to one of you.

DEALING WITH DIFFERENCES

It can help to anticipate some of the potential sticking points.

For example, if one spouse earns significantly less than the other, has trouble finding work because of a move, or doesn't work outside the home, resolving what that means for your relationship is essential.

If financial independence is important to you, you may want to keep a credit card and a bank account in your own name. Your spouse may feel the same way, but it's also possible that he or she may misunderstand your wishes or even see them as suspect.

Different experiences growing up are likely to impact the way each of you expects a family to manage its money. Ideally, you'll discuss why you feel as you do and find a compromise, even if it's not what either of you thinks is ideal.

The bottom line is that differences in your attitudes about money won't just work themselves out. They have to be resolved together.

Updating Details

Marriage requires more paperwork than you might imagine.

If you thought getting a marriage license was a hassle, just wait. There's lots more paperwork ahead. Some of it may have to be completed within a specific timeframe. The rest you should take care of as soon as possible simply to be done with it.

The driving factor, in some cases, is whether a name change is involved. If that's the case, it means updating government-issued documents, such as a driver's license, passport, and Social Security records as well as insurance contracts, employment records, credit cards, and individually owned financial accounts.

ENROLLING IN DEERS

As a service member, you're automatically registered in the Defense Enrollment Eligibility Reporting System (DEERS). When you marry, you must sponsor your new spouse for enrollment within 90 days unless he or she is also a member and

DEERS REGISTRATION

Service member needs:

☑ DD FORM 1172

Spouse needs: ☑

Certificate of Birth

Together you need: ☑ Certificate of Marriage

Each partner needs two forms of ID:

☑ SOCIAL SECURITY / STATE ID — 0001-01-0001 JOHN J. DOE

☑ SOCIAL SECURITY / STATE ID — 0001-01-0001 JANE T. DOE

THE NAME GAME
Be careful when you make airline or other travel arrangements from the day you get married until your identifying documents, like a driver's license or a passport, match the names on the tickets. It's no fun going on a honeymoon alone.

already in the system. If you have other eligible dependents as a result of the marriage—such as stepchildren—you should register them at the same time. Being enrolled entitles your family to healthcare insurance, childcare, eligibility for transfer of education benefits under the Post-9/11 GI Bill, and an ID card for access to the PX and commissary.

You'll have to complete a DD Form 1172 and provide the required documentation for each person. That always includes at least two currently valid IDs, including one issued by a state or federal government. For a new spouse, for example, you'll need your marriage certificate plus his or her birth certificate, Social Security card, and photo ID. The documents must be originals or certified copies.

Once your new family members are part of DEERS and have their Uniformed Services ID cards, you or they can update information by logging into MilConnect at https://milconnect.dmdc.osd.mil/milconnect or calling 800-538-9522. Each person's record must be updated individually.

UPDATING BENEFICIARIES

As promptly as possible after your wedding, you and your new spouse will want to update the beneficiary information on your individual life insurance policies, investment accounts, and retirement accounts, including IRAs.

You are typically required to name one or more beneficiaries when you purchase

policy or open an account. The issuing company, in turn, is legally required to pay benefits or transfer assets to the person or entity you've designated.

If you named a parent as beneficiary of your SGLI policy when you joined the military and don't update the information when you marry, that parent would receive the policy's death benefit, potentially leaving your spouse in financial difficulty. The same would be true of a TSP account or IRA with a parent beneficiary.

Issuers and sponsors provide clear, generally uncomplicated, instructions for making beneficiary changes. But they don't require those changes or prompt you to make them if your situation changes. It's up to you to take the initiative.

If you die without naming a beneficiary, the TSP distributes the assets according to a **statutory order of precedence**. If you're married, they go to your spouse. If not, the assets go to your children and their descendants, or, if you had no children, to your surviving parents, or finally to your estate.

OPENING ACCOUNTS

Unless you've decided to keep your finances totally separate, one of the first things you'll want to do is open joint checking and savings accounts or retitle existing individual accounts as joint accounts. It's usually fairly easy.

Check with the financial institution you plan to use about the documentation and process requirements. A valid government-issued photo ID and Social Security card may be all you need. If those documents haven't been updated to reflect a name change, however, you may need to present an original or certified copy of your marriage certificate as well.

Often you can handle the process online, though appearing in person may mean faster approval.

In joint accounts, the owners are typically **joint tenants with right of survivorship (JTWROS)**. This means each owner has access to the money in a joint account. Either one can write checks, make online payments and transfers, and withdraw.

If one owner dies, the surviving owner of a JTWROS account automatically becomes the sole owner, with immediate access to the money in the account without waiting for the will to be probated or the estate settled.

In community property states, there's a similar provision for accounts with rights of survivorship.

MERGING OTHER ASSETS

With a few exceptions, such as retirement savings accounts, you can own most assets jointly—including investment accounts, real estate, and cars—as many married couples do. Other couples maintain individual ownership of investments and other assets they inherited or purchased before marriage.

There are solid financial and emotional reasons for either approach. The key is to discuss each spouse's preferences and come to a mutually acceptable resolution. You may find it helpful to ask an attorney or financial adviser for his or her perspective.

SPOUSAL IRAS

If your spouse isn't earning income, another benefit of getting married is that you can open a traditional or Roth **spousal individual retirement account (IRA)** with any financial institution that offers IRAs. Though the contribution, which can be up to the annual limit each year, comes from your earnings, the account belongs to your spouse. He or she can choose and manage the assets, name a beneficiary, and have an independent source of retirement income.

Wills and Other Documents

Documents that govern transfer of assets and medical care must be legally sound.

If you're married, each of you should have a **will** explaining how you want your assets to be distributed after your death. Remember, though, that anything jointly owned with right of survivorship, from a checking account to a house, passes directly to the surviving owner and isn't included in a will.

You should identify an **executor**—your spouse, parent, sibling, or close friend—who will be responsible for carrying out the wishes expressed in your will. If you have young children, you'll also want to name a **guardian** who will care for them until they reach 18 in case a surviving parent isn't able.

WILL SPECIFICS

A will, which must be signed and witnessed in keeping with the laws of the state where it's executed, remains in effect until you update or replace it. To keep your will timely, though, you should review it every four or five years and at any significant life change. If you do make changes, the new will must be signed and witnessed to make it legal. Then the previous will should be destroyed.

A will may seem unnecessary when you're young and healthy and most of your possessions fit in the trunk of your car. And even without a will, your surviving spouse will, in most cases, be legally entitled to your assets. But the process of resolving any potential conflicts about what should happen to them must be handled through a state court and can be painfully slow and frustrating.

Your will should be kept in a secure place where it can be readily accessed if necessary. For example, you might leave the original signed and witnessed copy in a sealed envelope with your executor while keeping an unofficial copy for reference in your personal files along with a note about where to find the original.

LIVING WILLS

Unlike a will, which explains how you want your assets to be distributed after your death, a **living will** is a legal document that expresses your preferences for end-of-life medical care.

Among the topics a living will typically covers are whether you would want to be resuscitated, put on life support, or given food and water if you were unable to communicate your wishes in situations where such treatment might keep you alive. It's not something you decide lightly, or without consultation with your spouse and others whose judgment you respect.

Most professional caregivers opt to prolong life when possible. So a living will—also known as a **healthcare directive** or **advance directive**—is especially important if you don't want such measures taken on your behalf.

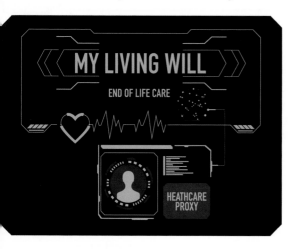

HEALTHCARE PROXIES

At the same time you create a living will, you'll want to establish a **durable power of attorney for healthcare**, also known as a **healthcare proxy**. This document gives the agent you name the right to make healthcare decisions on your behalf. That person—often your spouse, another family member, or a close friend—should be willing to discuss the responsibility he or she is taking on, agree to respect your wishes, and be trusted to make decisions that you would have made yourself.

It's common for the attorney who draws up your will to create your living will and healthcare proxy at the same time. You should be sure that your spouse and family know these documents exist and where to find them. You'll want to review your living will and proxy every four or five years and update them if necessary. Unless the documents are fairly current, they may be more vulnerable to dispute.

POWERS OF ATTORNEY

There are situations in which you or your spouse may be unavailable or unable to handle the day-to-day management of the family's affairs, either because you are deployed, on temporary assignment, seriously ill, or injured. In anticipation of that possibility, each of you can grant a **durable power of attorney (POA)** that meets DoD requirements to your spouse or someone else you trust to act as your agent. With a POA, that person can sign documents that require your signature, handle real estate and investment transactions, and, in effect, stand in for you in financial and legal matters.

Working with an attorney—often at the same time he or she draws up your will and living will—helps to insure that the POA meets state legal requirements. You specify the authority you're granting and the period it will be in effect, recognizing that it ends at your death. You can always change or revoke the power, change the agent, or add an end date.

Your agent should have a copy of the POA and know how to obtain an official version if it's required.

There are risks with POAs, including the potentially long-lasting consequences of bad decisions, whether intentional or inadvertent. For example, bank accounts could be emptied or valuable assets sold. And there's little oversight to ensure a POA is not abused. The key is to select an agent you trust.

Changing Stations

There's financial support for moving your household and settling in.

Moving is a fact of military life. Typically every two to four years you receive a new assignment and relocate to a new duty station, taking your family with you. The DoD pays for these **permanent change of station (PCS)** moves, typically through entitlements and reimbursements.

When you know a move is imminent, you can get a head start by contacting the relocation assistance specialists at your Military and Family Support Center. It also pays to go to planmymove.militaryonesource.mil, where you can create a personalized checklist to guide you through the process. For your first PCS move, using it is probably essential. Even if it's not a first move, a refresher on organizing the transfer can help smooth out any possible glitches.

You can also download "It's Your Move," an extremely detailed handbook of the moving process, at www.ustranscom.mil/dtr/part-iv/dtr_part_iv_app_k_1.pdf. Among other things, it explains how these moves vary by service branch.

COVERED COSTS

The biggest expense of a PCS move, in most cases, is the cost of shipping your household goods.

You can use packers and movers contracted by the DoD, choose a **personally procured move (PPM)**, better known as do-it-yourself (DITY), or split the difference with a partial DITY combined with a DoD move. With a DITY, you can collect up to 95% of the government's estimate for your move if you follow the rules and keep good records.

There are arguments for and against each approach. Generally, it's a matter of balancing the comparative cost—to the extent it can be predicted—with red tape and the labor expended.

The DoD also reimburses other PCS travel and relocation costs.

A **per diem** for meals and lodging en route to the new duty station is based on the number of authorized travel days. You are also reimbursed for mileage if you drive.

A **dislocation allowance (DLA)** is designed to help pay for unreimbursed moving costs. It helps, but it probably won't cover everything you spend.

A **temporary lodging expense (TLE)** covers up to three days lodging if you're leaving government quarters or up to ten if you're moving out of other housing. These nights can be spent either at the post you've leaving, the one you're going to, or split between the two.

When your PCS move takes you overseas or to Alaska or Hawaii, there is a **temporary lodging allowance (TLA)** of up to 60 days after arrival (or 10 days before departure) while you arrange for housing.

Since PCS moves are a fixture of military life, it's a good idea to establish a dedicated PCS savings account that you can tap into to cover moving expenses that may pop up.

CHANGING JOBS

If you're a military spouse who works outside the home, a PCS move means more than packing up the household, getting the family settled, and adjusting to a new location. It also means finding a new job.

That can be complicated if your profession requires you to have a state license before you can be employed. That's the case with teaching, nursing, physical therapy, selling real estate, and others. While licenses can't normally be transferred, many states are working to increase license portability and expedite the licensing process for military spouses.

Once you know where you'll be living, you can check that state's licensing rules. A good source of information is the Minnesota Spouse Licensure Portability Examination at https://reachfamilies.umn.edu/research/document/13865.

In addition, if you're in a new state as the result of a PCS move, your service branch can reimburse licensing and certification costs up to $500. Each branch handles the process a little differently, so you'll have to investigate how to apply. For more information, you can call Military OneSource at 800-342-9647 to contact a Spouse Education and Career Opportunities (SECO) career coach.

USING A CREDIT CARD

Using a credit card rather than cash to pay for reimbursable relocation costs can be a good idea. You're responsible for submitting receipts for these expenses, and having them listed on your credit card statement helps to insure you won't overlook some major ones. Of course, you'll have to pay the credit card bill, even if you haven't received the reimbursement that's coming from the DoD. Not paying at least the minimum balance due has serious consequences, not only professionally, but because of the negative impact on your civilian credit report.

FINDING HOUSING

If you won't be living in government quarters at your new posting, you'll receive the basic allowance for housing (BAH) or overseas housing allowance (OHA) based on average housing costs in the area, your rank, and family size.

To get a sense of what's available, either in privatized on-post housing or in rental properties off post, search the new installation's website for a link to housing or

log on to the Automated Housing Referral Network at www.ahrn.com and the DoD website www.homes.mil.

Remember that the BAH you're entitled to is based on the ZIP code of your duty station and not of the community in which you choose to live. In urban areas in particular, there may be substantial differences in the housing costs from one neighborhood to another. As you think about where to live, you may decide to move to a higher cost area either because it has an excellent school system that would save the expense of private education, or entails a shorter commute.

If you're tempted to buy rather than rent, the bottom line should be what makes the most financial sense based on the career path you currently anticipate.

Deployment Readiness

If you're prepared, it's easier to make it over the financial hurdles.

Deployment is a fact of military life. How often it affects you, what your assignment is, and how long you're away can vary considerably, based on your branch, your unit, and your position. But you always have to be prepared for the possibility of shipping out.

That means you need a **deployment financial plan**. This plan's scope has a shorter time frame than your longer-term financial plan—and it's much more granular. It should anticipate all the financial matters that are likely to arise during the time you're away and establish a process for ensuring they're handled effectively.

EMERGENCY FUNDS

You'll want to be sure your **emergency fund** is fully stocked. If the account balance has only two months rather than six months of living expenses, you may want to add to it if you can.

The reality is that unanticipated— and costly—things can go wrong with your car, your home if you own one, or the appliances your landlord doesn't provide. You want your family to have as much cushion as possible.

It's comforting to know there is a backstop. Each service branch's Military Relief organization provides emergency financial assistance to military families, usually in the form of interest-free loans. However, your authorization as the service member is required before help will be provided. You can ask your branch society about preauthorizing access before you deploy.

The American Red Cross works with the relief organizations to provide financial assistance in emergencies for things such as travel, food, and burial if necessary. For more information, you can contact the organization at 877-272-7337 or www.redcross.org.

FAMILY CARE PLAN

If you have one or more children and are single or half of a dual military couple, you're required to submit a **Family Care Plan** to your unit commander for approval. Though the details vary by branch, the plan must include a will naming a guardian for the children, and a special power of attorney naming the guardian as agent for the duration of your deployment. You must also have SGLI or other group life insurance and evidence that the children are enrolled in DEERS and have valid ID cards.

DEPLOYMENT CHECKLIST

Before you deploy, you'll want to be sure that:

- Your dependents' ID cards won't expire while you're gone and the information in DEERS is up to date.
- Everyone has a valid passport that's not close to expiration.
- Your car registration and inspection are up-to-date.
  - Your credit and debit cards won't expire, especially those you'll be taking with you.

UPDATE YOUR PAPERWORK

The first step in creating a deployment plan is ensuring that all your critical legal and financial documents are up to date.

Review your will—or create one—and the beneficiary designations on your TSP account, other retirement plans, and your life insurance contract.

Ensure that your DD Form 93, "Record of Emergency Data," including page 2 which names your beneficiaries, is up to date.

Sign a power of attorney to authorize your agent to act on your behalf in your absence. You can specify an end date for the authorization if you prefer and sign the document just before you deploy. In most cases, you'll also need to complete IRS Form 2848, "Power of Attorney and Declaration of Representative" to authorize your spouse or another person to sign and file your federal tax returns. If state income taxes apply, you should check those signing and filing requirements as well.

Single parents should name a guardian for their minor children. They should have a written agreement with the children's caregiver, ensure the caregiver will have access to installation services and medical records, and that he or she is authorized to make medical decisions on their behalf.

The legal services office on your installation can help you prepare or update your documents free of charge. Or you can find free legal advice by contacting the American Bar Association's ABA HomeFront at (www.americanbar.org/groups/legal_services/milvets/aba_home_front/).

At the same time, you should consolidate your important military documents, your marriage license, family birth certificates, property deeds, loan agreements, and other legal paperwork in a secure place. Remember, too, that it's essential for your spouse, partner, or other responsible person to know where to find them.

OTHER DEPLOYMENT RESOURCES

As you make your plan, you'll want to incorporate the resources that the DoD, the service branches, Military OneSource and other institutions make available before, during, and after deployments.

If you and your spouse or partner would welcome help in preparing your financial plan, you can contact a financial specialist or personal financial manager through your installation's Family Support Center (FSC).

Every branch uses an ombudsman or readiness group to oversee a network of support services for the families of deployed members. These resources include FSCs, school liaison officers, Child Development Centers, and chaplains. These ombudsmen also serve as conduits for important communication between the unit and the families at home. You can find contact information for each service branch in the Resources section.

If you'll be renting your home while you're deployed, seek help in drawing up a lease to protect your interests. Be sure to include a requirement for renters' insurance.

And if you or your spouse, partner, or designee needs help completing and filing tax returns, that support is available from a legal services office or Military OneSource.

On the Home Front

You want things to go smoothly for the ones who remain at home.

Keeping your household bills paid during deployment is a priority. But how the payments are made is something you'll need to work out. For example, for married couples or long-term partners, should the deployed member be responsible or should the spouse or partner at home? For single members, is it better to handle bill payment yourself or ask a family member or good friend to help out?

Obviously no one solution will work for everyone. But there are some things that apply in general. Chief among them is that the more you collaborate on handling household finances, and the clearer it is who will pay the bills, the better the process will work.

GET A BILL PAY PLAN IN PLACE

If you have advanced warning of your departure date, it's probably a good idea to make any changes in your customary financial routines before you leave. That will give you time to work out the kinks.

Electronic access to your financial records, including your Leave and Earnings Statement (LES) and checking account, and the ability to authorize electronic payments or transfers with a phone, tablet, or computer should make it relatively easy to keep on top of what's happening in your accounts.

Depending on the nature of your deployment, though, there may be times when you don't have regular secure access, which will affect your ability to make timely payments yourself. That's something that should factor into your planning.

If your spouse or partner will assume responsibility for much or

BILL PAYMENT STRATEGIES

Though you probably won't use all the techniques for bill paying mentioned here, some combination of them may work best for you. In fact, it may turn out that certain changes you make to how you manage your household finances during deployment will continue after it ends.

Here are some steps you may take:

✔ Make an inclusive list of what has to be paid, weekly, monthly, or quarterly. Review bank and credit card statements for the past 12 months for obligations you may have missed.

✔ Indicate which bills come in the mail and which are delivered electronically.

✔ Arrange to pay certain bills by allotment or through an automatic bill pay arrangement with your credit union or bank. This approach works best for bills where the amount is set, such as a car payment, rather than one that varies, such as a credit card bill.

✔ Authorize certain payees to debit your account, either automatically or with monthly consent.

✔ Be sure you have overdraft protection.

✔ If you'll be renting your home, notify your insurer and confirm your coverage will continue.

all bill paying, he or she will need access to a joint checking account into which earnings are deposited regularly to cover the household bills.

He or she should also have access to your LES, and enough familiarity with what it reports, to monitor it effectively.

CREDIT CARDS

You also need to think about how you'll use credit cards during deployment. You might decide that you'll be the only one using the card(s) you take with you while your spouse, partner, or financial stand-in uses different ones—ideally cards held in that person's name.

This way, you can notify the card issuer that you're out of country, and that the card may be used unexpectedly.

As a safety precaution, you might consider putting an active duty alert on your credit accounts. With the alert in place it's harder to open new accounts in your name or make changes to existing accounts without verifying the request with you directly. That helps protect you against identity theft and fraud. There's no charge, and the alert is active for a year.

To enroll, contact one of the three national credit-reporting companies—Equifax, Experian, or TransUnion—and that company will share the information with the others.

PLAN FOR YOUR EXTRA PAY

If your deployment means extra pay, and if you're eligible for the family separation allowance, you'll want to have a plan for that money. Saving and investing should be at the top of your list, especially if you can participate in the DoD's **Savings Deposit Program (SDP)** that pays 10% guaranteed interest.

You might also want to set aside a portion to pay off debt, especially high-interest credit card debt. But it probably makes less sense to prepay a mortgage loan when you can earn a much higher rate with an SDP account.

You don't want to use it to make major purchases, like a home or car, that require payments over time since the extra pay will stop when the deployment ends.

HOUSING DURING DEPLOYMENT

Another question is whether your family stays on or near the installation where you've been living or moves when you deploy, perhaps to be closer to other family members.

Emotional security may be the primary concern. If you have school-aged children, maintaining their routines can be very important. Living near others also coping with deployment may be valuable. But having family nearby, especially if access to childcare is important for a working spouse, could outweigh the benefits of staying put.

You'll also want to consider whether moving will affect access to TRICARE and other military benefits and what the cost of the move itself would be.

If you're single and don't have children, there's less to consider. It's usually smart to terminate your lease and store your possessions while keeping your renters' insurance in force.

Tax Benefits

Tax planning can make the system work for you, not against you.

Nobody likes paying income taxes. But the military provides some benefits that supplement your income but don't increase your taxes.

While tax is due on your base pay, a substantial amount—often 25%—of your total compensation isn't taxable. Combat and hazardous duty pay and some bonuses are partially or totally tax-exempt. So are most military allowances and benefits, including the basic allowance for housing (BAH), family separation allowance (FSA), dependent care assistance, education benefits, and moving and storage allowances.

And while the savings aren't exclusive to military families, you can reduce your current taxes by making tax-deferred contributions to a traditional TSP account. Based on your income, you may qualify to deduct your contribution to an IRA. And earnings in most retirement and education savings accounts are tax-deferred and may, in some cases, be tax-free at withdrawal.

REDUCING YOUR TAX BILL

It's important to be familiar with the IRS vocabulary before you file your return so you don't miss any opportunities to reduce your tax bill.

You add or subtract **adjustments** to or from your gross taxable income to find your **adjusted gross income (AGI)**. That's the starting point for determining what you'll owe.

You subtract **deductions** from your AGI to find your taxable income. Most taxpayers take the standard deduction, which is a fixed dollar amount based on filing status.

You subtract **credits** from the tax due, reducing the amount you owe dollar for dollar. Some credits are refundable, which means that if the credit is more than the tax you owe, the IRS refunds the difference to you. Most credits have AGI limits and other restrictions, but they can save you money.

KEY INCOME TAX FACTORS

The federal income tax you owe depends on two factors: your filing status and your tax bracket. You choose a filing status that accurately reflects your family situation. Your bracket—one of seven, with tax rates from 10% to 37%—depends on your taxable income.

If you're not married, you file as a single or head of household. If you are married, you can file jointly, as most couples do, or separately. While filing jointly doesn't always mean you owe less tax, it does make you eligible for certain tax benefits that are reduced or eliminated if you file separately.

Each bracket includes a certain amount of income and is taxed at a specific rate. If your income crosses three brackets—10%, 12%, and 22%—you pay 10% on income in the first bracket, 12% on the next, and 22% on the rest. The highest rate at which you pay is called your marginal rate. But the actual rate you pay is always lower than your marginal rate.

Filing Status & Your Tax Bracket

[10%] [24%] [35%]
[12%] [32%] [37%]
[22%]

CHILD TAX CREDIT

CHILD AND DEPENDENT CARE TAX CREDIT

AMERICAN OPPORTUNITY TAX CREDIT (AOTC)

LIFELONG LEARNING CREDIT (LLC)

EARNED INCOME TAX CREDIT (EITC)

MAKING THE MOST OF CREDITS

There are several substantial tax credits that you may be entitled to take.

The **child tax credit** lets you subtract up to $2,000 for each qualifying dependent child 16 or younger. Up to $1,400 is refundable. There's also a nonrefundable credit of $500 for qualifying adult dependents.

The nonrefundable **child and dependent care tax credit** lets you subtract between 20% and 35% of the amount you spend on childcare or care for an incapacitated spouse or parent so that you can work. The cap is up to $3,000 for one qualifying dependent and up to $6,000 for two or more. But you need to check the age and other restrictions.

When you pay tuition and fees for one or more of your dependents enrolled at least halftime in a degree- or certificate-granting program, you may be eligible for the **American Opportunity Tax Credit (AOTC)**. The credit, which can be up to $2,500 a year for each eligible student, is 40% refundable. You can't take this credit for amounts you paid for with tax-free withdrawals from college savings plans.

The related **Lifelong Learning Credit (LLC)** can be used for a wider range of education programs. But you recover a smaller percentage of what you spend since the maximum credit is 20% of the first $10,000 of qualifying expenses, or $2,000. The LLC isn't refundable.

The **Earned Income Tax Credit (EITC)** benefits working people whose income is below the maximum taxable earnings based on the number of dependent children. Many military families qualify for this refundable credit.

WITHHOLDING

Taxes must be withheld from your taxable pay to prepay most of the tax you'll owe when you file, usually by April 15 for the previous tax year. DFAS uses IRS Form W-4, which you submit when you join the military and can update on myPay as your family situation changes, to determine how much to withhold for you.

You'll want to estimate the number of withholding allowances correctly, adjusting for your spouse's earnings, if any, and any credits you expect to claim. You can use the IRS calculator at www.irs.gov/individuals/tax-withholding-calculator.

Having too little withheld means you'll owe money and maybe a penalty. But having too much withheld means the government is holding money on which it's not paying interest that you could otherwise use or invest. It's not a smart way to save, despite the fact that a tax refund may feel like a gift.

FINDING TAX HELP

- Military OneSource's MilTax provides free tax services, including tax preparation, filing software, and access to tax consultants with experience in preparing military returns.

- There's free tax preparation for simple returns and filing assistance in SJA/JAG offices.

- IRS Publication 3, *Armed Forces Tax Guide* is a valuable resource.

Adding Life Insurance

You can supplement your SGLI coverage with term or permanent protection.

Life insurance isn't optional if you have a family who is dependent on your income. It's the way you can provide for their financial security if you should die. That's why low-cost Servicemembers' Group Life Insurance (SGLI) is such an important benefit.

In fact, it may be all the insurance you need right now. But if you're considering additional coverage, the younger and the healthier you are, the more likely you'll be able to find a policy at favorable rates. Knowing how different types of life insurance work can help you can make better choices.

SPOUSAL INSURANCE

In most cases it's important, especially if you have young children, for both parents to have life insurance. If both spouses are earning income, the family cash flow depends on both. If one dies, it could be difficult to continue to cover living expenses and meet other financial obligations.

In addition, if a stay-at-home parent should die, life insurance would make it possible to hire childcare and household help to keep the family functioning.

Family SGLI is one alternative if you're on active duty and have SGLI yourself. The maximum coverage is $100,000, provided you're insured for at least that much. Premiums vary by the insured's age and are deducted from your pay.

But if you investigate other providers, you may be able to find commercial term insurance that costs less for similar or greater coverage. Or you might look into declining term, which would pay a larger benefit in the early years of the policy, when your children are young and need more care, and a gradually smaller one until the policy expires at the term's end.

TYPES OF INSURANCE

TERM INSURANCE

There are two categories of life insurance: **term** and **permanent**, or **cash value**.

Term insurance is simpler and less expensive, at least initially. A policy covers you for a specific term, or period of time, from as short as one year to as long as 20 or 30. When the term ends, you can extend your coverage for another term if the policy is **renewable**, as most are. When you renew, you don't have to demonstrate you're in good health.

However, at each renewal, the premiums on commercial insurance increase because you're older, increasing the risk you'll die during the term. And, at some point, typically between 70 and 80, you may face prohibitive premiums or not be able to renew at all.

TERM VS. PERMANENT

If you're not certain whether term or permanent insurance is right for you, you'll want to research the pros and cons of each and find the answers to these questions:

- What are the comparable costs of the death benefit you need?
- Is a cash value account an effective way to save for your goals or is investing the difference between the premiums on a term and a permanent policy more effective?
- Is there any reason to think you may be less insurable in the future, typically because of health issues, than you are now?

N INSURANCE PORTFOLIO

One approach you may consider is using a combination of insurance policies to meet different needs. For example, if you have a mortgage, you might buy a declining term policy, similar to the one insuring a

PERMANENT INSURANCE

Permanent insurance combines a death benefit with **cash value account** funded with part of each premium you pay. Account earnings are tax deferred and included in the death benefit when it's paid.

You may be able to borrow against the policy's cash value. But any amount that hasn't been repaid at your death reduces the death benefit. If you end your policy before you die or stop paying the premiums, the insurer subtracts outstanding loans, outstanding interest, and fees, and returns the balance, called the **cash surrender value**, and no death benefit is paid.

If you're considering permanent insurance, the traditional choice is **whole life**, or straight life. You're covered until you die, or in some cases until you turn 100 or 120, and premiums remain the same for the life of the policy. Other types of permanent insurance, such as **universal life**, give you added flexibility for paying premiums or increasing the death benefit, but you pay higher fees and administrative costs.

Convertible term is a hybrid. You can turn your term policy into a permanent policy with the same death benefit, usually without having to demonstrate that you're in good health. The premiums for a convertible plan are usually higher than for regular term with the same death benefit but not as high as for a permanent policy.

stay-at-home parent while the children are young.

The policy could be timed to end about the time your mortgage will be fully paid. It's likely to be much cheaper than mortgage life insurance. And, if you should die, it would provide money to cover a major obligation.

You might use a similar term policy to cover your children's post-secondary education costs or any goal with a specific timeframe.

Or, if you were willing to take the risk of a fluctuating death benefit based on investment performance that's a feature of a variable permanent policy, you might buy that in addition to a conventional term policy.

HOW MUCH DO YOU NEED?

The key with insurance is to have enough, but not more than you need, and never more than you can comfortably afford. If you don't pay the premiums and let the policy lapse, the coverage ends.

To help find the right balance, you can use a life insurance calculator—the VA provides a good one at www.benefits.va.gov/insurance/introCalc.asp—to analyze your needs. The VA calculator helps you to incorporate the DoD and VA benefits your survivors would receive if you died as it guides you through a process that helps you:

1. Estimate outstanding financial obligations and one-time expenses
2. Calculate your survivors' income needs as a percentage of the family's current spending
3. Account for family goals, such as higher education, or long-term security for special-needs children
4. Estimate the income your existing assets could provide
5. Determine whether you need additional insurance, and, if so, how much

> **ALERT:**
> You'll find more on pages 64-65 on the basics of life insurance, and on pages 120-121 about converting SGLI to a new policy when you separate from service.

Property Insurance

The right insurance will protect you and your property from a variety of risks.

Burned homes, stolen property, wrecked cars, and injured people. You can protect against such losses—known as **perils** or **hazards**—by purchasing mortgage, renters, and car insurance.

Typically, you purchase a **policy** that insures you against specific risks and pay **premiums** to keep the policy in force. If you have a covered loss, you file a claim, and, if the insurer agrees, it compensates you for any loss that exceeds your **deductible**, up to the policy's limit. A deductible is the out-of-pocket amount you pay before the insurer begins to pay. Usually, the higher your deductible, the lower your premiums.

Covered losses are paid in one of two ways. If you have an **actual cash value** policy, you're reimbursed for what something was worth when it was damaged or lost. Better policies, though, offer **replacement value**, or what it would cost to repair or replace your insured property.

Keep in mind that making lots of claims can boost your premium or may even result in having the policy cancelled.

HOMEOWNERS INSURANCE

If you own a home, you need **homeowners insurance**. For one thing, mortgage lenders require it. But you'd want this protection anyway because if your home were damaged or destroyed, you'd lose the place you live in as well as what you paid for it.

Insurance companies require you to cover your home for at least 80% of its replacement cost, an amount determined by the insurer. It's actually wiser to insure for 100% of that amount. The policy will cover the home's contents and other structures on the property based on a formula the insurer uses.

You can add liability coverage, which protects you against lawsuits for injury or damage for which you may be liable. To learn more about the types of insurance, you can download a copy of A *Consumer's Guide to Home Insurance* at www.naic.org/prod_serve_publications.htm. NAIC is the National Association of Insurance Commissioners.

BEWARE OF MORTGAGE LIFE

What you don't need is mortgage life insurance, which promises money to pay your mortgage if you should die. It's much more expensive than a term life policy covering the loan amount.

RENTERS INSURANCE

If you're renting, you should think about **renters insurance**. It's a very affordable way to protect your personal property against loss or damage. It also provides liability protection if someone is injured in your home and may cover temporary lodging if your unit is uninhabitable.

Your landlord's insurance covers the structure itself, but not what's in it. So if a leaky roof floods your living room, you aren't responsible for repairs to the ceiling, floor, and walls, but you will have to replace or repair your damaged property. In fact, you may find that the lease you sign with your landlord requires that you have renters insurance.

Some insurers limit coverage on valuable items, but most other losses, even cash in some cases, are protected. Your

FIRST, RESEARCH PROVIDERS

You should always check an insurer's financial reputation with a national rating company. Also check complaints that have been filed with the state's insurance commissioner and online reviews that include multiple complaints about customer service.

A+

THE COST OF COVERAGE

What you pay for property insurance depends on the characteristics of the property you're insuring, the amount of coverage you want, and the insurer you choose. But other factors matter as well:

- Your credit history
- The deductible you choose
- Your history of filing claims, and, in the case of homeowners insurance, the history of claims filed on the home

- Security systems protecting the property
- Other policies you have with the same insurer, especially when you insure your real estate and vehicles with the same company

With auto insurance, the type of car, your age, your driving record, where you live, and the distances you drive regularly all impact the cost of coverage.

property is insured even if it's not physically in your home, though the amount you can recover depends on your policy.

If you live in government quarters, you're covered by government insurance for damaged or stolen property as well as for liability. However, the coverage tends to be minimal, so having additional renters insurance is probably smart.

VEHICLE INSURANCE

Vehicle insurance typically includes different types of coverage.

Collision covers damage when it's caused by an encounter with another vehicle or object. **Comprehensive** covers losses other than a collision, such as fire, weather, or vandalism. With cars, you may also want to add full glass-damage coverage with no deductible. Collision and comprehensive coverage is optional in most states but collision may be required if you have a vehicle loan or lease.

Bodily injury liability, property damage liability, and **personal injury**

protection are required in all 50 states, though different minimums apply. It's generally smart to have more than the required protection in case you're sued for substantial amounts because of a serious accident. You can also add an **umbrella policy** that covers all types of liability up to a limit you feel is right, often in the $1 million to $5 million range.

Uninsured and **underinsured motorist** coverage protects you and other drivers permitted to use your car if it's damaged by an uninsured or underinsured driver.

WHERE TO BUY INSURANCE

You can buy insurance from local insurance agents, directly from insurance companies, from online sites that provide competitive bids, or through your financial institution. Many insurers offer discounts and other benefits to members of the military. So be sure to ask.

Family Health Insurance

Nobody can afford to be without comprehensive healthcare coverage.

Good health insurance is essential but can be expensive. That's why TRICARE is so important to your financial security as well as your health. It provides low-cost—sometimes no-cost—healthcare programs, prescriptions, and dental plans for members of the uniformed services and their families.

Service members, who are required to enroll in **TRICARE Prime**, act as sponsors for their eligible dependents, who have a choice between TRICARE Prime and **TRICARE Select**.

Understanding the differences between these plans and choosing the one that will best meet your needs may take a little time. But it's time well spent.

The place to start is the TRICARE website, at www.tricare.com. It provides detailed descriptions of the plans, a tool for comparing them, and decision trees to help you narrow down your choices.

HEALTH INSURANCE OVERVIEW

When you have health insurance through your employer, as you do with TRICARE, you often have a choice of plan categories. There are two main types—**managed care** and **point-of-service**.

A managed care plan may be either a health maintenance organization (HMO) or a preferred provider organization (PPO).

An HMO employs doctors and other health providers and may own the hospitals you use.

Typically, there are limited or no out-of-pocket expenses. A PPO assembles a network of hospitals, doctors, and other providers who have agreed to accept the payment the insurer presets for each service. You're charged a fixed-dollar amount, called a **copayment**, or copay,

MANAGED CARE PLANS
HMO OR PPO

TRICARE Prime

TRICARE PLAN OPTIONS

TRICARE Prime is a managed care plan, more like a HMO than a PPO. There are specific networks of providers—doctors and other healthcare professionals—hospitals, and other facilities in what are called Prime Service Areas. You're assigned, or may be able to select, a primary care manager (PCM) in your Prime Service Area who provides most of your care, refers you to specialists when needed, and files claims on your behalf.

If you stay within the network and always have a PCM referral to see a specialist, most costs are fully covered.

There are no deductibles and usually no copays for dependents whose sponsor is an active duty member. Copays do apply for dependents of Reserve and National Guard members.

There is a point-of-service (POS) option with TRICARE Prime that allows you more flexibility to choose providers and facilities outside the network, but it carries a stiff price tag. You'll have to meet a deductible before TRICARE begins to cover your costs. Even then, it will cover only 50% of the allowable cost for the service, which you can count on being substantially less than the actual charge.

SUPPLEMENTAL INSURANCE?

Before you buy a supplemental health insurance policy, you'll want to research the advantages and limitations to be sure the benefits you'll actually receive are worth the cost. See a list of questions to ask at https://www.tricare.mil/Plans/OHI/SuppInsurance.

If you'd like further guidance, you can contact a Beneficiary Counseling and Assistance Coordinator (BCAC) using the search function at www.tricare.mil/bcacdcao.

US FAMILY HEALTH PLAN

There's a TRICARE Prime option called **US Family Health Plan (USFHP)** that's available in six areas of the United States. It may provide more flexibility at lower cost than the other options.

You select a primary care provider from a network of doctors affiliated with the participating healthcare system in each region. That doctor coordinates your care, provides referrals to specialists, and helps schedule appointments. There are no enrollment fees or out-of-pocket costs for active duty family members, though those costs apply to Reserve and National Guard families.

You can find a list of who is eligible and where those areas are at www.tricare.mil/Plans/HealthPlans/USFHP.

for each visit to your primary doctor and a slightly higher one if you see a specialist. In most HMO and PPO plans, visits to doctors or facilities outside the network aren't covered.

A point of service (POS) plan allows you to use any provider you wish. After you've paid an annual **deductible**, the insurer pays a percentage of the cost of each service, based on what it determines to be the **allowable cost**. You pay the rest. Your share is called **coinsurance**

or **cost share**. However, the allowable cost is almost always less than the actual cost of the service. So, in addition to your cost share, you could owe the difference between what your plan pays and the actual bill.

POINT-OF-SERVICE

TRICARE Select

TRICARE Select is a PPO. There's a network of approved providers, any of whom you can see without a referral. For some treatments, though, you may need authorization, or preapproval, from the regional contractor to be eligible for coverage.

You pay an annual deductible before TRICARE begins to pay its share. Each time you see an in-network provider or use other services, such as an ambulance, you're responsible for a copay and TRICARE pays the rest. But if you see an out-of-network provider, TRICARE will pay 80% of what it determines to be the allowable cost. Then you pay a cost share of 20%

of the allowable cost plus any difference between what's allowed and the provider's actual charge.

Copays are generally small, but can be increased from year to year. Cost shares can be substantial. You can check current costs at www.tricare.mil/Costs/HealthPlanCosts/TS.

Neither Prime nor Select charge premiums and both have a catastrophic cost feature that limits the amount families pay out-of-pocket annually. Out-of-pocket costs depend on when the sponsor joined the uniformed services, whether before or after January 1, 2018.

TRICARE

Cost and flexibility in choosing providers are key considerations in selecting a plan for your dependents.

TRICARE is managed by the DoD Defense Health Agency and provides coverage worldwide, in three separate regions: East and West in CONUS and Overseas. Each region has a contractor who assembles the caregiver network, handles enrollment, referrals, and other paperwork, and provides healthcare information.

You enroll in the TRICARE region in which you're stationed. If you're transferred to a new PCS in a different region from the one in which you're currently enrolled, you and your dependents must update the information in DEERS and re-enroll.

PLAN ELIGIBILTY

If you're an active duty member, your spouse, children younger than 21, and others who qualify as your dependents, are eligible for TRICARE. As a member of the Reserve component, you're eligible for TRICARE Reserve Select, a comprehensive healthcare plan that allows you to see any provider.

ENROLLING IN A PLAN

You enroll in TRICARE using the Beneficiary Web Enrollment website at www.dmdc.osd.mil.milconnect.

NATIONAL GUARD OR RESERVE

If you're a National Guard or Reserve member, your family is eligible for TRICARE as well, though the benefits for which they qualify and their plan options depend on your current military status. You can download *TRICARE Choices for National Guard and Reserve Handbook* on the TRICARE website for detailed information on healthcare options.

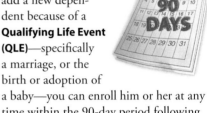

When you add a new dependent because of a **Qualifying Life Event (QLE)**—specifically a marriage, or the birth or adoption of a baby—you can enroll him or her at any time within the 90-day period following the QLE. At the same time, you can make changes in the coverage of all other family members if you choose.

If your family members are already enrolled, you can change their coverage for the next calendar year only during the annual **Open Season enrollment period** each fall. For example, you could switch them from TRICARE Prime to Select, or from Select to the US Family Health Plan. If you don't make any changes, they'll be automatically re-enrolled in the plan they're already in.

If your child is a full-time student in a qualifying program, younger than 23, and attending an institution located in the same TRICARE region where you're enrolled, he or she is eligible for coverage. Student status must be reflected in DEERS. Your challenge may be figuring out how care will be provided if TRICARE is the primary insurer but the school isn't located near a TRICARE-authorized provider.

If you have a disabled child, that child remains eligible for TRICARE after turning 21, provided the disability occurred before his or her 21st birthday.

If you have an unmarried child who is younger than 26, not a fulltime student, and not eligible for an employer-sponsored health plan, he or she is eligible for **TRICARE Young Adult** coverage. The child must choose a plan and pay monthly premiums and other costs determined by the plan and your military status.

When you retire, you and your family can still be insured through TRICARE, with the same options that were available before retirement. Then, when you're eligible for Medicare at 65, enrolled in Parts A and B, and paying Part B premiums, you're automatically enrolled in **TRICARE for Life**. Medicare pays its share of the services it approves, and TRICARE for Life pays the balance due directly to the provider.

Remember, to be covered under TRICARE for Life, your spouse must also be 65, enrolled in Medicare Parts A and B, and paying Part B premiums. Until then, he or she can continue to be covered by a conventional TRICARE plan.

CHOOSING A PLAN

For many families, the most challenging part of enrolling in TRICARE is selecting the best plan for them. The debate typically focuses on whether cost or flexibility in choosing providers is more important. It's an issue, at least in part, because you can't change plans during the year even if it becomes clear at some point that a different plan would have met your needs better.

You can compare your plan options at www.tricare.mil/Plans/ComparePlans, though you'll need to crosscheck a number of linked webpages to get the whole picture.

LOSING COVERAGE

If you or a family member are no longer eligible for TRICARE, the **Continued Health Care Benefit Program (CHCBP)** is designed to keep you insured until you're enrolled in a civilian plan. CHCBP provides the same coverage as TRICARE Select, but you do pay a monthly premium.

The coverage for you and your eligible dependents lasts 18 to 36 months, depending on your status:

FORMER CATEGORY	SCENARIO	LENGTH OF COVERAGE
Active Duty service member	Released from active duty	Up to 18 months
Full-time National Guard member	Separated from full-time status	Up to 18 months
Member covered by the Transitional Assistance Management Program (TAMP)	Loss of TAMP coverage	Up to 18 months
Selected Reserve member covered by TRS	Loss of TRS coverage	Up to 18 months
Retired Reserve member covered by TRR	Loss of TRR coverage (before age 60)	Up to 18 months
Dependent spouse or child	Loss of TRICARE coverage	Up to 36 months
Unremarried former spouse*	Loss of TRICARE coverage	Up to 36 months*

Source: https://tricare.mil/chcbp

You can find more detailed information about eligibility and coverage on the contractor's website at www.humanamilitary.com/beneficiary/benefit-guidance/special-programs/chcbp.

COORDINATION OF BENEFITS

If your non-military spouse has health insurance as a job benefit, that insurer pays its share first and then TRICARE may pick up the balance. Active duty personnel can't have insurance other than TRICARE.

Unremarried former spouses may qualify for additional coverage.

Other TRICARE Coverage

TRICARE provides prescription drugs plus vision and dental checkups.

Most TRICARE Prime and Select plans, including the US Family Health Plan, include prescription drugs for all enrolled family members. Coverage is the same in all plans, though USFHP insurance is provided through your local network rather than by the TRICARE Pharmacy Program. Routine annual eye exams are covered as well, and families can purchase dental insurance through the TRICARE Dental Program.

WHAT'S A FORMULARY?

TRICARE, like other healthcare insurers, creates and regularly updates a list, called a **formulary**, of the generic and brand name drugs it covers. Effectiveness, safety, and cost are among the factors that

FOLLOW PRESCRIPTION RULES

You must follow the rules for filling certain prescriptions or you risk not qualifying for coverage. For example, some drugs require prior authorization, and some can be obtained only by a specific method, such as home delivery. For more details, you can download the *TRICARE Pharmacy Program Handbook* at https://tricare.mil/CoveredServices/Pharmacy/Drugs

determine which drugs are included.

TRICARE covers at least part of the cost of the drugs in its formulary, all of which have passed Federal Drug Administration (FDA) testing. It also pays a portion of certain specialty medications and some non-formulary prescriptions, which it lists separately. Drugs that aren't in these lists aren't covered.

THE FORMULARY IS DIVIDED INTO FOUR CATEGORIES OR TIERS BASED ON PRICE:

	Generic drugs are the least expensive. A generic drug is sold using its chemical name. It may have the same chemical composition as a specific brand-name drug and, if so, works the same way.
	Brand-name drugs tend to cost more. Manufacturers price their drugs to help recover their research, development, and marketing costs before a generic version comes to market.
	**Covered non-formulary** drugs, which can be very expensive, are available through the plan because they meet a medical necessity.
	**Non-covered** drugs are available only if you pay full price.

Your prescription will be filled with a generic rather than a brand-name drug if a generic is available. At your doctor's request, there's a process for gaining approval for using the brand-name instead. But if approval isn't granted, and you want the brand-name version anyway, you'll pay full price.

FILLING YOUR PRESCRIPTIONS

There are four ways to fill prescriptions.

You can use a **military pharmacy** to get up to a 90-day supply of most formulary medications at no cost. Non-formulary medications aren't available.

With **TRICARE pharmacy home delivery**, you can get up to a 90-day supply of formulary drugs sent to a US, APO, or FPO address and have prescriptions automatically refilled. Some non-formulary drugs are covered only in this way. While there's no cost for active duty members, there's a small copay for a generic drug and a larger copay for a brand-name drug when dependents fill prescriptions.

There are **TRICARE retail network pharmacies** throughout CONUS and US territories. You can fill prescriptions and get up to a 30-day supply of drugs. There is a copay each time—somewhat larger than the copays for home delivery—but the pharmacy files the paperwork and receives payment from TRICARE.

If you use an **out-of-network pharmacy**, you pay full retail price for the prescription's cost and file a claim for reimbursement. The amount you get back is subject to a deductible and a 50% out-of-network cost share. Similarly, if you fill a prescription in a retail pharmacy overseas, you pay the cost and file a claim for reimbursement.

VISION CARE

Most TRICARE plans provide routine annual eye exams for a sponsor's spouse and children, though the coverage varies by plan. Adult children in TRICARE Young Adult as well as retired members and their families are covered as well.

Glasses and contacts aren't covered in most cases, although active duty and retired members do qualify to have these prescriptions filled.

With TRICARE Prime, you don't need a referral to see a network provider for the exam. But out-of-network visits without a referral are treated as POS expenses.

With TRICARE Select, you can use any TRICARE-authorized optometrist or ophthalmologist without a referral. But retired members, their families, those enrolled in TRICARE for Life, and young adults are not covered for eye exams.

With USFHP, your coverage allows you to find an eye doctor through your plan.

More comprehensive coverage is available through the **Federal Employees Dental and Vision Program (FEDVIP)**. You can enroll during the fall Open Season period or after a QLE, though QLEs in FEDVIP may differ from TRICARE QLEs. There's more information at www.benefeds.com.

DENTAL INSURANCE

The TRICARE Dental program provides comprehensive dental insurance worldwide for military families whose sponsor is an active duty, National Guard or Reserve member. It's not included in TRICARE Prime or Select, so you have to enroll separately through Beneficiary Web Enrollment at https://milconnect.dmdc.osd.mil by clicking on the "Benefits" tab.

You don't need a referral to see a dentist, but if you use one in the United

Concordia network, you will pay less than if you use one that's out-of-network. In addition, network dentists file your claims, saving you time.

Because the program is voluntary, there's a monthly premium, which you can arrange to have paid automatically from a linked account. There's also a cost share for each visit. While it may seem expensive, regular dental care is essential to overall good health. Putting it off or skipping it altogether is always a bad idea.

Childcare Benefits

Parenthood is expensive, but there are ways to offset some costs.

When you and your spouse are thinking about having a child, your decision probably won't be based on how becoming parents will affect your budget. But anticipating the financial implications of starting a family is important for a number of reasons.

If you're both working, either as service members or one as a service member and the other in a civilian job, one key issue is whether one of you will leave the work force to be a full-time parent. That may have been the plan all along, in which case you may have already factored the loss of one income into your plans. If not, now is probably the time to think about the adjustments you may need to make.

Or, if you both plan to continue to work when your parental leaves end, the availability and cost of childcare is a major factor. It's probably unlikely that you'll

have family close by to fill in the gaps, as civilian families may.

Also, if you're not comfortable with the maternity care your TRICARE plan provides, you'll need to investigate the cost of prenatal and obstetric care from an out-of-network provider.

MILITARY CHILDCARE SYSTEM

Through its military childcare system, the DoD provides the largest employer-sponsored childcare program in the country. There's a weekly fee for each child, with the amount based on the total family income as reported on your most recent income tax return. The government not only pays the majority of the program's costs but provides fee assistance when needed so that children of eligible service members can participate.

Each branch maintains its own childcare programs, and they vary from installation to installation. But the regulations that govern them and the standards they are expected to meet are essentially the same.

Child Development Centers (CDC) are accredited day care centers for children from six weeks to five years old. Some centers offer extended hours, weekend hours, and respite care.

Family Child Care (FCC) provides care by certified providers in private homes for children between two weeks and 12 years old. There can be no more than six children younger than eight or two children younger than two in the home at any one time.

School-age Care Programs (SAC) cover children in kindergarten through sixth grade before and after school, on days when school is not in session, during school holidays, and over the summer.

CHILDCARE RESOURCE

If your child doesn't have access to on-base childcare, you may be able to find a place in a neighborhood program through Child Care Aware of America. The organization, which has built a network of licensed childcare providers in support of each of the service branches, is also the administrator for the military fee assistance program for eligible families and pays the childcare providers directly.

You must select from a list of participating private providers and have a statement confirming space isn't available on your installation. Only single-parent families, families where both parents work, or families where one works and the other is a full-time student are eligible.

You can find the details about what's available through your branch and area by visiting the organization's website at https://usa.childcareaware.org/ or calling 800-424-2246.

CHILDREN WITH SPECIAL NEEDS

If you have a dependent with special medical or educational needs, he or she must be enrolled in the Exceptional Family Member Program (EFMP) to take full advantage of the services your branch provides. EFMP ensures that your family member's access to appropriate medical and educational services is considered during relocations.

For help in navigating the enrollment process, you can contact the EFMP family support center on your installation. The center can also be a resource for finding local services and support you may need and applying for the benefits and entitlements that are available.

You can also download the extremely valuable *EFMP Quick Reference Guide* at: https://download.militaryonesource.mil/12038/MOS/ResourceGuides/EFMP-QuickReferenceGuide.pdf

Looking to the future, you can meet with a Military OneSource special needs consultant who can assist you in establishing financial and estate plans that provide for the current and long-term needs of your special-needs dependent.

For example, you may want to establish a special-needs trust. Or you may open an **Achieving a Better Life Experience (ABLE)** account. Earnings are tax-free at withdrawal if they're used to pay qualified disability expenses of your special-needs dependent who is the designated beneficiary. ABLE income doesn't affect eligibility for Supplemental Social Security Income (SSI), Medicaid, and other public benefits.

USING WIC

If you're pregnant or have one or more children under five, you may want to investigate the US Department of Agriculture's Special Supplemental Nutrition Program for Women, Infants and Children or WIC. Based on your family's base pay and household size, you may qualify for this assistance, which pays for the nutritious foods on the program's list at commissaries or other grocery stores.

Paying for Higher Education

Military programs can make education affordable for your whole family.

Education beyond high school—whether at a college or university, technical or vocational school, or through an apprenticeship, training, or certification program—is probably essential to your children's future financial security. But the cost of providing a head start doesn't have to be a drain on your bank account.

That's because you can take advantage of a range of benefits for military dependents, allocate a portion of what you're saving to tax-advantaged plans, and potentially transfer some or all of your Post-9/11 GI Bill education benefit, as described in the following pages.

APPLYING FOR FINANCIAL AID

Most parents pay for higher education with a combination of savings, scholarships or grants, current income, and, if necessary, loans. Scholarships and grants, which don't have to be repaid, may be based on merit as defined by the school or organization providing the money, or on need.

If your child will be applying for any financial aid—including scholarships and grants as well as loans—you'll have to complete the **Free Application for Federal Student Aid**, or **FAFSA**. You should plan on having it ready as soon as possible after October 1 for the following academic year. Much of the information the form asks for can be automatically transferred from your tax return using the IRS Data Retrieval Tool (IRS DRT).

HELPFUL INFORMATION

You can find useful information about paying for college at the Consumer Financial Protection Bureau at www.consumerfinance.gov/ paying-for-college/ and under the Education & Employment tab at www.militaryonesource.mil.

Shortly after you file, you'll receive a student aid report (SAR) providing your **expected family contribution (EFC)**. Schools where your child applies use this figure to determine how much aid they may offer. But remember, offers are rarely final, and negotiation often pays off.

OFFICER TRAINING

If one or more of your children is interested in a military career, he or she might seek admission to the Air Force Academy, Annapolis, Coast Guard Academy, or West Point or enroll in a college or university that has a ROTC scholarship program offered by the Army, Air Force or Navy. Either way, in exchange for a commitment to serve in the armed forces for a contracted number of years, most if not all costs of an undergraduate degree are covered.

BENEFITS FOR SPOUSES

As a military spouse, you have access to a number of education benefits. For example, several colleges and universities offer scholarships specifically for military spouses interested in pursuing academic degrees. Other scholarships are available through individual states and more through the family relief societies of each of the service branches.

The DoD's **Military Spouse Career Advancement Account (MyCAA) Scholarship** program provides up to $4,000 in tuition assistance for

MILITARY SCHOLARSHIPS

You can find a variety of scholarships specifically for military dependents.

The **Fry Scholarship** provides Post-9/11 GI Bill benefits of up to 36 months of post-secondary education to children and surviving spouses of service members who died in the line of duty after September 0, 2001. If a beneficiary is also eligible for **Dependents Educational Assistance (DEA)**, he or she must choose between the two.

Scholarships for Military Children awards, which are merit based, provide $2,000 a year for college-related costs,

eligible spouses of active duty, Reserve, and National Guard service members in pay grades E1-E5, W1-W2, and O1-O2.

You can use the money at any academic institution that participates in the program to obtain an associate's degree, license, certificate, or certification that will help you find a job in what are described as **portable occupations** in rapidly growing, high-demand career fields. The scholarship can't be used to cover other costs associated with attending school, such as childcare, or for non-career related education.

You can find more information about careers and participating schools at www.militaryonesource.mil/mycaa.

The **Joanne Holbrook Patton Military Scholarship Program**, sponsored by the

excluding room and board. Recipients must enroll fulltime in a four-year undergraduate degree program or a two-year program from which they can transfer directly to complete a bachelor's degree. They're eligible for up to four years of support, though they must reapply each year and keep their grades up.

Individual commissaries award the scholarships, with each commissary that receives qualified applications providing at least one. A related program, **Heroes Legacy Scholarships**, provides needs-based scholarships for children one of whose parents died or was disabled on active duty on or after 9/11.

For eligibility and application information for these and other scholarships, check the Military OneSource website (www.militaryonesource.mil) for an article called "College Scholarships for Military Children and How to Apply" or visit www.militaryscholar.org. You can also schedule a no-cost confidential education consultation online at Military OneSource or by calling 800-342-9647. And check https://studentaid.gov/understand-aid/types/military.

TAKING A SHORTCUT
Students may be able to reduce the cost of education and speed up progress toward a degree by transferring credits earned in the past or by passing qualifying tests through the **College Level Examination Program (CLEP)**.

National Military Family Association, provides small scholarships—on average $1,000—to spouses with valid military IDs. You can use the money toward the cost of certifications, licenses, academic degrees, continuing education units, and other career-related costs.

The DoD's **Spouse Education and Career Opportunities (SECO)** website is a valuable resource for finding scholarships to help finish an undergraduate degree, preparing for admissions tests such as the GMAT for master's degree programs, or finding continuing education courses required to maintain a license or certification.

Saving for College

Federal and state governments encourage you to save by providing substantial tax advantages.

If you're saving for your children's education, you should have a plan now for accumulating what you'll need before each of your children is ready to enroll.

Fortunately there are a number of programs that encourage you to save by providing tax-deferred growth, tax-free withdrawals, and sometimes other tax benefits. Among the most useful are those that share the 529 label—529 college savings plans, 529 state prepaid tuition plans, and the 529 private college prepaid plan—and Coverdell education savings accounts (ESAs).

Remember, though, that return on these investments is not guaranteed, so you may realize less than you'd hoped or expected to have. But that shouldn't deter you.

You may also realize tax savings by paying college expenses with interest you earn on certain US savings bonds. You can find information on how to buy these bonds and the rules that apply at www.savingsbonds.gov.

COLLEGE SAVINGS PLANS

Each 529 college savings plan is sponsored by an individual state and managed by the financial institution the state chooses.

When you open an account, you designate a beneficiary for whom you'll use the money to pay **qualified higher education expenses (QHEEs)**, such as tuition, books, and fees, at an accredited post-secondary school. If your beneficiary doesn't use the

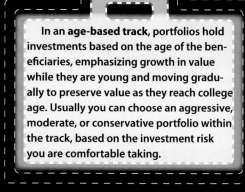

In an **age-based track**, portfolios hold investments based on the age of the beneficiaries, emphasizing growth in value while they are young and moving gradually to preserve value as they reach college age. Usually you can choose an aggressive, moderate, or conservative portfolio within the track, based on the investment risk you are comfortable taking.

THE TRACK SYSTEM
When you contribute to a 529 savings plan account, the plan manager pools your money with contributions of other plan participants and invests it in the portfolio you choose from among those the plan offers. Usually those portfolios are grouped into two separate tracks.

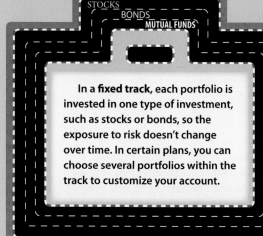

In a **fixed track**, each portfolio is invested in one type of investment, such as stocks or bonds, so the exposure to risk doesn't change over time. In certain plans, you can choose several portfolios within the track to customize your account.

money, you can use it for anyone in his or her extended family, including yourself and your spouse.

Since every state offers access to a 529 plan, you have the flexibility to choose the one that best meets your criteria. In fact, you can open more than one 529 for the same beneficiary, since in most cases neither you nor the beneficiary has to live in the sponsoring state to participate in its plan. But, using a home-state plan may have tax advantages.

In choosing a plan, you'll want to consider its:

- Investment options
- Reputation for producing strong returns
- Fees and expenses
- Possible state income tax deductibility
- Contribution limits, including who can contribute

EDUCATION SAVINGS ACCOUNTS

You open an ESA with a financial institution, just as you would an individual retirement account (IRA). You name the beneficiary and choose the investments for the account, which gives you more control over how your money is allocated than you have with most 529 plans.

There are limitations, though. The annual cap on contributions is $2,000 for each beneficiary. There are also income caps on who can contribute, and the beneficiary must be younger than 18 when you open the account. He or she must also use the money before turning 30, though you can change the beneficiary to anyone else in the same extended family if the original beneficiary is not going to use the money.

ANOTHER POSSIBLE USE

You can use ESA savings and up to $10,000 a year in 529 plan savings to pay for K-12 expenses. Of course that money won't be available to cover the costs of higher education.

MAKING CONTRIBUTIONS

You and others can contribute after-tax money to all college savings plans, either in a lump sum or installments, an approach that might fit more easily into your spending plan. With 529 plans, you can contribute up to the annual tax-exempt gift limit—$15,000 in 2020 or $75,000 once every five years—for each beneficiary without having to file a gift tax return. A couple can gift twice that amount—$30,000 in one year or $150,000 every five years.

YEARLY CONTRIBUTION CAPS		
ESA	$2,000 plus income caps	
529 Plans	Single	$15,000 or $75,000 once every 5 years
	Couple	$30,000 or $150,000 once every 5 years

TAKING WITHDRAWALS

Withdrawals from 529 college savings plans and ESAs are tax-free if they're used to pay the beneficiary's QHEEs. Your plan provides an annual statement detailing your contributions, earnings, and withdrawals. It's up to you to match expenses with withdrawals when you file your federal income tax return each year. If withdrawals exceed QHEEs, taxes on that amount, plus a 10% tax penalty, are due.

PREPAID PLANS

You may also want to consider a **529 prepaid tuition plan**. It lets you lock in some or all of the cost of future undergraduate tuition and mandatory fees at any of the schools included in the plan.

Each plan—offered by only some states and by a consortium of private colleges—differs, so you have to investigate the ones that might be of interest. With most state plans, either you or the student must be a resident of the state.

Despite the potential tax and other benefits, there are some drawbacks. If you withdraw, the refund is minimal. There's no guarantee your child will be admitted to or want to attend a participating school. It's also possible you could realize a stronger return with a different approach.

Transferring Your GI Bill Benefit

Sharing your entitlement makes education a family affair.

One way to cover the costs of higher education is to transfer the education benefits of the Post-9/11 GI Bill to which you're entitled to your spouse, your dependent children, or both.

However, your transfer request must be submitted and approved while you're on active duty, and the number of transferrable credits could be limited by the DoD or the Department of Homeland Security.

TRANSFERRED TIME

If your full benefit of 36 months is eligible for transfer, you can assign them to one dependent or divide those months as you wish among your eligible dependents.

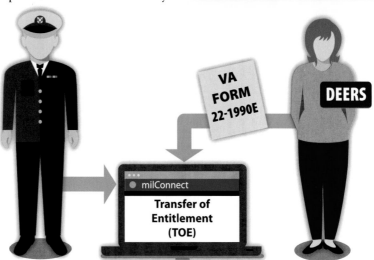

CHECK YOUR ELIGIBILITY

You qualify for the transfer option if you're an active duty or Selected Reserve officer or enlisted member who meets one of these criteria:

- Six years of service on the date of approval plus your agreement to serve four more years in the armed forces from the date of the transfer request
- At least ten years of service on the date of approval plus your agreement to serve the maximum amount of time that you're allowed

A rule ending eligibility if you have served more than 16 years on active duty or in the Selected Reserve has been passed but not implemented.

MAKING THE TRANSFER

If you're eligible, you can initiate the benefit transfer as soon as you have one dependent. You can later adjust your benefit allocation if you choose, without an additional service obligation.

For example, if, after serving six years, you're married but have no children, you can transfer your benefits to your spouse. When you do have children, you can reallocate the benefit to include them.

To allocate, modify, or revoke transferred benefits, known as a **Transfer of Entitlement (TOE)**, while you're on active duty, you use the Transfer of Education Benefits link on the milConnect website at www.dmdc.osd.mil/milconnect/. After separating from service, you can revoke a TOE, modify the number of months you've allocated, or set a timetable for use. But you can't add beneficiaries.

If you have questions, you can contact the VA Education Call Center at 888-442-4551 or the appropriate career counselor or personnel center for your service branch. There's a list of contacts and other detailed information at www.benefits.va.gov/gibill/post911_transfer.asp

USING THE BENEFIT

To be eligible to use a TOE, family members must be enrolled in DEERS. When they're ready for a post-secondary program, they submit VA Form 22-1990e either online or by mail to the VA regional processing office. They can choose among colleges and universities, non-college degree granting programs, apprenticeships, vocational flight schools, correspondence schools, and national testing programs. The dollar value of their benefit is linked to the program they choose.

Your spouse may use TOE at any time after it's approved, whether you remain on active duty or separate from service. A child may use the benefit only after you've completed ten years of service. He or she must have a high school diploma or be at least 18 to qualify and must use the credits before turning 26.

WHAT THE BENEFIT PAYS

The Post-9/11 GI Bill education benefit pays the full cost of in-state tuition at a public college or university directly to the school for the equivalent of four academic years. If you have several children, you might allocate the full benefit to just one or split it to help cover expenses for several of them.

The Harry W. Colmery Veterans Assistance Act of 2017 allows the transfer of Post-9/11 GI Bill benefits to surviving eligible dependents if a service member, veteran, or another dependent with unused transferred benefits has died.

If your child enrolls in a public institution, the school must offer the in-state rate regardless of your family's legal or current residence. If he or she enrolls in a private institution, the VA will pay the national maximum, which correlates with the highest public school tuition the program covers. These payment caps change annually, on August 1.

The transferred benefit may also pay a monthly housing allowance for the months that school is in session. Your spouse isn't eligible for the allowance while you're on active duty but may be if you're separated from service. Children do qualify for the allowance, whatever your status, if they're enrolled on a more-than-halftime basis.

The allowance a student receives is based on the school's ZIP code, not where the family lives. The amount is more limited, though, if the child is enrolled in an exclusively online program. In that case, it's half the national average paid to students attending conventional schools.

THE YELLOW RIBBON PROGRAM

Children using a TOE to attend a participating private college or university are eligible for the Yellow Ribbon Program, just as if you were using the education benefit yourself.

Under the program, schools agree to waive some or all of tuition that exceeds what the VA will pay under the Post-9/11 GI Bill. For example, suppose tuition at a participating college was $45,000. If the GI Bill was paying $24,476 which was the rate for the 2019-2020 academic year— the college might waive $10,000. The VA would match that with another $10,000, so you'd be responsible for tuition of just over $500 ($45,000 − ($24,476 + $20,000) = $524).

There are cautions. Your child must be admitted to the college or university before applying to the highly competitive program and there's no guarantee that even a highly qualified applicant will be approved. It's probably worth checking with the school about its record of supporting military dependents.

Avoiding Scams

To protect your identity and your assets, vigilance is critical.

Con artists cheat American consumers out of billions of dollars each year by targeting people they see as vulnerable, including service members and their families.

PHONY PROBLEMS

A classic scam starts with a phone call about a problem that needs your immediate attention:

- A caller pretending to be from the Red Cross might alert you that a family member has been injured and needs immediate treatment.
- A caller claiming to be from a law firm says you're in trouble for not showing up for jury duty, not paying a tax bill, or not responding to a traffic summons.

The caller always offers to help if you provide a credit or debit card number or send a money order or prepaid debit card to an address the caller provides. Don't believe it. The problem is a fabrication and your money will be stolen.

INTERNET SCAMS

The internet offers a world of scamming possibilities, including phishing. In this scheme, the identity thief sends an email with a link to a website that looks official and may replicate a site you use, such as a financial institution. If you click on the link and log on, your data goes directly to the scammer, providing access to your account.

Other internet scams claim to offer prizes, trips, huge discounts, or access to a large sum of money that's yours simply by providing your bank or credit union account information or a small down payment. Just remember, if a deal sounds too good to be true, the chances are it's a scam.

AFFINITY FRAUD

Affinity fraud occurs when a dishonest person plays on your affiliation with a group—such as your military unit, a house of worship, social club, support group, or veterans' group— as a way to win your confidence, either to sell you something worthless or trick you into handing over cash.

The scammer may in fact be a member of the group, or just pretending to be. He or she may even be someone you know and like. But if anyone wants access to your personal information, offers to handle your money, or suggests making changes to your legal documents, like a deed to property, don't do it.

Affinity fraud is one the most difficult scams to protect yourself against because the threat is coming from someone you believe to be an ally.

LOANS TO AVOID

Among the most common financial traps are various types of loans and cash advances—such as payday, or fast cash, loans—that con artists use to prey upon military personnel and their families who are under financial pressure.

Advance-fee loans are typically promoted as easy money that's available to anyone who needs it. But there are danger signs that should alert you to a scam.

SOCIAL MEDIA

LIMIT YOUR POSTS ON SOCIAL MEDIA

Many scammers depend on information shared on social media to victimize their targets effectively. These bits of information—about friends, family, events, interests, travel plans, and purchases—enable identity thieves to put together amazingly complete personal profiles of potential victims and determine the most convincing way to approach them.

The clearest is that the lender says you're approved but must pay an upfront fee by money order or wire transfer before you can get the loan. That's almost a guarantee you'll never get it—and you won't get the fee back either.

Spot financing, sometimes called yo-yo loans, allows you to take possession of a vehicle before the financing the dealer promises has been finalized. If the dealer can't get a financial institution to approve the loan, you'll be told you have to agree to a larger payment, return the car, or have it repossessed.

Even with a legitimate car loan, be sure you understand how much it will cost you and be sure you can afford the monthly payments. If you can't, chances are the car will be repossessed and you'll lose what you've spent to date and the car as well.

Car title loans are short-term secured loans of between 25% and 50% of a car's value. They can be arranged quickly, but they're very expensive, with an upfront fee that may be as high as 25% of the loan amount. That's an APR of 300% and there may be other fees as well. If you can't repay what you owe, you'll be talked into rolling the loan over for an additional fee. If you default, the lender can repossess your car.

SPOT FINANCING

CAR TITLE LOAN

DEFENSIVE MOVES

The people who are trying to trick you are persistent and ruthless, extremely clever, and constantly refining their techniques and use of technology. How can you defend yourself?

1. Be suspicious of anyone who contacts you and wants personal information or money. Don't be fooled by official-sounding names, impressive titles, appeals to your patriotism, or desire to help others.
2. Be especially wary if the person urges you to act immediately and warns you

not to share the information with others—two telltale signs of a scam.
3. Never, ever, share vital personal information—credit card or PIN, military ID, or your Social Security number—online, on the phone, or in person with someone you can't prove is requesting the information legitimately.
4. If you're uncertain about a request or an action you're asked to take, talk with your base legal office. The advice is free and can save you a lot of money and grief.

Ending Relationships

State law and military regulations impact your divorce settlement.

The end of a marriage almost always means major financial adjustments. That's because in legal—though not emotional—terms, divorce is about dividing up property and, if there are children, resolving issues of custody and support.

Divorce is regulated by state law, and court settlements generally reflect local practice. There's no uniform national standard or consistent definition of what's equitable. What that means is unless you can agree to mutually acceptable terms that the court will ratify, you can never be certain of how your divorce will be resolved.

And, because you've been a military family, your divorce will be impacted by the complex DoD regulations that apply to retired pay and survivor benefits, access to TRICARE, and other privileges including base access.

You and your spouse should work with separate attorneys experienced in handling military divorce since the rules are different from those for civilian couples. Without this expertise, you or your spouse risk what may seem to be an inequitable resolution.

LEGAL ASSISTANCE

When divorce is inevitable, your first step should be contacting the base legal assistance office, a service that's free wherever you live. To avoid a conflict of interest, the same officer can't advise you both.

Legal assistance officers can't represent you in court but can provide valuable advice on the legal and financial documentation you'll need, the paperwork

DIVORCE STATS
About 90% of all divorces are settled out of court, and only about 15% of divorces involve alimony, typically paid by the spouse with more assets and income.

the military requires, and where to file the divorce petition. It can be in one of three states:

- Where the non-military spouse lives
- Where the service member is stationed
- Where the service member maintains legal residence

THE 10/10 RULE

The **Uniformed Services Former Spouse Protection Act (USFSPA)** governs the rights of a former spouse to a portion of a member's retired pay. It authorizes, but doesn't require, state courts to treat retired pay as property rather than income in a divorce proceeding so it can be divided for settlement purposes. The former spouse is entitled to a maximum of 50% of its value, but a number of factors influence the actual division. The length of the marriage is one. Whether or not the spouse has a comparable retirement plan may be another.

THE 20/20/20 RULE

The USFSPA also provides certain benefits, including lifetime healthcare coverage and commissary, exchange, and other on-base privileges, if the 20/20/20 rule is met and the former spouse doesn't remarry before turning 55. The rule requires that:

However, the state that may be advantageous for one party may not be so for the other.

HOUSING ISSUES

If two service members divorce and share legal and physical custody of their children, one but not both members will receive BAH at the dependent's rate. A parent is entitled to that rate only for the period the child is in his or her physical custody.

FAMILY SUPPORT

Each service branch has a policy requiring service members to provide support to the family after a legal separation if there's no agreement or court order. You should be aware of one that affects you:

- Army Regulation 608-99, "Family Support, Child Custody and Paternity"
- Chapter 15 of Marine Corps Order P5800.16A, "Marine Corps Manual for Legal Administration"
- Chapter 15 of Naval Military Personnel Manual 1754-030, "Support of Family Members"
- Air Force Instruction 36-2906, "Personal Financial Responsibility"

The act also provides a way for the former spouse to receive direct payments from DFAS if the marriage meets what's known as the **10/10 rule.**

The rule requires that the couple must have been married for ten years or more that overlap with at least ten years of service counted toward the member's eligibility for retired pay. If the rule is met, the direct payments are required. If it's not, he or she is still entitled to the income but not a direct payment.

If the 10/10 rule applies, the former spouse must file a court order stating the percentage of income to be received and requiring DFAS to make the payments, along with DoD Form 2293. If the filing isn't made in a timely fashion or lacks required information, direct payments may not be possible.

If you're still on active duty at the time of the divorce, individual courts may use different methods of calculating the percentage of retired pay to which the former spouse is entitled and must state the method it used in a court order.

There are several payment alternatives including:

- An upfront buyout calculated on net present value
- A deferred distribution in which the share is calculated at divorce but not paid until the member retires
- A reserve jurisdiction, where the share is calculated at retirement

- The couple was married for at least 20 years when the marriage legally ended.
- The member has, based on service, accrued at least 20 years of eligibility for retired pay.
- At least 20 years of marriage have overlapped with 20 years of creditable service.

There's also a 20/20/15 rule that applies when the first two conditions have been met but the marriage and the creditable service overlapped by just 15 years. In that case, the former spouse is eligible for TRICARE for one year after the divorce but doesn't qualify for base privileges.

Former spouses who aren't eligible for TRICARE may buy CHCBP for at least 36 months and in some cases indefinitely if they qualify.

Dividing Assets

If both of you are willing to negotiate, you may avoid a protracted battle.

Though one or both of you may be angry or hurt that your marriage is ending, you need to focus on resolving your financial affairs as quickly and as equitably as possible. You should decide what you want and what you're willing to give up, and be prepared to negotiate.

In evaluating your marital assets, you may discover that substantial amounts are in your retirement plan accounts, such as the Thrift Savings Plan (TSP), IRAs, and 401(k)s or similar civilian plans.

If you both have retirement plans, you may each agree to keep your own. But if only one spouse has a retirement account or one that's much larger, the other spouse can claim a share. But the process for dividing TSP account assets differs from those of other plans.

DIVIDING A TSP ACCOUNT

If a TSP retirement account is to be divided by court decree or a court-approved property settlement agreement, the non-military spouse's attorney must provide TSP with a **Retirement Benefits Court Order (RBCO)**. The order must meet the plan's specifications, so it's essential that it be done correctly. Otherwise, the TSP won't review it.

If the RBCO requires a payment to the non-military spouse, it must be for an exact dollar amount or a fraction or percentage of the account value as of a certain date. The TSP will honor an order that requires future payment if the present value of that entitlement can be calculated to be paid currently.

The RBCO can also ask that the account be frozen so that assets can't be withdrawn or borrowed. If the TSP determines the order is qualified and a payment is required, it will explain how the amount will be calculated and when it will be paid.

SURVIVOR BENEFITS

When you retire from the military, you have the option of purchasing a **Survivor Benefits Plan (SBP)**, the equivalent of an annuity, to be paid to your surviving spouse when your retired pay ends at your death. You also identify the base amount of the SBP, from as little as $300 to 100% of retirement pay, of which the survivor will receive 55%.

If the plan has been purchased before the divorce, the decree nullifies the existing beneficiary designation. You may voluntarily name your former spouse as beneficiary within one year from the date of the divorce or be compelled to do so by court order addressed to the retirement pay center. That order may also specify the required base amount.

The SBP cannot be split among adult beneficiaries. But it can be used to provide annuities to minor or disabled children in addition to a spouse or if a spouse dies.

DISABILITY PAY

If you receive VA disability compensation, your disability pay is not taxable and doesn't have to be divided with a former spouse.

Retirement Benefits Court Order (RBCO)

THRIFT SAVINGS PLAN

MAKING FINANCIAL CHANGES

Whether you initiated the divorce or not, there are some ways to help you reduce potential financial problems that could arise:

✔ Make copies of all legal and financial documents and give copies to your attorney or a friend.

✔ Establish separate checking, savings, and credit card accounts immediately. If your existing assets are jointly held, you can ask your lawyer's advice about withdrawing from them to open your own account.

✔ End powers of attorney (POA) you have granted your estranged or former spouse, as well as any other authority to make decisions on your behalf.

✔ Make a new will. Existing wills are sometimes but not always voided by a divorce.

✔ Designate a new beneficiary for insurance policies, civilian pensions, retirement accounts, and any other assets that pass directly to a beneficiary.

✔ Cancel joint equity lines of credit and freeze joint brokerage accounts. Otherwise you might end up with more debt or fewer assets than you expected.

✔ Ask your lawyer about how to handle ownership of real property that's currently held jointly.

✔ Evaluate the long-term implications of dividing assets, including the tax consequences. For example, if you receive a capital asset, such as a house, you may owe all the capital gains tax if the house is eventually sold.

✔ If you can work things out amicably, consider an escrow account or joint account requiring both signatures to pay family expenses until the divorce is final.

SOCIAL SECURITY

If you were married ten years or longer before you divorced, you'll be eligible for your former spouse's Social Security benefit when you reach retirement age if it's larger than yours would be. You make this arrangement directly with the Social Security Administration. Your former spouse is not involved, and his or her benefit is not reduced by the amount paid to you. This could be a valuable income booster that you don't want to overlook.

DIVIDING PENSIONS

Federal law requires the court in the state where the service member legally resides to divide a military pension in divorce, something courts in other states could, but may not be required, to do. In those states, the service member could agree to the division as part of the settlement.

SCRA PROTECTION

If you're on active duty, SCRA protects your legal right to delay responding to papers that are served on you or demands to appear at scheduled court hearings. A 90-day delay is standard, which can be extended if your situation requires it.

SCRA

Leaving the Military

Your emotions are likely to be a mix of excitement and unease.

When your next move isn't to a new duty station but to life in the civilian world, you should be prepared for some dramatic changes whether you're retiring or separating voluntarily or involuntarily.

If you're planning a move to the civilian workforce, you'll need to adjust to the fact that, unlike in the military, published pay scales and a clearly defined path to promotion aren't typical. Neither are tax-free benefits to help defray everyday living costs.

Personally it may hard to move from a built-in community of colleagues and friends with shared experiences to a new and perhaps initially alien environment. But there are resources and programs to smooth the way. It's up to you to take advantage of them.

ENROLLING IN THE VA

There are certain things you have to do before you leave the military, and a fairly strict time frame for completing them. One of the most important is enrolling with the VA for access to the healthcare benefits and disability compensation for which you may be eligible. You use VA Form 10-10EZ, "Enrollment Application

for Health Benefits," which you can download at www.va.gov, request by phone (877-222-8387), or pick up at your local VA medical center.

MOVING OUT

If you're leaving the service voluntarily, the DoD will normally cover the expense of moving your household from your last duty station to a new location within 180 days of your separation. However, you must be returning to your home of record or moving to a destination that's an equal or shorter distance. If your new home is farther away, you're responsible for the additional cost of the move.

If you are leaving the service involuntarily but in good standing, these distance limits don't apply to your moving costs and the time limit is extended to one year.

This may be the time you decide to buy a home if you've lived in government quarters or in rental properties while on active duty. So you'll need to explore the costs of buying and owning a home that you can afford and how the **VA Loan Guaranty program** can help.

It's worth noting that the strength of your credit report will have a major impact on qualifying for a mortgage loan or being able to rent a home that meets your needs. Your credit history is equally important to being hired for a job for which you're qualified. So if you have substantial outstanding debt, it's often a good idea to pay off as much as you can while you're still receiving your military salary.

FINANCIAL CONSIDERATIONS

If you're uncertain about the direction your post-military career will take, you may want to investigate the fastest growing occupations and those with the highest projected growth rates. The *Bureau of Labor Statistics Operational Outlook Handbook* (www.bls.gov/ooh/) is a good place to start. It covers those topics as well as the education and training that various jobs require, along with their median salaries.

You'll want to look not only at the current average pay in careers that interest you, but at the potential for growth over time. In some jobs, what you earn changes relatively little over a multi-year career, while in others seniority and experience are more likely to be rewarded.

You'll also have to be realistic about the income you'll need to live comfortably as a civilian. It's almost certainly more than your military pay because of the supplemental benefits you'll now have to pay for yourself. They include some potentially costly ones: housing and, unless you're retiring or have a service-connected disability the VA covers, healthcare. Even good employer health plans generally require you to pay part of the premium and some out-of-pocket expenses.

WORKING FOR YOURSELF

An alternative is to work for yourself. If that appeals to you, you might begin by checking out the **Small Business**

Administration **(SBA)**. It has an Office of Veterans Business Development that offers a variety of programs, including a learning center, an outreach program, and, as part of the DoD Transition Assistance Program (TAP), a two-day course called Boots to Business. If you have a service-connected disability, The Veterans Corporation (TVC) can be a valuable resource. You can find more information at www.veteransbusinessservices.us/.

If you need money to start a business, you should check with the SBA, your state's office of veteran's affairs, and private-sector lenders with military affiliations.

LONG-TERM PLANNING

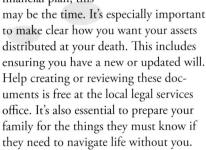

If you haven't incorporated estate planning into your financial plan, this may be the time. It's especially important to make clear how you want your assets distributed at your death. This includes ensuring you have a new or updated will. Help creating or reviewing these documents is free at the local legal services office. It's also essential to prepare your family for the things they must know if they need to navigate life without you.

This includes the benefits for which they would be eligible, such as life insurance, and, if you're retiring, the Survivor Benefit Plan (SBP), which would help provide long-term financial security.

ESSENTIAL READING
You should check out the annual edition of *Federal Benefits for Veterans, Dependents and Survivors* (www.va.gov/opa/vadocs/Fedben.pdf) for a detailed account of available benefits. You can also learn about your separation and transition benefits on the Military OneSource website (www.militaryonesource.mil) under the Benefits and Resources tab in the main menu.

Transitioning

There's lots of assistance available if you capitalize on the opportunity.

If the transition from military to civilian life were easy—just a new address and a new job description—it wouldn't be as unsettling as it is for so many of the 200,000 service members who experience it each year.

To eliminate the hard stop between being a member of the military one day and a civilian the next, the DoD has redesigned the **Transition Assistance Program (TAP)** to make transition an integral part of the military life cycle and smooth the path to civilian life.

The program mandates individual initial counseling and individual transition plans (ITPs) as well as pre-separation counseling to be completed at least 365 days before transition. There's also a push to align service experience more directly with post-military career goals.

The capstone of the transition process is an evaluation, to be completed by your commander or the commander's designee at least 90 days before separation. It must certify that you've met career readiness standards and that your transition plan is viable.

TRANSITION GPS

The TAP curriculum called **Transition GPS**—for Goals, Plans, Success—is a mandatory three-day interagency program offered by the DoD, the VA, and the Department of Labor (DOL). Its focus is providing information on financial planning, career decision-making, education, certification, training resources, and veterans benefits.

The first day covers, among other topics, the Military Occupational Code (MOC) Crosswalk, which is designed to help you align your military skills, training, and experience with civilian job opportunities. The second day is an overview of VA benefits and the third, from the DOL, provides employment workshops keyed to levels of career readiness.

There are also four optional two-day tracks to supplement GPS: Two are from the DOL, one on employment and the other on vocational training, one on higher education from the DoD, and one from the Small Business Administration (SBA) on entrepreneurship.

Transition Assistance Program TAP

TRANSITION RESOURCES

When you're anticipating a move to civilian life, the transition program website at www.dodtap.mil, service branch websites, whose web addresses are listed in the Resources section at the end of the book, and https://benefits.va.gov/tap are your primary resources.

To get a head start, you may want to download the ITP checklist, DD Form 2958, at https://wdr.doleta.gov/directives/attach//TEN/TEN-10-14-Attachment-1_Acc.pdf and the Pre-Separation Counseling Checklist, DD Form 2648, at www.esd.whs.mil/Portals/54/Documents/DD/forms/dd/dd2648.pdf.

The GPS curriculum is provided in classroom settings, but it can also be accessed online through Joint Knowledge Online (JKO) at https://jkodirect.jten.mil if you're unable to attend in person. The program is also available to spouses, who are encouraged to participate. If you're not retiring, you have continuing access to the JKO site for 180 days after separation.

CREDENTIALING

You can follow up on the MOC Crosswalk information provided in the GPS curriculum on your own. Each service branch has a credentialing website where you can determine if you've met the standards for certain civilian jobs during your military career. There's also a tool on the VA eBenefits website at www.ebenefits.va.gov that will help you capitalize on your military experience to bolster your civilian credentials.

You can find additional credentialing information online at www.acinet.org or www.dantes.doded.mil/index.html.

VA BENEFITS

To take advantage of the VA benefits to which you're entitled as a veteran, you must enroll in a VA eBenefits Premium account. Click on Register at the top of the eBenefits homepage (www.ebenefits.va.gov/ebenefits/homepage) and follow the instructions.

The eBenefits homepage also provides a benefits overview and access to both a comprehensive *VA Benefits and Services Participant's Guide*, which you can download at www.benefits.va.gov/TAP/docs/VA-Benefits-Participant-Guide.pdf# and *Federal Benefits for Veterans, Dependents,*

≡eBenefits

and Survivors, updated annually, which you can download at www.va.gov/opa/publications/benefits_book.asp.

ESSENTIAL DOCUMENTS

To be eligible for most VA benefits and services and to participate in federal and state veterans' programs, you need a copy of **DD Form 214, "Certificate of Release or Discharge from Active Duty."** You'll want to be sure all the information is correct before you separate, as it's hard to make changes later. As backup, you might want to give a certified copy of the form to your local veterans' center.

You'll also need DD Form 2586, "Verification of Military Experience and Training (VMET)," which you should be sure to obtain before leaving your final assignment. You'll need this information to create a resume and evaluate the skills you have to offer employers. The timing is important because you need a current CAC, DFAS myPay PIN, or DS Logon to access the form.

Since you'll need DD214 in the future, you'll want to be sure you have the original and a number of certified photocopies.

TERMINAL LEAVE

If you have unused leave, you may decide to use that time before you transition out. You can use it to look for a job, find a new home, or take a vacation before you start a new job or enroll in an education program. All active-duty benefits apply during leave, including your BAH, BAS, and TRICARE coverage. Alternately, you can sell back your unused leave, but that terminates BAH, BAS, and TRICARE earlier.

MORE RESOURCES

You may also want to check out:

- **DoD SkillBridge**, which provides opportunities to build resumes through internships and apprenticeships with industry partners within 180 days of discharge while drawing a military salary (https://dodskillbridge.usalearning.gov)

- **Break Line**, which provides transition for veterans pursuing technology careers through interactive learning, mentorships, and access to interviews (https://breakline.org)
- **American Corporate Partners**, to find a civilian mentor in the corporate world (www.acp-usa.org)

Finding a Job

Few things are more challenging than launching a new career.

As you begin your search for a satisfying civilian career, you'll want to hone your ability to explain how your service skills and experiences qualify you for the jobs you're seeking. The way you position yourself is often key to success.

MAKING CONNECTIONS

Finding the job you want depends, in the vast majority of cases, on effective networking that helps you make personal connections with employers looking for someone with your skills.

It's important to reach out to former colleagues already in the civilian marketplace, to friends, and relatives, and to veterans groups at companies who may know about job openings for people with your skills and interests. You'll want to think about which of your contacts can best act on your behalf by introducing you to a potential employer, passing along your cover letter and resume, or writing letters in support of your applications. The wider the network you establish, the better the opportunity for success.

You'll also want to investigate veteran-friendly employers and jobs where veterans have preference, including federal agencies and all DOL-funded programs. If you apply for these positions, be sure you make your eligibility for preferential consideration clear. Preference doesn't guarantee you'll be offered a job, but there's no downside in highlighting your veteran status.

RESUMES AND COVER LETTERS

When you apply for a job, you need a resume and a cover letter. They have the same goal—to secure you an interview.

A resume highlights your experience, skills, education, and training in a recognizable format. There's an excellent discussion of all aspects of resume creation, including samples of common resume styles at www.careeronestop.org/Veterans/JobSearch/ResumesAnd Applications/resume-styles.aspx. This website, sponsored by the DOL, also features a comprehensive **Veteran and Military Transition Center**.

Or, for a federal government job, you may want to check the resume builder at https://gogovernment.org/writing-your-federal-resume.

You can use the same resume for jobs that require similar experience and skills but you should plan to adapt it to emphasize specific strengths you have for particular jobs. For example, you might highlight your leadership experience for one employer and your technology or financial skills for another.

Your cover letter creates a critical first impression. The goal in writing it is to set you apart from other candidates and point out the skills you have that make you the right choice for the job. Each cover letter should be different, focused specifically on the position for which you're applying, and on the

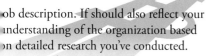

ob description. If should also reflect your understanding of the organization based on detailed research you've conducted.

You can be pretty sure that a generic, one-size-fits-all letter won't produce the result you want.

Before sending the letter and resume, be absolutely certain there are no spelling or grammar errors and that you've checked the spelling of the potential employer's name and organization. It's a good idea to have the letter and resume proofread by someone else. It's notoriously easy to miss your own mistakes.

TAKING A FEDERAL JOB

If you move from active duty to a job with the federal government, you can use a **Military Service Credit Deposit** to convert the years you accumulated toward a military pension to years of civil service. That makes you eligible to accrue leave time more quickly, retire earlier, and receive a larger retirement annuity.

For example, if you resigned from the military after ten years, began a civil service career, and chose after a year to convert, you'll have eleven years of seniority and credit toward retirement instead of one.

There are conditions, however, and a cost. You must apply within two years of being hired to avoid paying interest on the value of the credit you're depositing. The conversion itself, which typically takes about six months, must be completed before you retire from the civil service. Though the process varies somewhat among federal departments, it's always handled through the HR department and requires a copy of DD214 to establish your eligibility.

JOB SEARCH SITES
Good places to start your job search are the Veterans Employment Toolkit, at www.va.gov/vetsinworkplace/veteransresources.asp, the Veterans' Employment and Training Service (VETS) at www.dol.gov, and the US Chamber of Commerce Hiring Our Heroes at www.hiringourheroes.org. You can also check:
www.usajobs.gov
www.va.gov/careers-employment
https://helmetstohardhats.org
www.proudtoserveagain.com

What you pay, either by check or payroll deductions, is 3% of your military earnings. You use Form RI 20-97 to request that your service branch calculate your time and earnings to facilitate the conversion. Then your new agency's benefits department can compute what you owe. Once the conversion is complete, you want to be sure to have official verification for your records as proof of payment.

You can use the DFAS calculator at www.dfas.mil/civilianemployees/military-service/militaryservicedeposits/estimator.html to determine whether conversion makes financial sense for you, as it often does.

If you've retired from active duty, the story is different. In that case, you must waive your military pension to convert your credits, though you retain the medical and other benefits to which you're entitled. If you're accumulating credits for retirement from the Reserve component, however, a pension waiver isn't required.

Insuring Your Health

Your healthcare choices depend on when and how you leave the armed forces.

When you retire or separate from service, which is considered a **Qualifying Life Event (QLE)** like marriage and the birth of a child, you have 90 days to enroll in a new healthcare plan or purchase temporary coverage.

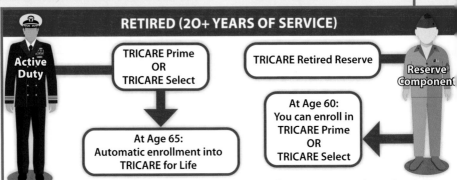

RETIRED (20+ YEARS OF SERVICE)

Active Duty

TRICARE Prime OR TRICARE Select

At Age 65: Automatic enrollment into TRICARE for Life

TRICARE Retired Reserve

At Age 60: You can enroll in TRICARE Prime OR TRICARE Select

Reserve Component

RETIRING FROM ACTIVE DUTY

When you retire, you can reenroll in TRICARE Prime (including the US Family Health Plan if available) or TRICARE Select within 90 days and keep your coverage intact. If you miss that deadline, you can request retroactive enrollment within 12 months of your retirement date. If you miss that deadline too, you have to wait for the next Open Season to enroll.

Between 90 and 180 days before you retire or start terminal leave, you should complete DD Form 2807-1 and schedule your Separation History and Physical Examination (SHPE) to establish your complete medical history and current health status.

Your coverage will change somewhat as a retired member, and your costs will increase. But unless you have compara-ble or better insurance through a civilian employer's plan, those changes are probably not significant enough to make you look elsewhere for coverage.

When you enroll in Medicare at 65 and pay Part B premiums, you'll automatically be enrolled in TRICARE for Life. For more information on how that works, check www.tricare.mil/Plans/HealthPlans/TFL and review the description of coverage in Chapter 4.

If you're a retired Reserve component member enrolled in TRICARE Retired Reserve (TRR), that coverage ends when you turn 60 and you become eligible for TRICARE Prime or TRICARE Select. You can enroll when your retired status is reflected in DEERS.

Retired members and their eligible dependents may also use FEDVIP to purchase dental and vision coverage.

ENROLLING FOR VA BENEFITS

You, and every veteran, should enroll for VA health benefits in addition to the health insurance you buy after separation or the TRICARE coverage you are eligible for as a retired or disabled member.

Your non-military spouse and dependent children aren't eligible for VA healthcare, however, unless you have a permanent and total disability.

It's easy to enroll online at www.va.gov/health-care, where you can learn about the benefits and find a list of the documents you'll need to complete the application.

Unlike Medicare, which provides the same benefits for all participants, VA benefits are based on who you are, what you need, and sometimes your income. You'll be assigned to one of eight priority groups based on factors like service-

The VA

WHAT THE VA COVERS

The VA does provides comprehensive care for eligible veterans, including:

- Basic preventive services including health exams and immunizations
- Inpatient hospital services, including surgery, acute and specialized care, cancer care, and other services

- Emergency services
- Mental health services to treat PTSD, MST, and other needs
- Assisted living and home healthcare
- Prescriptions
- Therapy and rehabilitation

VA healthcare services may be free or you may be assessed a fee based on your income level, disability rating, and military service history.

Retired members and members who separate from service because of service-connected disease or injury may receive healthcare services from both TRICARE and the VA. In most cases, TRICARE is the primary provider, though the VA may provide some services TRICARE doesn't, such as hearing aids or inpatient care for certain injuries or diseases.

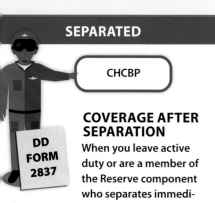

SEPARATED

CHCBP

COVERAGE AFTER SEPARATION

When you leave active duty or are a member of the Reserve component who separates immediately after active duty, you're eligible for temporary healthcare coverage. Your eligible dependents will also be covered.

The Continued Health Care Benefit Program (CHCBP) provides health insurance for you and your spouse and dependent children after you're no longer eligible for TRICARE. The coverage is the same as TRICARE Select, including prescriptions, though you do pay a premium for this program. You can learn more about the coverage at www.humana-military.com.

CHCBP will cost much more than you've been accustomed to paying, but it protects you until you're able to secure coverage through a civilian employer or an individual policy. That's important because it will cover large medical bills that you may incur and means you can't be denied treatment for not having insurance.

In addition, CHCBP ensures that your pre-existing conditions will continue to be covered. If there is a gap of 63 days or more when you don't have health insurance, you may have to wait as long as 18 months after enrolling in a new plan for those conditions to be covered.

If you are involuntarily separated from the military, are demobilized, or agree to become a member of the Selected Reserve immediately following release, you may qualify for the Transitional Assistance Management Program (TAMP), which provides 180 days of premium-free coverage. You can check with your service's personnel department for the eligibility rules or find them at https://tricare.mil/tamp.

connected disabilities and where and when you served.

There are enhanced benefits available for five years after discharge if you have served in a combat zone since November 11, 1998. You should be notified of your status less than a week after enrolling. You'll receive a *Veteran Health Benefits Handbook* that details the services available to the group to which

you're assigned and a Veterans Health Identification Card (VHIC).

If you're not approved or believe you qualify for a higher priority, you can appeal. For information, download a brochure from the Board of Veterans' Appeals detailing the process at www.bva.va.gov/docs/Pamphlets/How-Do-I-Appeal-Booklet--508Compliance.pdf.

Insurance After SGLI

Separating from service requires a new approach to life insurance.

When you leave the military, you leave behind the life insurance coverage you've had through SGLI. But what you don't leave behind is the need to provide financial security for the people who depend on you if you're no longer around to provide it yourself.

You have some time to decide on new insurance because SGLI is automatically extended for 120 days after separation with the same death benefit as your existing policy. But before that period ends, you need to arrange for new coverage for yourself and also for your spouse if he or she is covered through **Family SGLI (FSGLI)**.

You have three alternatives: converting your SGLI policy to a **Veteran's Group Life Insurance (VGLI)** policy, converting to a permanent policy from an insurer affiliated with the VA, or choosing a new insurance provider for a term policy. In making the decision, you'll want to use a life insurance calculator like the one at www.benefits.va.gov/insurance to calculate the amount of coverage you need. You'll also want to be sure you can afford a policy's premiums before you buy.

CONVERTING YOUR POLICY

VGLI, like SGLI, is a term policy with maximum coverage of $400,000. Initially, the VGLI death benefit cannot be more than your existing SGLI death benefit. But, if you're not at that maximum when you convert, you can gradually increase your coverage in $25,000 increments until you reach the limit.

VGLI is **renewable** which means you can extend your coverage annually without having to demonstrate that you're in good health. But the premiums aren't level, or the same for your lifetime, as SGLI premiums are. They increase every five years.

Alternately, you can convert your SGLI policy to a **permanent policy**—but not a

term policy—offered by one of the commercial insurance companies affiliated with the VA program within 120 days from the date you separate. Choosing one of these policies provides the opportunity to increase your coverage beyond the $400,000 cap set by VGLI. But as with

LIFE INSURANCE WHILE IN SERVICE

most permanent policies, the premiums are likely to be higher initially.

A spouse who has a FSGLI policy may convert it to an individual permanent policy with one of the affiliated insurance companies within 120 days of the date that family coverage ends. Another alternative is choosing a commercial term policy. A non-military spouse isn't eligible for VGLI.

TIMELY CHOICES

As long as you convert to a permanent policy with an affiliated company within 120 days of separation, you don't have to answer questions about your health. That's important if you have health problems, which can make it difficult or sometimes impossible to purchase a good policy at a reasonable price.

To be sure there's no gap in your insurance, you should act within the 120-day window. But if you choose VGLI, you have an additional 120 days—240 in total—to convert without passing a physical examination and a total of 485

TERM OR PERMANENT INSURANCE

In deciding whether to buy term or permanent insurance as you separate or retire from service, you'll want to consider the following questions:

- Do you have mortgage payments and tuition bills that life insurance would help cover?

- How will your insurance needs change as your mortgage is paid off and your children have finished school?

- Would a large life insurance policy provide better protection for your surviving spouse than income from the Survivor Benefit Plan (SBP)?

A helpful resource is the *VA Life Insurance Handbook*, which you can find at https://www.benefits.va.gov/insurance/ins_publications/asp.

You might also seek free objective advice from your installation's Financial Management Program, Military and Family Support Center, or Military OneSource.

LIFE INSURANCE AS A VETERAN

TERM LIFE INSURANCE   VS.   PERMANENT INSURANCE

 Convert to VGLI

 **Convert to a permanent policy offered by an affiliated commercial insurance company**

 Compare and choose your own term policy

PARTICIPATING INSURERS
Companies that offer permanent policies for SGLI conversion are listed at www.benefits.va.gov/insurance/forms/SGL_133_ed2019-07.pdf. However, not all of them offer the conversion option in all 50 states.

---

days from separation to purchase policy.

The VA has developed a detailed worksheet that helps you compare VGLI with other policies you're considering. You can find and print the document at www.benefits.va.gov/insurance/vgli_rates_compare_vgli.asp.

CHOOSING A NEW TERM POLICY

If you decide that term life insurance meets your needs better than permanent and are in good health, you shouldn't have any trouble finding competitive bids for the coverage you want. You can check online, work with your financial institution, or contact an insurance agent.

You'll want to compare the policies you're considering carefully. Be sure to check each insurer's financial standing based on ratings from independent rating agencies, such as AM Best, Fitch, and Moody's, and to investigate its reputation for customer service.

You might want to ask if the policies offer an **accelerated benefits option**

(ABO), as VGLI does, that allows you early access to a portion of the death benefit if you are terminally ill and need the money to cover your healthcare costs. And, if you have a potentially dangerous hobby, like scuba diving or flying, you might ask if the insurer would pay if that hobby caused your death.

AN INSURANCE PORTFOLIO

Buying insurance doesn't have to be an either/or proposition. You can combine a term policy with a permanent one, with one supplementing the other or earmarked for a specific use. For example, with a term policy, you can gradually reduce the amount of coverage as you get older and your financial obligations decrease. That reduces the cost while still providing a benefit to help your survivors with immediate costs.

Buying a Home

Leaving the military may be the perfect time to buy a home.

If you've lived in government quarters or rental properties throughout your military career, you and you spouse may decide that you want to buy or build a home of your own. If you've chosen a community where you plan to put down roots and one or both of you have well-paying government or civilian jobs, buying may fit more comfortably into your budget than it has before. And, as a veteran, you can usually take advantage of the **VA home loan guaranty** even if you've used it before.

MORE ABOUT VA LOANS
For information on comparing buying with renting, how the guaranty works, and how you qualify, see pages 72-73.

PLANNING AHEAD
At least six months before you begin looking for a mortgage loan, log onto to www.annualcreditreport.com to check your credit report at one of the three credit reporting agencies.

You want to be sure there are no red flags that might make a potential lender hesitant to offer you a loan. Major concerns include being 30 days or more late with credit payments, having large credit debts, or defaulting on a loan.

If you have a weak history, you may be offered a much more expensive loan or turned down altogether. But if there's a mistake or if your SCRA protections were ignored during a deployment, contact the credit rating agency where you found the problem to have it corrected. There are clear instructions on the site explaining what to do.

THE COSTS OF BUYING
Before you begin to search actively for a home, you'll want to be sure you can cover the costs of buying.

Perhaps most important is the question of a **down payment**—the amount you pay out-of-pocket to reduce what you borrow. Unlike most loans, those with a VA guaranty don't require cash up front. But there are good reasons to make a down payment if you can. By reducing what you need to borrow, you can reduce your mortgage payments substantially.

You'll also need enough cash on hand when the purchase is finalized to pay the closing, or settlement, costs, including legal fees and title insurance. Although a VA guaranty limits these costs, you may owe more than the national average, which is 2% of the loan amount, if you're buying in an area with high real estate taxes.

Other costs you should anticipate include buying appliances and furniture, regular maintenance, essential repairs, and potential improvements.

QUALIFYING TO BORROW
If you've decided to buy, you want a lender who offers a competitive **annual percentage rate (APR)**. A quick

LOAN

DOWN PAYMENT

WHAT A PITI

In addition to the principal, or amount of the loan, and interest, your monthly mortgage loan payment will almost certainly include 1/12 of your local property taxes and 1/12 of your annual homeowners insurance premium. Together, principal, interest, taxes, and insurance are known as PITI.

nternet search at sites like www.bankrate.com will give you a sense of what the current range is. Other factors that influence the cost of borrowing are the size of the loan and its term. The shorter the term—say 15 rather than 30 years—the less expensive borrowing is, though the larger your monthly payments are likely to be.

You might also investigate a hybrid, or multiyear, mortgage that offers an initial fixed rate for a specific period, such as ten years, and then becomes adjustable. The initial rate will be lower than a regular fixed rate, meaning smaller monthly payments and easier qualification. That can be a real plus for first-time homeowners.

Potential lenders consider your credit history, income, and **debt-to-income ratio (DTI)** in evaluating your application. DTI measures all your outstanding debt, including PITI, in relation to your income. As a rule, it's harder to qualify with a DTI above 41%, and 36% is the preferable limit.

LENDER RESPONSE

Within three business days of receiving your mortgage loan application, the lender must provide a good faith **loan estimate** of the total cost of borrowing to clarify what you'll owe and make it easier to compare offers.

Just before you finalize the purchase you'll receive a **closing disclosure**, which you'll want to check carefully. The terms should match your most recent loan estimate. You can find samples and tips on what to look for on these forms on the Consumer Financial Protection Bureau website (www.consumerfinance.gov).

FIXED OR ADJUSTABLE?

One decision you'll have to make is whether to take a **fixed** or **adjustable** rate loan. With a fixed rate, your monthly

payments remain the same for the life of the loan, making it easier to budget. With a variable rate, which may be lower initially, your payment is adjusted up or down, typically annually, to reflect changes in interest rates. If your monthly payment increased substantially, as it could, you might find you couldn't afford it and risk defaulting.

DISABILITY HOUSING GRANTS

The VA also provides special housing benefits for veterans with permanent and total service-connected disabilities. These benefits include:

- The Specially Adapted Housing (SAH) Grant and the Special Housing Adaptation (SHA) Grant provide funding to construct, modify, or purchase a home that enables you to live independently or accommodates your disability.
- The Temporary Residence Adaptation (TRA) Grant provides interim financial support for a disabled veteran residing in a family member's home.

You can learn more about these benefits at https://www.benefits.va.gov/homeloans/adaptedhousing.asp and apply by filling out VA Form 26-4555 at www.ebenefits.va.gov or calling 1-877-827-3702 for a claim form.

Disability Compensation

There are many types of disabilities, but also many disability benefits available.

If you're a veteran with an injury or disease that was caused or aggravated on active duty or active duty training, you may be entitled to VA disability compensation. You may also qualify if you were injured or had a heart attack or stroke during inactive duty training. In most cases, you must have been honorably discharged or be a retired veteran to receive these payments.

This tax-free benefit covers a wide range of physical and mental health issues, including conditions that arise only after you've left the military, provided the VA determines them to be service connected.

The compensation you'll receive depends on the nature and severity of your disability. And having dependents—a spouse, children, or parents—usually increases your benefit amount. As a rule, your payment will also be adjusted for times you couldn't work because of your disability or related illness.

MULTIPLE DISABILITIES

If you have two or more disabilities, the VA uses a special formula to calculate a combined rating. The formula is not cumulative. The highest rating establishes a base on which the second rating is calculated, which then becomes the new base for rating the next less severe disability. The final rating is then rounded up or down to the nearest 10%.

For example, a 50% rating plus a 20% rating does not equal a 70% rating. Instead, the disabilities are arranged in their order of severity. The rating would be 60%.

There's a detailed explanation at www.benefits.va.gov/compensation/rates-index.asp.

DISABILITY RATINGS

You must apply for disability compensation to have the VA consider your case. Applying also ensures that your dependents will be eligible for the VA benefits to which they're entitled.

If your claim is approved, the agency assigns a rating of 0% to 100% in 10% increments. Generally, the more severe your disability, the higher the rating will be. That means more compensation and makes you eligible for additional benefits.

If you receive a 0% rating, your disability does not qualify for compensation However, it leaves open the possibility of receiving a higher rating at some future point should your condition worsen or result in a related illness.

DISABILITY INFORMATION
The various types of disability compensation, eligibility requirements, and payment amounts, along with an explanation of the claims process, can be found under the Compensation tab at www.benefits.va.gov/compensation/types-compensation.asp.

Table I-Combined Ratings Table
[10 combined with 10 is 19]

	10	20	30	40	50	60	70	80	9
19	27	35	43	51	60	68	76	84	92
20	28	36	44	52	60	68	76	84	92
21	29	37	45	53	61	68	76	84	92
22	30	38	45	53	61	69	77	84	92
23	31	38	46	54	62	69	77	85	92
24	32	39	47	54	62	70	77	85	92
25	33	40	48	55	63	70	78	85	93
26	33	41	48	56	63	70	78	85	93
27	34	42	49	56	64	71	78	85	93
28	35	42	50	57	64	71	78	86	93
29	36	43	50	57	65	72	79	86	93
30	37	44	51	58	65	72	79	86	93
31	38	45	52	59	66	72	79	86	93

CHANGES IN DISABILITY RATINGS

Your disability rating is not necessarily permanent, and the VA has the right to reexamine your claim. If they do, they will send a Notice of Reexamination with an appointment time and date. You should be sure to attend since the VA can reduce or terminate your disability payments if you don't.

The reason for the reexamination, which generally occurs several years after your initial rating but can occur at any time, is for the VA to determine if the initial rating no longer applies because your condition has worsened, improved, or disappeared. After the reexamination, the VA may recommend increasing or decreasing your rating, leaving it as it is, or terminating it.

In some cases, your rating may be protected, depending on several factors, including the type of disability, how long you've had the rating, and your age. For example, if your disability is considered permanent or total, you are unlikely to be reexamined.

If the VA decides to change your rating, they must officially notify you. If your rating is lowered and you don't agree, you have 30 days to appeal the decision and up to 60 days to submit evidence that the decrease was unwarranted.

HAVE A COLA

To ensure that the purchasing power of your disability benefits isn't eroded by inflation, the VA makes annual cost-of-living adjustments, or COLAs, using the same rate that determines the change in Social Security benefits.

AID AND ATTENDANCE

Recognizing that more severe disabilities create exceptional hardships for veterans and their families, the VA also provides Special Monthly Compensation (SMC). Essentially, SMC pays a higher rate of compensation for veterans who are housebound, need help performing everyday functions, or who are living under circumstances that require another person to provide constant care.

This benefit, which is commonly referred to as aid and attendance, can be paid to the veterans, as well as to their spouses and parents.

SPECIAL DISABILITY CLAIMS

The VA recognizes that certain service-connected disabilities not officially listed as covered, or rated, may require special care. So it provides compensation to help veterans cope with these circumstances. As examples, you may qualify for disability coverage to buy or modify your vehicle to enable you to drive, or to replace clothing damaged by prosthetic devices.

TAX RELIEF

If you're a veteran who is eligible for retired pay and VA disability pay, you must waive a portion of your retired pay equal to the amount of your disability compensation. Since retired pay is taxable and disability compensation is tax exempt, you actually come out ahead.

However, the waived amount is restored if you qualify for Concurrent Retirement and Disability Pay (CRDP), which is taxable, or Combat Related Special Compensation (CRSC), which is not. If you qualify for both payments, you'll receive the one that's most beneficial, though you can change to the other if you wish.

You can compare the programs at www.dfas.mil/retiredmilitary/disability/comparison.html.

Combat-injured veterans who receive **disability severance pay (DSP)** owe no tax on the one-time lump-sum payment even if they later receive VA disability compensation.

Disability Claims

You can file your claim months before you leave the military, at separation, or when a disability appears.

Filing a disability claim is not simple. You use specific procedures before and after you leave the service. There are several options for filing new or supplemental claims if your disability worsens. And if you have to appeal a claims decision, there are multiple steps.

Learning what and when to file before you start the process can save time, reduce frustration, and may help you secure disability payments sooner. For more information, go to www.va.gov/disability/how-to-file-claim/.

FULLY DEVELOPED CLAIMS
You can often expedite the claims process by filing a Fully Developed Claim. You'll need to file VA Form 21-526 EZ, submit all your supporting evidence, certify there's no additional evidence related to the claim, and take any medical exams the VA requires. The VA can, with your permission, request records and information on file with federal agencies, though it saves time if you submit these with your claim.

BEFORE SEPARATION

| 365 DAYS | 180 DAYS | 90 DAYS |

BEFORE LEAVING THE SERVICE
If you believe you have a medical condition that was caused or made worse by your active duty service, you can file a disability claim before you separate from service.

180- 90 days before separting, you can file a claim through the Benefits Delivery at Discharge (BDD) program. You must have a known separation date, be on full-time active duty, and not file a claim that requires special handling.

Fewer than 90 days before you separate you can file a **fully developed** or **standard claim** along with supporting documents, such as a doctor's examination and medical test reports, as evidence to support your claim.

FILING A DISABILITY CLAIM
You can speed up the application process by gathering the evidence you'll need to support your claim, including:

✔ Your discharge papers (DD214 or separation documents)

✔ Records of treatment you received while serving, including at a nonmilitary facility, are extremely important

✔ Medical or hospital records and test results, whether from the VA or a private provider

✔ Supporting statements from people who can speak to your condition

You can file your claim online, by mail, or in person. If you need help with an initial filing or an appeal, you can work with a specially trained and accredited representative or a Veterans Service Officer (VSO). There's no fee for help with an initial filing, though agents and attorneys may charge for subsequent work. You can find help at www.ebenefits.va.gov/ebenefits/vso-search.

FILING AN APPEAL

If the VA denies your claim or you disagree with a decision the VA makes, you have the right to appeal within a year from the date you're notified of its action.

To appeal, you'll need to follow the procedure in effect on the date you received the decision. If that was on February 19, 2019, or after, there's a streamlined four-step process you can pursue:

 Step 1: File a Supplemental Claim that provides new evidence supporting your case for disability compensation using VA Form 20-0995.

Step 2: Request a Higher-Level Review with a senior reviewer, who will determine, based on the evidence you originally provided, whether a different decision is warranted. You can choose to schedule an informal call with the reviewer. Use VA Form 20-0996.

 Step 3: Request a Board Appeal with a Veterans Law Judge under the Rapid Assessment Modernization Program using VA Form 10182. You can ask the judge to review your case based on the evidence previously submitted or request a hearing to discuss your case and introduce new supporting evidence.

Step 4: If you disagree with the Board's decision, you can file another Supplemental Claim with new evidence or **appeal to the US Court of Appeals for Veterans Claims** within 120 days of the Board's decision.

You can find more information at www.va.gov/disability/file-an-appeal/

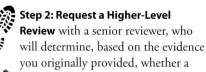

AFTER SEPARATION OR RETIREMENT

365 DAYS

DISABILITIES THAT ARISE LATER

As a general rule, you have a year after separation to claim a disability. But some conditions that appear later may qualify if the VA determines they're service connected.

Chronic diseases such as arthritis, hypertension, or ulcers that appear within a year after you're discharged and are rated at least 10% disabling are presumed to be service connected. So are diseases, including tuberculosis, multiple sclerosis, and others, even if they appear more than a year after you've left the service.

There are different time limits for disabilities resulting from tropical diseases, exposure to radiation, certain herbicides, contaminated water, and being a prisoner of war.

A full list of covered illnesses and the time frames that apply appear in Title 38, Code of Federal Regulation, 3.09(a). Remember, though, the longer you wait to file a claim for these disabilities, the more complicated the process is likely to be.

TYPES OF CLAIMS

In addition to your initial claim, you can file follow-on claims if your condition worsens or your circumstances change. In either case, you'll need up-to-date evidence, such as a new medical report, to support your claim.

You file an **increased claim** to increase your disability rating and receive higher monthly payments.

You file a **new claim** to increase your disability benefit, receive special monthly payments, or shift to Individual Unemployability status if you are unable to work because of your disability.

If you develop a new disability that's linked to one already covered, you file a secondary claim to increase your benefit. For example, you may develop heart disease as a result of high-blood pressure.

TRACKING CLAIMS AND APPEALS

You can track the status of your claim or appeal by signing in at www.va.gov/claim-or-appeal-status/.

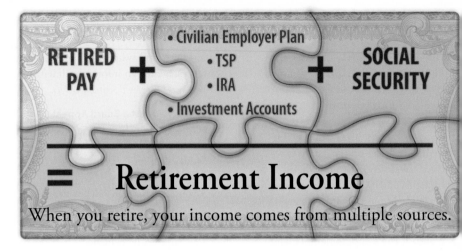

Retirement Income

When you retire, your income comes from multiple sources.

If you served at least 20 years on active duty, accumulated the equivalent qualifying service in the Reserve component, combined the years you spent on active duty with qualifying service in the Reserves, or have a qualifying medical disability, you're eligible for lifetime retired pay.

You can supplement your retired pay with compensation from a civilian job in either the public or private sector. Your post-retirement earnings don't reduce your retired pay, and, if they're substantial,

you can increase the amount you're investing in a new employer's retirement savings plan or an individual retirement account (IRA) or taxable account to bolster your long-term financial security. When you reach 59½ you can begin to take TSP withdrawals. If the account is tax-deferred, you'll owe income tax on the amounts you take out. But if it's a Roth account, withdrawals are tax-exempt if the account has been open at least five years.

But if you don't need the TSP money to live on, you may want to leave it in your account to continue to compound.

RETIRED PAY BEGINS

RETIRED PAY

If you retire from active duty, your first retired pay is direct deposited to your account of record on the first business day of the month following the month you retire. But that's contingent on DFAS having your complete retirement package including a correct DD Form 2656.

If you retire from the Reserves, your retired pay begins when you turn 60 even if you retire earlier.

DD FORM 2656

LEGACY HIGH-3

To find your pension, your retirement pay base is multiplied by 2.5% (0.025) for each year of service (YoS).

Pay Base x (YoS x 2.5%) = Monthly Income

EXAMPLE

If your pay base was $9,000 and you had 25 years of service you'd be entitled to a monthly income of $5,625.

$9,000 x (25 x 0.025) = $5,625 a Month

The amount you receive each month if you retire from active duty is calculated using a formula that includes:

- **Retired pay base**, which is determined by your average base pay (excluding allowances and special pay) during the 36 continuous months it was the highest, or your High-3

COLA

COST OF LIVING ADJUSTMENTS

Your retired pay is adjusted each year on January 1 to reflect the impact of the annual **cost of living adjustment (COLA)** to which you're entitled. In most cases, the amount of the COLA, which varies from year to year, is equal to the percentage increase in the third-quarter Consumer Price Index (CPI) the previous year. If the CPI is flat or decreases, the COLA will be zero.

The same COLA is applied to the incomes of survivors of members who died on active or inactive duty as well as survivors of retired members who participated in the SBP. Over time these COLAs have the potential to increase your income substantially.

RETIRED PAY PROBLEMS

If you have problems with your retired pay, you should contact Retired and Annuitant (R&A) Pay, the DFAS agency for retired members and eligible surviving spouses. The number is 800-321-1080. If you have questions about disability ratings and entitlements, contact the VA at 800-827-1000. If the issue is offsetting and overlapping entitlements, contact both agencies.

- The number of years you served

- A multiplier determined by whether you are a member of the **Legacy High-3** system (2.5%) or the **Blended Retirement System (BRS)** (2%) which became effective January 1, 2018

You can use the calculators at https://militarypay.defense.gov/Calculators/ to estimate your retired pay based on the system of which you're a part. Remember, though, that because retired pay is taxable, federal and state taxes, if any, will be withheld from your gross pay, as well as medical and dental premiums if applicable, and **Survivor Benefit Plan (SBP)** premiums if you participate in the plan.

SOCIAL SECURITY INCOME

Since you contributed to Social Security while you drew military pay, you're entitled to your full Social Security benefit when you reach what's considered full retirement age (FRA). That age has increased gradually from 65 for anyone born before 1938 and tops out at 67 for anyone born in 1960 or later.

You can begin taking benefits at 62, but unless you need the money it's generally better to wait until you reach your FRA or, ideally, until you turn 70. If you begin to collect at 62, your benefit is permanently reduced. Another reason to wait is that the money you make at a civilian job before you reach your FRA will reduce your benefit by $1 for every $2 or $3 you earn once you exceed the low thresholds set by Social Security. The reduction doesn't apply once you reach your FRA, no matter how much you earn. And, if you wait to collect, your benefit increases 8% a year every year after you reach your FRA until you turn 70, when the benefit is the most it can be.

Your spouse can claim Social Security based on his or her own earnings record or, if you're receiving benefits, collect 50% of your FRA if that amount is higher. If your spouse begins taking benefits at 62 or any time before his or her FRA, the benefit is permanently reduced.

If you die, your spouse is entitled to his or her own benefit or to yours, whichever is higher. The longer you've waited to take your benefit, the higher your benefit will be, and the more income it will give to your spouse. A surviving spouse living in the same household is also eligible for a one-time death benefit of $255.

A percentage of your Social Security benefit may be subject to tax, depending on your income.

Reserve Retirement

You need to accumulate at least 50 points a year for 20 years to retire from the Reserve component.

If you serve in the National Guard or the Regular Reserves or transition to the Inactive Ready Reserve (IRR) after leaving active duty, your eligibility for retired pay is determined by the points you accumulate on an annual basis rather than the actual number of years you serve.

Specifically, you need 20 qualifying years of service, sometimes described as *good years.* Those are the years in which you earn at least 50 points for your participation and for various activities you performed during the year on both active and inactive duty. The greatest number of points you can earn in a year is 365, which would occur, for example, in a year you spent on active duty.

All the points you earn count, even if in some years they're fewer than the 50 required for a qualifying year.

KEEPING TRACK OF YOUR POINTS

Retirement points are credited on an annual basis over the course of each year, which begins on the first day you join and ends on the day prior to your anniversary date. For example, if you join on April 22 of one year, your anniversary year runs through April 21 of the next year.

Your service branch should maintain records of the points you have accumulated and notify you when you have qualified for retired pay. However, it's

HAVING A GOOD YEAR
In a typical Reserve unit you collect 15 points for annual participation, another 15 points for annual training, and 48 points for monthly drills, for a total of 78 points. That makes it a good year. You earn additional points for activities such as being in an Honor Guard and completing correspondence courses.

smart to review your points on a regular basis, which you should be able to do on the personnel section of the branch's website. It's especially important if you've had an interruption in service or mobilization, or you've engaged in an activity that earns retirement points. In fact, it's a good idea to print out and keep paper copies of your annual retirement point summaries in your own files.

PARTIAL YEARS OF SERVICE

If you have a break in active service, you may be credited for a partial year of service that will count towards the 20 years you need to qualify for retired pay. To get the credit you must have earned enough retirement points in the days you served which, when computed proportionally, would be equal to or greater than 50 points. Partial qualifying years are counted in figuring the total qualifying years you need to collect Reserve retirement pay. You can find a detailed explanation in DoD Instruction 1215.07.

My Annual Retirement Plans

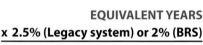

CALCULATING YOUR RETIRED PAY

The amount of retired pay to which you're entitled depends on your equivalent years of service and is calculated in three steps.

1. **Equivalent years** are determined by dividing your total number of points over the 20 or more years of your qualifying service by 360, which is the equivalent of 12 military months.

2. The result is multiplied by the appropriate multiplier—2.5% if you're part of the Legacy system and 2% if you're part of the BRS—to find your **retired pay multiplier**.

3. Your retired pay multiplier is multiplied by your High-3 **retirement pay base** to find your monthly retired pay.

	Total Number of Points
EQUIVALENT YEARS	360 (12 military months)

x 2.5% (Legacy system) or 2% (BRS)
= **RETIRED PAY MULTIPLIER**
x **High-3 Retirement Pay Base**
= **MONTHLY RETIRED PAY**

Retiring Before Age 60

RESERVE HEALTH PLANS

If you retire from the Reserve Component before turning 60, you and your dependents are eligible to purchase TRICARE Retired Reserve although not for other TRICARE plans.

When you turn 60, you're eligible for the same TRICARE health benefits that are available to other retired members. The plans for which you're eligible—Prime, Select, US Family Health Plan or TRICARE for Life—depend on where you live and, in the case of TRICARE for Life, whether you are 65 and enrolled in Medicare Parts A and B. Your spouse will also qualify for TRICARE for Life at 65 if he or she is enrolled in Medicare Parts A and B.

If you participate in a TRICARE plan, your children who are younger than 26 but don't qualify for coverage under the family plan may purchase TRICARE Young Adult.

RETIREMENT READY

You can retire as a Reserve or National Guard member as soon as you have enough qualifying service. But unlike members who retire from active duty, you're generally not eligible to receive retired pay until you turn 60. And payment is not automatic. When you're eligible you must request that the payments begin.

There is an exception, though, if you're a member of the Ready Reserve and have been recalled to active duty or called to active service in response to a national emergency since January 28, 2008. In that case, the age at which you're eligible for retired pay is reduced three months for every cumulative period of 90 days in which you serve in either of these capacities.

You can increase your retired pay if, when you're eligible to retire, you join the Retired Reserves. That's because the base pay for your rank when you turn 60 will be higher than it was at the time you retired, thanks to annual pay increases and COLAs. So your High-3 retirement base pay, one of the factors that determine retired pay, will be higher. However, as a member of the Retired Reserves you could be called back to active duty or called up to the Ready Reserves.

Managing TSP Investments

The more your account earns, the more secure your retirement.

If you contributed to a TSP account while you were on active duty or a member of the Reserve component, you have another potential source of retirement income when you leave the work force for good. The more effectively you manage your account, the greater that income has the potential to be.

A DIFFERENT ROLLOVER OPTION

Unless you take a job with the federal government, you won't be able to make additional contributions to your TSP account after you separate or retire. But, if you accumulate assets in a civilian retirement plan, you're entitled to move those

LEAVING THE MILITARY

TSP accounts are portable, which usually means you have three choices when you separate or retire. You can:

- Leave the accumulated assets in your TSP account
- Roll the assets over to an IRA

alternatives offer, the comparative cost of the accounts, and how strongly you feel about consolidating your retirement assets into a single account. You'll find TSP is a strong competitor based on its low cost and investment options, though an IRA or employer plan may offer more investment choices.

- Move the assets to a new employ-

er's plan, if the plan accepts rollovers What's best for you will depend on the investments the

You also have the right to take a lump sum distribution in cash, though that's rarely smart. You will owe taxes on the full withdrawal when you file your tax return for the year. If you're younger than 59½, you may also be liable for a 10% tax penalty.

TAPPING YOUR ACCOUNT

When you're eligible to withdraw from your TSP account, you can find a detailed discussion of your options at https://www.tsp.gov/PlanningTools/LivingInRetirement/withdrawalStrategies.html. You'll also find a retirement calculator to help you decide how to receive the income to which you're entitled.

TSP LIFE ANNUITY

After you leave the uniformed service or another federal government agency, you can choose to purchase a TSP life annuity with $3,500 or more of your vested account balance. The annuity will provide guaranteed monthly payments for your lifetime in addition to your retired pay and any other income you may have. If you have a joint annuitant—typically but not necessarily your spouse—the payments will continue as long as either of you is alive.

There are advantages and drawbacks to life annuities, so you may want to consult a qualified financial adviser deciding whether or not to purchase one.

assets into your TSP account when you leave that job. A retirement plan doesn't usually accept rollovers once you're no longer contributing to the plan, so it's worth serious consideration if you like what TSP offers.

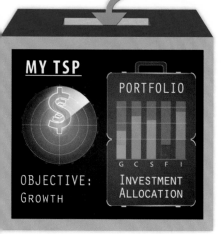

REVIEWING TSP INVESTMENTS

You don't have to do anything to leave your account in the TSP. But you may want to take a look at the way your money is invested. Like many people, you may have never adjusted the way your account is allocated even though your financial situation has probably changed.

Taking another look can work to your advantage, especially if you are heavily invested in the G Fund, which invests in a portfolio of short-term US Treasury securities. Its advantage is that you won't lose money. But you're very likely to lose buying power since the fund's return after adjusting for inflation and taxes is very modest. Similarly, if you're in a lifecycle (L) Fund, the fund will invest more conservatively as time passes. Of course, you can always stick with those funds if your inclination is to protect the assets you've accumulated.

But if you're financially more secure now than when you opened the TSP account, or if you're collecting retired or disability pay while working at a civilian job, you may be ready to take a bit more investment risk in the hope of realizing a better return. In that case, you may consider investing in a combination of the plan's C, S, and I stock funds.

CHOOSING A ROTH

If you continue your contributions to your TSP account because you've moved to a new federal government position or earn Reserve component income, you may want to put future contributions into a Roth account rather than a traditional tax-deferred account. You can authorize this change on the TSP website or by calling 877-968-3778 to use the automated ThriftLine or talk to a representative.

Unlike contributions to a tax-deferred TSP account, your contributions to a Roth account are not tax-deductible and don't reduce your taxable income. But a Roth account provides more flexibility in the future.

Specifically, you'll be able to take totally tax-exempt withdrawals after you're at least 59½, provided the account has been open at least five years. Tax-exempt income means lower income taxes and more money in your pocket during retirement. Tax-exempt withdrawals are required when you turn 72, but you could roll over your TSP Roth balance to a Roth IRA. There, withdrawals are never required, and your assets can continue to compound.

If you qualify for matching contributions—up to 5% of your pay each year—from your new agency to your TSP account, the matching funds will go into a tax-deferred account that mirrors the investments in your Roth account.

TAX ON WITHDRAWALS

If any contributions to your TSP account were made with tax-exempt pay earned while serving in a combat or hazardous duty zone, the rules governing what portion of a withdrawal is taxable are complicated. You may want to consult an experienced tax adviser to be sure you're filing correctly.

Estate Planning

You can't control future events, but you can plan for them.

Your estate is an entity that's created at your death, with a legal and a tax identity that's different than yours. The financial and personal assets that are included in your will are transferred to the estate, as are your debts.

It's the job of the executor whom you've named in your will to transfer the estate assets to their new owners in keeping with the wishes you've expressed in the will. The **executor** also pays the estate's bills and settles other unresolved issues.

The executor acts under the supervision of the **probate court** in the state where your will is filed at your death. In most cases, the process works smoothly, but there can be delays if the estate is complicated or your will is contested.

You can simplify the executor's task if you review and update your will, perhaps every five years or so, to be sure it's timely. If you've moved to a different state since the last update, it's often smart to have a new will executed there.

ACCESS TO YOUR RECORDS

One of the best things you can do for those who will survive you is to leave orderly financial records that detail the money coming into your checking and savings accounts, amounts that are automatically debited, bills that you pay regularly, and any outstanding debts owed by you or to you.

You'll also want to have a primary checking account that's either held jointly with right of survivorship (JTWROS) or placed in a living trust. That way it won't be frozen at your death and your survivors will have access to the account balance.

You'll want to provide a list of retirement accounts, indicating those that will require annual required minimum distributions (RMDs).

You may also write a letter—known as a **memorandum**—with instructions for

disposing of certain assets and distributing personal belongings and other private property not mentioned in the will. In some states this memorandum is binding. But even where it's not, instructions like these can be a great help to the executor and surviving family members in carrying out your wishes.

Equally essential are detailed instructions for accessing online accounts and other digital assets. You may have a written record or use an online password manager. If you use a password manager, check to confirm that there will be a way for your executor or a family member to access your secure information after your death.

BEYOND THE WILL

Having a will is extremely important, even if many of your assets pass directly to a joint owner or beneficiary. But there are some things you'll want your survivors to know that you should clarify with them or explain in writing:

- Your wishes for final arrangements
- Where to locate your military service records
- The organizations to be notified of your death
- The jointly held assets that will have to be retitled in the name of the new owner
- The location of your will and other legal and financial documents and passwords for online accounts

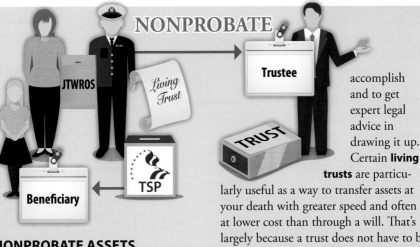

NONPROBATE

NONPROBATE ASSETS

Assets that are not transferred by your will are described as **nonprobate assets**. They include:

- Assets that were held as joint tenants with right of survivorship (JTWROS) and become the property of your joint owner
- Assets, such as a TSP account or a life insurance policy, which go directly to the beneficiary you named
- Assets you transferred to a trust to be transferred by the trustee to the trust beneficiaries

USING TRUSTS

You establish a **trust** to hold assets that you transfer to it and name a **trustee** to administer the trust and distribute its assets in keeping with your instructions. In many ways, a trustee's role is similar to an executor's, and they may be the same person.

To use a trust successfully, it's important to know what you want it to accomplish and to get expert legal advice in drawing it up. Certain **living trusts** are particularly useful as a way to transfer assets at your death with greater speed and often at lower cost than through a will. That's largely because a trust does not have to be probated, as a will does, or administered under court supervision.

These living trusts are **revocable**, which means you can change the terms as often as you wish, as you can with a will. And you can act as trustee of your own revocable living will, naming a **co-trustee** or **successor trustee** to assume control at your death.

A living trust is particularly advantageous if you own real estate in a state other than the one where you live. If those properties are distributed by your will, it could mean probate proceedings in more than one state.

Trust distributions are also confidential, unlike wills, where the bequests are public information. And while it is possible for a disgruntled beneficiary to take legal issue with a trust, it's much more difficult than contesting a will.

You can find information on wills, living wills, advance directives, and powers of attorney on pages 78-79.

Survivor Benefits

You can ensure that your spouse has lifetime income after your death.

Although your retired pay automatically stops at your death, you can provide guaranteed lifetime income for your spouse, and income for your minor children if you wish, by participating in the **Survivor Benefits Plan (SBP)**.

You must enroll in the program before your retirement date by completing Part III of DD Form 2656, "Data for Payment of Retired Personnel and SBP Elections and Eligible Beneficiaries." You need a witness to the completed form who must sign the document on the same day you do.

If you elect not to participate or choose less than the maximum benefit, your spouse must sign the form and have the signature notarized on or after the date you signed and before your retirement date.

HOW THE SBP WORKS

When you participate in SBP, you choose the amount of your retired pay that will be the base of the coverage. It could be the default amount, which is your full gross pay, or a smaller amount, but not less than $300. After your death, your beneficiary will receive 55% of the base amount you've chosen.

To pay for the plan, you agree to have pretax dollars deducted from your gross retired pay, reducing the income you receive each month.

If you became a member of the armed forces on or after March 1, 1990, and you retire after having served on active duty for at least 20 years, the cost of the SBP premium is 6.5% of the **base amount** you have selected. If you retire from the Reserve component, the premiums are calculated at the same rate but there's an add-on cost that depends on the beneficiary you name, whether you choose an immediate or deferred annuity, and the age difference between yourself and your spouse. A financial professional can help you clarify your options.

If you became a member before March 1990 or retire because of a disability, the premium can be calculated in one of two ways, which you can review on the DFAS website. You're entitled to choose the method that will cost you less.

If your base amount is your full retired pay, your spouse is the beneficiary, you've paid premiums for 360 months, and you're at least 70, your policy is considered paid up and no further premiums are deducted from your pay, but the coverage continues.

If you name your children as beneficiaries if your spouse dies or without naming a spouse, the premiums depend on your age and the age of your youngest child. You can check with your installation's SBP counselor for more information.

- SURVIVOR BENEFIT PLAN

SSN

e completed regardless of S

31. PLAC

r spouse by entering (FS

c. DATE OF BI
(YYYYMMDD)

uld consult a Survivor Bene
spouse and/or eligible d

previously made on the DD
ght to make a new election o

service make the electi
ular retirement not when
33a through 33c before
ck 33a. through 33c.)

ble to receive retired p

not make an election in Blo

BP Coverage (Do not ma
-regular retirement and did
election in Block 34

n RC-SBP.

SBP ADVANTAGES

✓ Provides monthly income rather than a lump sum that would have to be invested to produce lifetime income.

✓ Cost is relatively low.

✓ Premiums are paid with pretax income, unlike insurance policies, which you buy with post-tax income.

✓ Spouse can't outlive the benefit unless he or she remarries before 55.

✓ COLAs protect income value by offsetting inflation.

You could also name someone with an insured interest in your death, meaning a person who would suffer financially because of your death, though this option is very expensive. However, you can terminate this type of coverage at any time.

COLLECTING SBP BENEFITS

Your beneficiary becomes eligible for SBP income the day after your death. The death should be reported by calling DFAS at 800-321-1080 or by filling out a form on the DFAS website. Then, DFAS will mail the forms required to process the payment to the beneficiary's address of record. He or she should complete and return them along with a certified copy of your death certificate.

RESTRICTIONS APPLY

You should be aware that if you're married and decline SBP, you won't be able to cover your spouse, or a former spouse who's eligible, at a later time. Nor will you will be able to cover a new spouse if you later remarry after your current spouse dies or you divorce.

But if you're unmarried at the time you retire and marry at a later date, you can enroll in SBP, and name your new spouse within a year of the marriage and any children you may have within a year of their birth. You need to file DD Form 2656-6 and a copy of the relevant marriage or birth certificate with DFAS.

You can withdraw from SBP only if the VA determines you have a service-connected total disability. And you can cancel your participation in SBP only during the third year of retirement. In both cases, spousal consent is required.

ANOTHER PERSPECTIVE

There are cases when enrolling in SBP may not make financial sense, since the premiums do reduce your take-home retired pay. Issues such as your spouse's health or access to substantial financial assets from other sources will influence your decision, as will whether your children are young enough to benefit.

The reason spousal agreement is required if you decline the coverage, as it is in comparable civilian arrangements that provide lifetime income to a surviving spouse, is that survivor income provides financial security for a potentially vulnerable population.

Survivor Entitlements

DoD and VA benefits help see you through when your military spouse dies.

The death of a spouse is hard, no matter what the circumstances. You must go on with life for your own sake and the sake of your children. In addition to coping with emotional distress, a death often means confronting potentially complex financial and legal responsibilities, both as a survivor and quite likely as executor of your spouse's estate.

As a surviving military spouse, you don't have to cope alone. Your spouse's branch of service will designate an assistance officer—called a casualty assistance calls officer (CACO) in the Navy, Marines, and Coast Guard, a casualty assistance officer (CAO) in the Army, and a casualty assistance representative (CAR) in the Air Force. The officer will help:

- Secure all your entitlements and benefits
- File all the required claim forms and notifications
- Provide access to legal and tax advisers who can help prepare tax returns and explain the long-term consequences of the benefit-related choices you make
- Ensure you receive your new ID card

Your assistance officer will also connect you with your service branch's local family assistance support services and long-term management program.

INCOME BENEFITS
Surviving spouses may be eligible for some or all of these benefits:

Dependency and Indemnity Compensation (DIC) if your spouse died on active duty, as a result of a service-connected disability, or was permanently and totally disabled. DIC provides surviving spouses with a fixed monthly tax-exempt income, adjusted annually, plus an additional amount for each eligible dependent child until he or she reaches 18 or 23. The income continues for your lifetime provided you don't remarry before turning 57.

A tax-exempt **Death Gratuity** of $100,000 if your spouse died on active

EDUCATION BENEFITS
There are several benefits to help cover education costs for surviving spouses and eligible children. See pages 100-105.

ESSENTIAL REFERENCE
You can download the extremely useful Military OneSource *A Survivor's Guide to Benefits* at https://download. militaryonesource.mil/12038/MOS/ ResourceGuides/A-Survivors-Guide-To-Benefits.pdf.

duty, active or inactive duty for training, or within 120 days of release from active duty if the death was caused by a service-connected disability.

Monthly income from the **Survivor Benefit Plan (SBP)** if your spouse died on active duty or enrolled in the benefit plan at retirement and you don't remarry before 55. If you're also eligible for DIC, you'll have to waive a portion of your SBP income equal to the DIC income. This offset actually results in higher income overall since no income tax is due on the DIC portion but is on SBP income.

In addition, you'll be eligible for the Special Survivors Indemnity Allowance (SSIA). It's a small amount, but is adjusted annually by the same COLA that applies to DIC.

LIFE INSURANCE BENEFITS

If your spouse had one or more life insurance policies, the tax-exempt death benefits of those policies will be paid as a lump sum or in monthly installments to the beneficiary your spouse has named.

If you're the beneficiary of a SGLI or VGLI policy, you might want to take advantage of the financial counseling services.

- Military OneSource provides free financial counseling. You can call 800-342-9647 in CONUS or either that number or collect to 703-253-7599 if you are overseas.
- You might also contact Financial Point, which is paid for by the VA. You can call 888-243-7351 or email them at fcs@financialpoint.com.

INVESTING LUMP SUMS

You can rollover up to the full amount of the death gratuity and the SGLI death benefit—potentially a total of $500,000—into a Roth IRA, an education savings account (ESA), or a combination of the two within a year of receiving the money. This contribution dwarfs the caps that normally apply, allowing you to establish a strong base on which earnings can compound. And these rollovers don't prevent you from making contributions to these accounts in the future.

Earnings aren't taxed while they remain in the accounts. If the Roth IRA has been open at least five years and you're at least 59½ when you take money out, the withdrawals are totally tax-exempt. If you need money before turning 59½, the amount you rolled in, though not the earnings, can be withdrawn without tax or penalty.

However, the money in an ESA must be used to pay qualified education expenses for an account beneficiary before he or she turns 30 to be tax-exempt. Other withdrawals are taxable.

URGENT: DON'T LOSE IT
It is essential that you have a plan for saving and investing the insurance and other payments you receive. Remember that the money must be available for longer-term expenses, not only immediate needs.

OTHER BENEFITS

As a surviving spouse of active duty, retired, and some Reserve component members, you're eligible for:

- Social Security benefits
- The VA Home Loan Guaranty Program
- TRICARE for survivors of deceased veterans who died from a service-connected disability or were totally and permanently disabled
- Exchange and commissary privileges if your spouse was retired or death was service-connected
- Federal employment preferences

Glossary

Actively managed funds are mutual funds or exchange traded funds (ETFs) overseen by professional managers who buy and sell investments to achieve a specific objective, such as providing regular income or long-term growth in value. While actively managed funds may provide stronger returns than passively managed funds in some years, they typically have higher expense ratios because of their management and investment fees, which can erode any potential outperformance.

Adjustable rate mortgage (ARM) loans are used to finance real estate purchases. The rate at which interest on the loan is calculated changes over time, reflecting changes in a publicly reported financial index. The initial rate on an ARM is usually lower than for a fixed-rate mortgage of the same size and term. That makes it easier to qualify for a loan. But if interest rates rise, the monthly payments increase. Changes to an ARM's rate occur at preset times, usually once a year, and there are annual and lifetime caps on the percentage change.

Adjusted gross income (AGI) is calculated by subtracting certain adjustments, such as interest on education loans and contributions to IRAs, from your gross income from salary, investments, and other sources. AGI is used to calculate your taxable income and affects eligibility for certain tax credits and exemptions.

Affinity fraud occurs when a dishonest person plays on your affiliation with a particular group to win your confidence in order to gain access to your assets.

After-tax contribution is money from which income taxes have been withheld that you put into a tax-advantaged plan such as a Roth IRA, a Roth TSP account, or a 529 college savings account. These contributions are not taxed when they're withdrawn because the tax has already been paid.

Allotment is money that is deducted from your pay and direct deposited to accounts designated for specific purposes. Some allotments are discretionary, such as contributions to an IRA, and can be ended at any time. Others are nondiscretionary. If an allotment is required to meet a specific financial obligation, you can't end it.

Allowance is an amount the DoD pays to equalize your living costs and compensate you for certain expenses, such as relocation, food, housing, and separation from your family. Allowances are generally nontaxable, making the full benefits available to you. However, COLAs you receive while stationed in the continental United States are taxable.

American opportunity credit (AOC) is an education tax credit available for each of a student's first four years of eligible post-secondary study for a degree, certificate, or other recognized credential. Eligibility for the credit is based on the taxpayer's modified adjusted gross income.

Amortization is the gradual repayment of debt, such as a mortgage loan, over a period of time.

Annual percentage rate (APR) is the cost of credit expressed as a percentage of the amount you borrow. The APR includes interest and most fees for arranging a loan but does not include late payment fees or a credit card's annual fee, if any.

Annual percentage yield (APY) is the amount paid on a savings account or certificate of deposit (CD) expressed as percentage of principal. When the APY is higher than the nominal, or named, interest rate, the interest is compound, or being added to the principal.

Annuity is income paid on a monthly or other regular basis over a year. The income may come from a retirement pension plan, the survivor benefit program (SBP), or an insurance company from which you've purchased a tax-deferred or immediate annuity.

Approved charge, or allowable amount, is the amount an insurance company will pay for each medical procedure or office visit if you have fee-for-service health insurance. If the cost exceeds the approved charge, you are responsible for the excess charge in addition to a percentage, called a cost share or coinsurance, of the approved charge.

Asset is anything you own that has monetary value, such as money in checking and savings accounts, investments, your home and other real estate, the value of your life insurance policy, and personal property. Money you're owed is also an asset.

Asset allocation is an investment strategy for managing investment risk as you seek to maximize investment return over the long term. It involves dividing your investment assets on a percentage basis among different asset classes, such as stocks, bonds and cash equivalents. Allocations vary based on investor goals, time frames for achieving those goals, and willingness to take risk. Asset allocation doesn't guarantee a profit or ensure against losses in a down market.

Asset class is a category of investment, such as equity, fixed income, real estate, derivative investments, and precious metals. Each class has specific features that distinguish it from other classes and impact the way it behaves in the financial marketplace. For example, equities provide ownership and may increase or decrease in value over time, while fixed income investments repay debt plus interest on a specific schedule.

Automatic enrollment means that you're automatically included in an employer retirement savings plan, such as the TSP or a 401(k) plan, as soon as you become eligible. If you don't want to participate, you must opt out, or refuse, in writing. Your employer determines the percentage of salary you contribute and how your contributions are invested, though you have the right to change one or both.

Base pay, or basic pay, is the core salary you earn each month while on active duty. It increases progressively as you attain higher pay grades and accumulate years of service. Service members with the same pay grade and years of service earn the same base pay, regardless of service branch. Base pay does not include housing or other allowances or any special pay that is part of your total compensation.

Benchmark is a standard against which investment performance is measured. For example, a market index, such as the S&P 500, that reflects the movement of a certain segment of the stock market, is a benchmark for the performance of the stocks in that segment and the funds that invest in those stocks.

Beneficiary is someone you name to receive the assets in a retirement savings account, trust, or annuity, and the death benefit on a life insurance policy at your death. These assets are transferred directly to the beneficiary, not by your will. You also name a beneficiary for a tax-advantaged education savings account.

Bond is a fixed income investment that pays interest on the principal, or amount you invest, over a specific term and promises to repay the principal at maturity. Bonds, which are issued by corporations and governments, are often referred to as debt investments because investors are actually loaning money to the issuers.

Broker acts as an intermediary for a buyer or seller. Stockbrokers who work for broker-dealers buy and sell stocks, bonds, and other investments for their clients, usually in return for a commission.

Broker-dealer (BD) is a brokerage firm licensed by the Securities and Exchange Commission (SEC) to buy and sell investments for clients and for the firm's own account.

Budget is a spending plan for allocating your income to cover your essential expenses, such as housing, food, transportation, and savings, as well as discretionary expenses, on a monthly basis. With a budget, you can track how closely your actual expenditures line up with what you had planned to spend and make adjustments to prevent spending more than you earn.

Capital gain is the profit you make when you sell a capital asset, like a stock or real estate, for more than you paid to buy it. If you have owned the asset for more than a year before selling it, you have a long-term capital gain. If you hold the stock for less than a year, you have a short-term capital gain. Long-term gains are usually taxed at a lower rate than your ordinary income.

Cash advance is money you borrow on a short-term basis using your credit card at an ATM or from fast cash lenders, also known as payday lenders. You typically pay an upfront transaction fee and interest at a significantly higher rate that you pay on conventional loans or credit card purchases.

Cash equivalents are investments, such as certificates of deposit (CDs), US Treasury bills, very short-term bond funds, or money market accounts that can be redeemed, or converted to cash, easily and with little or no loss of value.

Cash flow is the movement of money into and out of a checking account. If you have more coming in on a regular basis than you spend to cover your expenses, you have a positive cash flow. But if your expenses are higher than your income, you have negative cash flow. A consistently negative cash flow results in serious debt.

Cash surrender value is the amount you receive if you cancel, or surrender, a permanent life insurance policy. The payment is a portion of cash value that accumulated tax-deferred in your account while you were paying the premiums, minus fees and expenses. Generally, you owe tax only on the portion, if any, of the cash surrender value that exceeds what you paid in premiums.

Casualty insurance, also known as property and casualty insurance, protects against damage, theft, or loss to your personal or real property, including your home, cars, and boats. This insurance generally provides liability and fraud protection. However, it typically excludes fire and flood insurance, which you must purchase separately. Premiums vary by location, by insurance provider, and by many other variables, including the amount of the deductible.

Catch-up contribution allows people 50 and older who participate in an employer-sponsored retirement plan or IRA to make additional tax-deferred contributions over and above the annual limits. The catch-up amounts increase from time to time based on the rate of inflation. You can make catch-up contributions regardless of how much you contributed in the past. If you have both an employer plan and IRA, you can make catch-up contributions to both.

Certificate of deposit (CD) is a time deposit account that pays fixed-rate interest for a specific term, typically three months to five years, though adjustable-rate and market-rate CDs may be available. You usually face a penalty of forfeited interest if you withdraw funds before your CD matures. CDs offered by banks or credit unions are federally insured for up to

$250,000 per account category, protecting you against financial loss.

Certified Financial Planner (CFP) has met the rigorous professional standards of the CFP Board of Standards, passed a certification exam, agreed to follow a code of ethics, and is required to act as a fiduciary, always providing advice that's in the best interest of his or her clients.

Closing costs are fees and other expenses you pay when you finalize the purchase of real estate, such as a home. The lender must provide you with a Closing Disclosure of these costs at least three days before the closing.

Coinsurance see Cost share.

Collateral is an asset that is used to guarantee a loan. For example, your home is collateral for a mortgage loan and your car is the collateral for an auto loan.

Community property is property acquired during a marriage in states where community property law applies. The couple owns the property equally, and in a divorce the value of the property must be divided equally even if the couple no longer lives in a community property state. The nine community property states are Arizona, California, Idaho, Nevada, New Mexico, Texas, Washington, and Wisconsin.

Compounding occurs when investment earnings are added to investment principal, creating a new, larger base on which future earnings may accumulate. As your investment base gets larger, it has the potential to grow faster. The longer your money is invested, the more you stand to gain from compounding.

Contributions are amounts you deposit in a tax-deferred or tax-exempt account either by having them withheld from your pay or through an allotment. Contributions may be made with pretax or after-tax income, depending on the type of account.

Convertible term is a type of term life insurance that can be converted or changed into permanent life insurance at times specified in the contract without requiring a health screening exam.

Copayment, or **copay**, is the fixed amount you pay for each office visit to an in-network provider for approved medical treatment when you're insured through a preferred provider organization (PPO). Copayments are often higher to see specialists, and there may be no copays for an annual physical, preventive care, or certain inoculations and tests.

Cost basis is the original price of an asset, which is usually what you spent to buy it, plus any commissions and fees that applied. In real estate, the cost basis also includes the value of improvements made to the property. You use the cost basis to calculate capital gains and capital losses, depreciation, and return on investment. If you inherit assets, your cost basis is the asset's value on the date the person who left it to you died (or the date on which his or her estate was valued).

Cost of living adjustment (COLA) is an increase in wages or other financial benefit designed to compensate for increased living costs. Most COLAs occur annually based on changes in a public index, such as the Consumer Price Index (CPI).

Cost share is the portion of an approved healthcare provider or hospital bill that you pay when you're covered by a fee for service plan. The healthcare insurer usually pays a larger percentage of the bill. Some policies cap your out-of-pocket expenses, so that the insurer covers 95% to 100% of the cost once you have met your out-of-pocket limit.

Credit generally refers to the ability of a person or organization to borrow money. That ability usually depends on an acceptable history of past credit use, especially repaying amounts due on time. Auto loans and mortgage loans are examples of installment credit, where the amount you've borrowed is fixed. Credit cards and other lines of credit are examples of revolving credit, where you have continuing access to the amount you can borrow, called your credit limit. Each time you repay an amount you owe, that amount is available to borrow again.

Credit cards provide cardholders with a line of credit that can be used to make purchases or pay for services, deferring payment until the payment due date on the next monthly billing statement. The card issuer, usually a bank or credit union, sets the credit limit and annual percentage rate (APR) for each cardholder based on his or her credit history. You can use this form of revolving credit without paying interest or finance charges if you always pay your outstanding balance in full and on time.

Credit history is the evolving record of how you use credit, including loans, lines of credit, and credit cards. Credit reporting agencies continuously collect this information and compile it into your credit report. Credit issuers, employers, insurers, and landlords, among others, use this information in evaluating the credit risk you pose. If you don't use credit and so don't have a credit history, it is difficult to obtain credit.

Credit limit, also known as a credit line, is the maximum amount of money you can borrow under a revolving credit agreement, such as a credit card or home equity loan. If you exceed the credit limit, you may owe a fee if you've agreed that the card issuer should honor purchases that exceed your credit limit.

Credit report is a summary of your financial history. Primarily, it shows the different types of credit you use, your record of paying the amounts you owe on time, and the portion of your available credit you are currently using.

Credit score is a number between 300 and 850, calculated using information in a credit report. Lenders use your credit score as a factor in deciding whether to give you a loan and the interest rate they will charge. Factors affecting credit score include paying on time, having limited amount of debt in relation to your credit limit, the types of credit you use, and how often you apply for new credit. You have multiple different credit scores at any one time depending on the companies calculating them.

Creditworthy describes a person or institution as an acceptable risk, with the means and the will to repay what they borrow, plus interest, or meet other financial obligations. The more creditworthy the borrower is, the more likely the lender will be to offer credit on desirable terms, including the lowest interest rate available.

Custodian is a person or organization responsible for ensuring safety and security. In investment terms, a custodian is a financial services firm that maintains electronic records of the assets in an account or has physical possession of these assets. For example, the company where you open an IRA account is the custodian of that account.

Death benefit is money a beneficiary collects from a life insurance policy if the insured dies while the policy is in force. Typically, the beneficiary receives the face value of the policy as payment, less any unpaid loans that have been taken against the policy. Social Security also provides a death benefit when an enrolled participant dies. So does the Department of Defense, which provides a death gratuity if a service member dies on active duty.

Debit cards can be used to make purchases by directly debiting the amount of the sale from a linked checking account or, in the case of a prepaid debit card, from the value loaded on the card. The cards can be used online, at a card reader, or at an ATM.

Debt-to-income ratio (DTI) is the relationship, stated as a percentage, between what you owe and your income. It's generally calculated by dividing your monthly debt—or what you must pay in a month—by your gross monthly income. DTI is a major factor in determining whether you qualify for credit and the terms under which it is offered.

Decreasing term life insurance is a life insurance policy in which the death benefit is gradually reduced over the term. The premiums are generally lower than with other types of commercial insurance, and this approach may be suitable when the insurance is being used to cover a comparably decreasing obligation, such as a mortgage loan.

Deductible is the amount a policyholder must pay out-of-pocket before an insurer begins to cover its share of a claim. As a general rule, the higher the deductible, the lower the annual premium will be.

Default occurs when a person or institution fails to repay a loan. If you are in default, you may lose any property that you used as collateral and you will damage your credit history and your credit score, making it more difficult to borrow in the future. In addition, creditors may sue you for the unpaid amount or arrange to have your wages garnished.

Defined benefit plan, often known as a pension plan, is an employer sponsored plan that pays eligible retired employees a lifetime income, usually on a monthly basis. It's the employer's responsibility to fund the plan. The pension amount is typically determined by years on the job and final pay, or sometimes by the average pay for the most recent three or highest three years. If your employer offers a pension plan and you qualify to participate, you're automatically enrolled.

Defined contribution plan is a retirement savings plan, such as a TSP account in the DoD's Blended Retirement System. Each participating employee has an account in the plan and contributes a percentage of earnings, which are automatically deducted from each paycheck. Employers may match a portion of these contributions. Employees choose among the investments offered by the plan and earnings in the account grow tax-deferred. In most cases, required minimum distributions are mandatory when you turn 72. In traditional tax-deferred accounts, contributions are made with pretax income and withdrawals are taxed at the same rate as ordinary income. In Roth accounts, contributions are made with after-tax income but withdrawals are tax-exempt.

Distribution is an amount a mutual fund pays its shareholders from either its investment income or capital gains it realizes. A distribution is also an amount withdrawn from a tax-advantaged account, such as a TSP account or IRA. These distributions are generally restricted before you're 59½ and may be required after you turn 72.

Diversification is an investment strategy for managing risk and strengthening return. To diversify, you buy investments in different asset classes and within each class. The mix you choose depends on your age, your risk tolerance, and your investment goals. The goal is to protect the value of your overall portfolio in case a single investment or market sector loses value. But diversification can't guarantee a profit or protect against losses in a down market.

Dividends are the portion of a corporation's earnings that it chooses to pay its shareholders, typically on a quarterly basis.

Down payment is a portion of the purchase price of a property that you pay up front in cash as part of the transaction. Typically, the down payment is the difference between the price and the amount you borrow.

Conventional mortgage loans generally require a down payment of 10% to 20%, but you may qualify for a VA or other mortgage that requires a small or no down payment.

Durable power of attorney gives a person, known as an agent, the right to make legal and financial decisions on behalf of the person granting the power. The agent—called the attorney-in-fact—has the right to buy and sell property and handle banking and investment accounts for the grantor. An agent with a durable power of attorney continues to have the authority to act if the grantor becomes incompetent. The grantor can specify the powers being granted, revoke the appointment, set an end date, or name a replacement agent at any time.

Early withdrawal occurs when money is taken from an account before the term is up or before the time permitted by law. For example, cashing in a certificate of deposit (CD) before it matures or taking a distribution from a tax-deferred or tax-free retirement savings plan before turning 59½ are considered early withdrawals. There is usually a penalty for early withdrawal, which is the loss of some or all the interest on the CD or a 10% penalty tax on earnings withdrawn early from a tax-deferred savings plan. However, with an IRA, this penalty is waived if the money is used to cover certain expenses, such as paying for higher education or buying a first home.

Earned income credit (EIC) reduces the income tax that qualifying taxpayers would otherwise owe. It's a refundable credit, so if the tax that's due is less than the amount of the credit, the difference is paid to the taxpayer as a refund. Eligibility for the credit requires that the taxpayer must work, earn less than the ceiling based on filing status and family size, and meet other conditions.

Earnest money is a cash deposit that a potential buyer makes to a seller to confirm a bid for, or offer to purchase, real estate. If the sale is not finalized within a specified period, the money is often but not always refunded. Earnest money, also known as a binder or a good faith deposit, is usually held in escrow until the contract of sale is signed, at which point it becomes part of the buyer's down payment.

Effective tax rate is the rate you actually pay on your taxable income. You find the rate by dividing the tax you paid for the year by your taxable income for the year. It is generally lower than your marginal rate, which is the rate you pay on the income that falls into the highest tax bracket you reach.

Emergency fund is an account, such as a savings or money market account, that can quickly be converted to cash to meet unbudgeted expenses, such as unexpected repairs or medical bills, or the loss of a job. The fund should be large enough to cover two to six months of living expenses and should be replenished as quickly as possible if some of the funds are used.

Equity is ownership of an asset, such as a stock you purchase in a company, shares you own in a mutual fund, and the percentage of your home on which there is no debt.

Escrow is an arrangement for holding assets, such as cash or securities, in a reserve account until the terms of an agreement are fulfilled. For example, if you make a down payment on a home, the money is held in escrow until it's transferred to the seller at the closing. Amounts you prepay in property taxes and insurance premiums as part of your regular mortgage payment are also held in escrow until those bills are due and are paid by the lender.

Estate includes everything you own in your own name, plus your share of anything you own with other people. Following your death, your assets, which may include cash, investments, retirement accounts, and real estate, are valued to determine the value of your gross estate. Any outstanding debts you may have, along with the costs of settling the estate, are subtracted to calculate the value of your taxable estate. Most estates, except those of exceptionally high value, are exempt from federal estate tax but state estate taxes may apply.

Exchange traded funds (ETFs) resemble mutual funds in some ways but are traded like stock on a public exchange. Rather than being sold and redeemed by the issuing company, as mutual fund shares are, ETF shares are sold by broker-dealers and traded in the secondary market. Most ETFs are passively managed and linked to a market index, which determines the fund's portfolio, though a limited number are actively managed.

Executor is the person or institution you name in your will to carry out the wishes you express in the will and settle your estate. The executor's duties include collecting and valuing the estate's assets, paying taxes and debts, and distributing assets to the people and organizations you've identified. The executor is usually a spouse, other family member, or close friend but may also be a lawyer or other professional.

Expense ratio is the percentage of a mutual fund or exchange traded fund's total assets that are deducted to cover operating and management expenses but not trading costs.

FDIC, an acronym for the Federal Deposit Insurance Corporation, insures bank deposits up to $250,000 for each depositor account in each bank. You may qualify for more than $250,000 coverage at a single bank if your assets are deposited in different types of accounts or are registered in different ways including individual, joint, business, and trust accounts, or in individual retirement accounts (IRAs). Investment products purchased through the bank are not FDIC insured.

Fee is an amount charged by a financial institution for providing a service or as a penalty for failure to meet certain account requirements, such as paying late, not paying the minimum amount due, or overdrawing your account. Fees vary by institution, and some may be capped by law.

Fee-for-service health insurance allows you to use healthcare providers of your choice. Most fee-for-service plans pay a percentage—often 70% to 80%—of the allowable amount, or what they will pay for each covered office visit or medical treatment after you have paid an annual deductible. You pay the balance of the approved charge as a cost share, plus any amount that exceeds the allowable amount. In many cases, you pay the full cost and file a claim for reimbursement from your insurance company.

Fiduciary is an individual or organization legally responsible for managing assets on behalf of someone else. The assets must be managed in the best interests of the asset owner, not for the personal gain of the fiduciary. Executors, trustees, guardians, registered investment advisers (RIAs), Certified Financial Planners (CFPs), and agents with powers of attorney all have a fiduciary responsibility.

Filing status is one of the five categories of taxpayer defined by the IRS. Your status is determined primarily by whether or not you are married or have dependents. You must use the status that most accurately describes your situation, though if you are eligible for two or more you may select the status that would require you to pay the least tax.

Finance charge is the interest you owe, plus any fees that may apply for obtaining credit, expressed as an annual percentage rate (APR). It does not include any late fees or penalties you may incur. With credit cards, in most cases, if you have paid the previous balance in full and on time, and you haven't taken any cash advances, there's no finance charge.

Financial adviser is a generic term for someone who provides financial advice. While there is no federal registration or oversight, people who serve as financial advisers may have some recognized credential, such as Certified Financial Planner (CFP), Chartered Financial Consultant (ChFC), and Accredited Financial Counselor (AFC). Advisers are available to service members and their families free of charge through Military OneSource and Family Support Centers.

Financial plan is a document that describes your current financial status, your financial goals and when you want to achieve them, and suggests money management and investment strategies to meet those goals. You use the plan to measure your progress and can update your goals and timeframe as your situation changes. There may be a one-time fee to have a plan created, or it may be included as part of your relationship with an investment adviser or financial planner.

Financial planners evaluate your financial situation and help you create an approach to help you meet both your immediate financial needs and longer-term goals. Planners identify appropriate investments and insurance and monitor your portfolio. They may have professional designations and certifications and may or may not be registered to sell investments.

Planners are available to service members and their families free of charge through Military OneSource and Family Support Centers.

Fixed-income investments, such as bonds and preferred stock, typically pay interest or dividends on a regular schedule and may promise to return your principal at maturity, though that promise is usually not guaranteed. Fixed-income securities provide regular income if you hold them to maturity, though their market price fluctuates over time.

Fixed-rate mortgage loan is a long-term loan that you use to finance a real estate purchase, typically a home. Initially the interest rate you pay may be larger than an adjustable rate loan of the same size and term. However, your borrowing costs and monthly payments remain the same for the term of the loan, despite any changes in market interest rates.

Foreclosure occurs when your lender repossesses your home because you have defaulted on your mortgage loan or home equity line of credit. In a foreclosure, you lose any equity you have built up in the home.

Fund of funds (FOF) is a mutual fund whose underlying investments are other mutual funds rather than individual stocks or bonds. A FOF tends to provide greater diversification than an individual fund by including many different types of investments. Such funds, including TSP's Lifecycle (L) Fund, reduce some of the burden of making investment decisions. However, FOF fees tend to be higher than you would pay by owning the underlying funds directly.

Garnish means an employer is ordered to withhold some or all of an employee's earnings and forward them to the court that ordered the withholding or to a payee. The court order follows a judgment against the employee in favor of a plaintiff who sued for unpaid debt or other financial damages.

Good faith deposit see Earnest money.

Grace period is the length of time you have to make a payment before it's considered late or delinquent. With credit cards, it's the number of days between the date a credit card issuer sends your billing statement and the date your payment is due. By law, it must be at least 21 days. There are grace periods of varying lengths for paying insurance premiums, personal and mortgage loans, rent, and repaying student loans. If you exceed a grace period, you may be subject to penalties, fees, cancellation, or other punitive actions.

Guardian is a person designated to be legally responsible for a minor child or others who are unable to care for themselves. You may name a guardian in your will to serve in that role if your child's other parent is unable or unwilling to do so.

Hardship withdrawal, legally known as a hardship distribution, occurs when you take money out of a qualified retirement savings plan, including the TSP, while you're still employed to cover an immediate and heavy financial need. Eligible needs are listed in the plan document and may include preventing foreclosure, funeral expenses, covering out-of-pocket medical expenses for yourself or a dependent, and paying college tuition for yourself or a dependent. If you're younger than 59 ½, you generally owe a 10% tax penalty plus income tax on the amount you withdraw.

Head of household is an IRS filing status that you can use if you are unmarried or considered unmarried under the tax law during the tax year, and you provide at least half the cost of maintaining a home for one or more qualifying dependents. Filing as head of household entitles you to take a higher standard deduction than filing as a single and qualifies you for certain deductions and credits that further reduce your tax.

Home equity line of credit (HELOC) lets you borrow against the equity you've built up in your home. In some cases, you begin to repay principal and interest as soon as you borrow against the line. But in other cases you repay only the interest for a specific period, often several years, and then begin to repay the principal. Because your home is collateral for the line of credit, you could lose it to foreclosure if you default.

Home equity loan, sometimes called a second mortgage, is secured by the equity in your home. You receive the loan principal, minus fees for arranging the loan, as a lump sum. You repay monthly over the term of the agreement, just as you do with your first, or primary, mortgage. While interest rates on home equity loans are generally lower than the rates on unsecured loans, you run the risk of foreclosure if you default on the loan.

Identity theft is the unauthorized use of your personal information, such as your name, address, Social Security number, or credit account information. Scammers steal your identity to make purchases or obtain credit, or they may use the data to apply for official forms of identification.

Immediate annuity is an insurance company product you purchase to provide income either for yourself or an annuitant you name. The payments generally begin right away or within the year. The most typical use for an immediate annuity is to provide regular retirement income.

Index tracks the movement, up and down, of a financial market, a number of markets, or the economy as a whole from a specific starting point. The change in an index is typically expressed as points and as a percentage over various periods of time from as short as 15 seconds to a year or longer. Indexes are often used as performance benchmarks against which to measure the return on investments that resemble those tracked by the index.

Index fund is a mutual fund or exchange traded fund designed to mirror, or replicate, the performance of a stock, bond, or other financial index. To achieve this goal, the fund purchases all—or a representative sample of—the securities tracked by the index and adjusts its portfolio of underlying investments only when the components of the index change. An index fund is also known as a passively managed fund.

Individual retirement account (IRA) is a tax-advantaged, personal retirement account. You choose the custodian, such as a bank, credit union, brokerage firm, or mutual fund company and select investments for your account from among those available through the custodian. There are annual contribution limits and restrictions on withdrawals before you turn 59½. Any earnings accumulate tax-deferred while they remain in the account. In a traditional tax-deferred IRA, you must begin to take required minimum distributions (RMDs) after you turn 72. The withdrawals are taxed at the same rate as your ordinary income. Withdrawals from Roth IRAs are tax exempt if your account has been open at least five years and you are at least 59½ when you start taking money out. Withdrawals from a Roth IRA are not required.

Inflation is a persistent increase in prices over time, reducing money's purchasing power. To maintain the same standard of living, your income must increase at a rate at least equal to the rate of inflation.

Installment loan is a loan that's repaid on a predetermined, usually monthly, schedule over a fixed term. The payments typically include a combination of principal and interest, which may be calculated at a fixed or variable rate.

Interest, calculated as a percentage of principal, is the amount you earn as income from a savings account, bond, or other fixed-income investment or pay on the outstanding balance of a loan or credit card.

Investment adviser is a financial professional who works for a registered investment advisory (RIA) firm and provides guidance to investors in making investment decisions. The adviser may also manage an investor's portfolio and provide financial planning advice. The adviser as a fiduciary obligation to always act in the client's best interest.

IRA rollover occurs when you move assets from an employer-sponsored retirement plan to an IRA or from one IRA to another. With a direct transfer, all the assets are moved from the old to the new account by the plan administrator or custodian and the earnings continue to be tax-deferred. If you withdraw the money from your account, your employer must withhold 20%. Unless you replace the 20% with money from other sources and deposit the full amount of the withdrawal in the new IRA within 60 days, you'll owe a penalty and taxes on any amount that was not deposited. That amount is considered a distribution and loses its tax-deferred status.

Joint tenants with right of survivorship (JTWROS) provides that if two or more people own property, including financial accounts, jointly and one of the owners dies, the deceased owner's share automatically becomes the property of the surviving owner or owners. Couples often own their homes as joint tenants with right of survivorship.

Laddering is an investment strategy that involves staggering the maturity dates of fixed-income investments so that they become due on a rolling basis rather than all at once. For example, instead of buying one $15,000 certificate of deposit (CD) with a three-year term, you buy three $5,000 CDs maturing one year apart.

Level term insurance is a life insurance policy in which your annual premium remains the same for the term of the policy, which may be as long as 20 years. The coverage stops at the end of the term. But if the policy is guaranteed renewable, you can often extend the policy for an additional term with evidence of good health, but usually at a higher premium.

Liability insurance pays claims if you are responsible for causing harm to people or damage to property. Liability policies cap, or limit, what they will pay, and there is also a deductible that you pay before the insurer begins to pay. Liability coverage typically covers auto accidents and hazards in your home, but there are specialized policies providing professional and business coverage.

Lien is a legal claim on an asset or property you have used as collateral for a loan. If you default on the loan, the lender, or lienholder, can repossess the asset. You can't sell or refinance an asset on which there's a lien until the lienholder has been repaid in full.

Lifecycle funds, sometimes known as target date funds, are generally intended to provide a source of retirement income starting at a specific future time, such as 2040 or 2050. Each lifecycle fund gradually shifts its investment focus from growth investments to income investments as the target date approaches. The college savings plans known as 529 plans also use lifecycle funds to accumulate savings to pay tuition and other education costs.

Lifetime learning credit is a tax credit that allows eligible taxpayers to reduce the income tax they owe by up to $2,000 a year for amounts they spent for qualified higher education expenses, such as tuition and fees. Eligibility is determined by modified adjusted gross income (MAGI).

Line of credit is a loan arrangement in which you pay interest on the amount of money you borrow rather than on your credit limit, or the total amount the lender determines you are eligible to borrow. Once you repay an amount you've borrowed, you can borrow it again. A line of credit on a credit card is usually unsecured, but with a home equity line of credit, your home serves as collateral against the amount you borrow.

Liquidity describes how quickly and easily you can convert an asset to cash with little or no loss of value. Examples of liquid assets are shares in a money market mutual fund and certificates of deposit (CDs), which you can redeem at any point though you may forfeit interest if you withdraw before the CD matures.

Living trust, also called an *inter vivos* trust, is a legal entity set up while you're alive to hold assets that you, as grantor, transfer to the trust. You name the beneficiaries and the trustee or successor trustee to carry out the terms of the trust. When the trust ends, which may be at your death, the assets are distributed directly to your beneficiaries in accordance with the trust's terms and aren't subject to probate, as is property transferred by a will. If a living trust is revocable, its terms can be changed. If it's irrevocable, they can't.

Living will is a legal document that describes the type of medical treatment you want—or don't want—if you are terminally ill or unable to communicate your wishes. To be valid, a living will must be signed by two or more witnesses and must meet the standards of the state where it is executed.

Loan is money a lender provides to a borrower, contingent on the borrower's promise to repay the principal plus interest. The loan, which may be secured or unsecured, must be paid off at the end of the agreed-upon term.

Loan estimate is a document a potential lender must provide within three days of your application for a mortgage loan. It reports the details of the loan you requested, including the proposed interest rate, monthly payment, and closing costs. It also provides estimates of the property taxes you will owe and property insurance costs.

Lump sum payment is an amount of money you receive all at once rather than in increments over a period of time. For example, you might receive the death benefit of an insurance

147

policy, or the full or partial value of your retired pay, as a lump sum. There are usually tax implications for some but not all lump sum payments that may eat into their value and reduce the amount you receive. Other lump sum payments, including insurance death benefits, are tax-exempt.

Marginal tax rate is the rate you pay on the portion of your taxable income that falls into the highest of the seven US tax brackets. Each bracket has a minimum and maximum amount, though those amounts vary by filing status. Some taxpayers have income in just one bracket, some in multiple brackets, and some in all seven.

Market capitalization is a measure of the value of a company calculated by multiplying the current share price of its stock by the number of either the outstanding shares (those held by stockholders) or floating shares (those actually available to trade). Market capitalization, or market cap, is used to categorize companies as small, mid-sized, and large.

Matching contribution is money your employer adds to your retirement savings account, such as a TSP account or IRA, usually as a percentage of the amount you contribute up to a cap, such as 5% of base pay.

Minimum payment due is the least amount you can pay on the outstanding balance of a line of credit without incurring a fee or other penalty or risking being in default. However, when you pay only the minimum amount due, the balance you owe is subject to a finance charge, which can increase the cost of borrowing substantially over time.

Modified adjusted gross income (MAGI) is used to establish your eligibility for certain tax or financial benefits, such as deducting your IRA contribution and qualifying to contribute to a Roth IRA. To find your MAGI, you add back some types of income and specific adjustments you may have taken to calculate your AGI. The items that must be added back vary by benefit and are listed in the worksheet in the IRS instructions for completing the form you use to calculate eligibility for each benefit.

Money market accounts are hybrid accounts that typically pay interest comparable to, or slightly below, the rate on short-term certificates of deposit (CDs) but permit a limited number of transactions each month. You must maintain a minimum balance or be subject to fees and potential loss of interest. The account balances are insured up to $250,000 by FDIC if they're in banks or by NCUSIF if they're in credit unions.

Mortgage loan is a long-term loan, typically between 10 and 30 years, which you use to finance the purchase of real estate, such as a home. As the borrower, or mortgagee, you repay the lender, or mortgagor, the loan principal plus interest, which may be calculated at a fixed or variable rate. When the loan is repaid in full, you own the property outright. But if you default on your payments, the lender may repossess the property. The VA guarantees mortgage loans to make it easier for service members and veterans to afford to buy a home.

Mutual fund is a professionally managed investment that pools the assets of many investors to invest in stocks, bonds, or a combination of stocks and bonds, depending on the fund's objectives. Mutual fund companies, also known as investment companies, offer a variety of funds, each with a particular investment objective. The objective, along with information about the fund's fees, the risks it poses, and the investments it owns, are explained in the fund's prospectus. A distinctive feature of mutual funds is that they sell as many shares as investors want to buy on a continuous basis and buy back any shares investors want to sell.

National Credit Union Share Insurance Fund (NCUSIF) insures credit union deposits up to $250,000 for each depositor account in each credit union. You may qualify for more than $250,000 coverage at a single credit union if your assets are deposited in different types of accounts or are registered in different ways including individual, joint, business, and trust accounts, or in individual retirement accounts (IRAs). However, financial products purchased through a credit union are not covered by the insurance.

Net asset value (NAV) is the dollar value of one share of a mutual fund or exchange traded fund (ETF). It is calculated by totaling the value of the fund's holdings plus money awaiting investment, subtracting operating expenses, and dividing by the number of outstanding shares. A fund's NAV changes regularly, though day-to-day variations are usually small. With a mutual fund, the NAV is reset at the end of each trading day, while with an ETF, the NAV changes throughout the day as shares trade on a public exchange.

Net worth is a snapshot of where you stand financially at a particular point in time. You calculate net worth by adding the total value of your assets, such as cash, investment and retirement accounts, and real estate, and then subtracting your liabilities, or what you owe in loans, credit card bills, and other obligations. If your assets are larger than your liabilities, you have a positive net worth. If the liabilities are larger, you have a negative net worth.

Nominal interest rate is the stated or advertised interest rate a bank or credit union pays on deposits or charges for loans. If interest is compounded, the annual percentage yield (APY) on deposits is higher than the nominal rate. And the actual annual percentage rate (APR) you pay will be higher than the nominal rate if you owe fees and other charges that apply to arranging a loan.

Note is a legal document a borrower signs, agreeing to pay a loan according to specific terms, such as interest rate and maturity date.

Ordinary income is income, including salary or wages and certain types of investment income including withdrawals from tax-deferred accounts, that's taxed based on your filing status and the tax brackets into which your taxable income falls. Other income, such as long-term capital gains and dividends on qualified equities, is taxed at lower rates.

Overdraft means withdrawing, or attempting to withdraw, by electronic transfer, debit card, or check, more money than the available balance in your checking account.

Overdraft protection ensures that all checks you write and electronic transactions you authorize will be paid, even if you spend more than your account's available balance. If you have a savings account linked to the checking account or an overdraft line of credit, the amount of money you overdraw is transferred from that account or line to cover the shortfall. You are generally charged interest on the overdraft amount and must repay it to avoid continuing interest charges. You must agree to overdraft protection for debit cards separately.

Par value is the face value, or named value, of a bond, usually $1,000 but $100 in the case of US Treasury issues. It's the amount you pay to purchase the bond at issue and the amount you receive when the bond is redeemed at maturity. Par is also the basis on which the interest you earn on a bond is figured. While par value typically remains constant, a bond's market value may fluctuate until the bond matures.

Passively managed refers to an index mutual fund or exchange traded fund (ETF) whose portfolio tracks an index, such as the S&P 500, and whose objective is to produce a return that mirrors the return on that index. Since the fund portfolio changes only when the make-up of the underlying index changes, these funds tend to have fewer transactions and generally lower fees than actively managed funds.

Payable-on-death (POD) is a way to title a bank or credit union account so that when you die, the assets pass directly to the beneficiary or beneficiaries you've named without having the assets go through probate. A similar type of arrangement, known as transferable-on-death, or TOD, is available in some states for securities and brokerage accounts.

Payday loans provide immediate cash for a short period without a credit check, for an upfront fee. The borrower authorizes a debit from his or her bank account for the amount of the loan. The lender debits the account on the maturity date, often the day the borrower is paid. However, many borrowers can't repay the loan in full on time and take another loan. The annual percentage rate (APR) on payday loans can exceed several hundred percent.

Many states forbid these loans entirely or cap the APR, and no member of the military may be charged an APR higher than 36%, though violations of these rules are common.

Pension is lifetime income paid to eligible retired employees. The amount of the pension usually depends on years of service and final or average earnings. The employer contributes funds to the defined benefit plan that will provide the pension, manages the assets, and pays the benefit, typically monthly.

Performance measures the total return an investment provides over a specific period. Expressed as a percentage, it can be positive, representing a gain in value, or negative, representing a loss. Performance over longer periods, such as one, five, or ten years, is a better indicator of overall strength or weakness of an investment than day-to-day results, which may be volatile in some cases. An investment is said to outperform when its return is stronger than that of its benchmark and to underperform if its results lag behind that benchmark. You can use past performance to review how an investment has reacted historically to changing market conditions, but there's no guarantee that those results will be repeated in the future.

Permanent insurance is a type of life insurance that remains in force as long as you live, or in some cases until you turn 100 or 120, provided you continue to pay the required premiums. A portion of your premium pays for the insurance and the rest goes into a tax-deferred cash value account in your name. You can usually borrow against the policy or terminate it and receive the cash surrender value. There are many types of permanent insurance. The most common and least expensive is called whole life or sometimes straight life. Others are universal life and variable life.

Phishing is a technique that identity thieves use to retrieve your personal information, such as passwords and account numbers, from the internet. They may send hoax emails claiming to be from legitimate businesses or establish phony websites designed to capture your personal information.

PITI is an acronym for principal, interest, taxes, and insurance—the four elements in a monthly mortgage loan payment. Lenders use PITI as a factor in determining whether you are eligible for a mortgage loan on a specific property at a competitive rate.

Portability means that you can transfer or roll over the assets that have accumulated in a retirement savings account, or, in some cases, the value of those assets, to another account in your name when you leave your employer. The assets remain tax-deferred. For example, the value of your TSP account is portable, so you can transfer that amount to an IRA or a different retirement savings plan if that plan accepts transfers. Health insurance may also be portable if you've had employer-sponsored group health insurance and move to a new employer who offers health insurance. The new group plan can't exclude coverage for preexisting conditions, provided there hasn't been a gap in coverage.

Portfolio is the collection of investments an investor owns. A diversified portfolio holds investments in different asset classes, and a number of different investments in each of those classes.

Power of attorney (POA) is a legal document that gives the person you name the authority to act for you as your agent or on your behalf. The power may be limited or special, durable, or springing, which takes effect only when you are no longer competent to act on your own. Individual states, most banks and credit unions, and the Department of Defense have rules governing POAs.

Pre-existing condition is a medical problem you have before you apply for health insurance. Provisions of the Affordable Care Act (ACA) of 2010 make it illegal to deny you coverage a for a pre-existing condition, refuse to treat it, or charge a higher insurance premium. However, there are exceptions for plans in effect before March 23, 2010, that were purchased individually.

Premium is the purchase price of an insurance policy or annuity contract. You may pay the premium as a single lump sum, in regular monthly or quarterly installments, or in some cases on a flexible schedule over the term of the policy or contract. The premium may be fixed for the life of the policy or change as you grow older, depending on the type of policy and its specific terms.

Prepayment penalty is a charge that may apply if you repay an outstanding loan balance in full before it matures. The penalty may be calculated in different ways, based on the terms of the loan. However, some loan agreements exclude a fee for early repayment, and prepayment penalties are illegal in some states. Where they are legal, a lender may offer to finance a loan at a lower interest rate if you agree to the prepayment penalty.

Pretax income, sometimes described as pretax dollars, is your gross income before income taxes are withheld. Contributions to a tax-deferred retirement account, such as a traditional TSP or 401(k), are deducted from your pretax income, reducing the income reported to the IRS and therefore your income tax bill.

Principal is a sum of money. It can refer to the amount you invest, an amount you borrow, or the face value of a bond.

Probate is the process of authenticating, or verifying, your will, generally through a local authority such as surrogate's court. After probate, your executor can carry out the wishes expressed in your will and settle your estate. If your will isn't legally acceptable or if it's contested, probate can take a long time and cost a great deal.

Prospectus is a formal written offer to sell an equity investment to the public. It contains a range of required information about the issuing company, its business plan, and the risks of making the investment. A mutual fund prospectus describes the objectives, fees, risks, holdings, past performance, and other details about the fund.

Real return is the return on an investment or investment portfolio that's adjusted to account for the impact of inflation. Real return is a useful tool for determining whether your returns are increasing your purchasing power or keeping it stable.

Realized gain is the profit you make when you sell an investment for more than your basis, or what you paid to buy it. In the case of an inherited asset, it's the difference between the amount you receive for selling and its value at the time you received it. You typically owe tax on realized gain unless the investment is tax-exempt, though long-term gains on certain assets you've held for more than a year are taxed at a lower rate that your ordinary income. However, if you have gains in tax-deferred accounts, the gain becomes part of the account value that will be taxed as ordinary income at withdrawal. If the value of the asset increases but you don't sell it, you have an unrealized gain.

Reallocate means to change the way your investment portfolio is divided, on a percentage basis, among specific asset classes. Typically, you reallocate to meet a specific objective, to reflect a change in lifestyle or family situation, or as you get older and nearer retirement. Lifecycle funds reallocate systematically over time, typically shifting from an emphasis on equity to an emphasis on fixed income investments as the target date approaches.

Rebalance means to adjust a portfolio's current asset allocation to align it more closely to your intended allocation. You may rebalance, for example, by increasing your fixed income holdings after a strong stock market performance leaves your portfolio more heavily invested in equities than you intended. If your actual allocation strays too far from the one you planned, you may be exposed to too much or not enough risk to meet your goals.

Refinance means to renegotiate a financial contract, such as a mortgage loan. The goal may be to modify the term of a loan, increase the principal, or reduce the interest rate to make the loan more favorable. For example, you may seek a lower rate and shorter term to reduce the cost of borrowing, or, if cash is tight, extend the term to make lower payments over a longer term even though that increases the overall cost.

Refundable credit is a tax credit that may result in a payment to you from the IRS if the credit to which you are entitled reduces your income tax to less than $0. In that case, some or all of the credit that you did not use to reduce your taxes is paid to you.

Registered investment adviser (RIA) is a firm that is paid for providing investment advice, generally as a percentage of the assets it manages for you, though other payment arrangements may be available. RIAs and their employees are bound by a fiduciary standard to recommend financial products that are in the best interest of each individual client.

Registered representatives, more commonly known as stockbrokers, are licensed to act on investors' orders to buy and sell securities and to provide advice about portfolio transactions. These investment professionals may be paid a salary, a commission on sales, or a fee based on a percentage of a client's account value.

Required minimum distribution (RMD) is the smallest amount you must take each year from your tax-deferred retirement savings plan or IRA once you've reached the mandatory withdrawal age, usually 72. If you take less than the required minimum in any year, you owe a 50% penalty on the amount you should have taken but did not. The administrator or custodian of your plan will normally send you a statement showing the end-of-year account balance, the RMD you must take, or both. You can calculate an RMD on your own using the account balance and a divisor based on your age that you can find in IRS Publication 590.

Return is the gain or loss on your investment principal. It is determined by the change in an investment's value, up or down, over a specific period, such as a year, plus any earnings the investment provides. A positive return means you end up with more money than you started with and a negative return means you end up with less.

Retired pay base is one of the factors in the formula for calculating retired pay. It is determined by your High-3, or your average base pay during the 36 continuous months your base pay was highest.

Revocable trust is a living trust whose terms can be changed at any time by the grantor, or person who establishes the trust and transfers assets and property to it. During the grantor's lifetime, he or she is entitled to any income the assets produce and owes taxes on the earnings. When the grantor dies, the assets pass directly to the beneficiaries named in the trust rather than by will, and so are not subject to probate. The grantor can choose to serve as trustee of the trust during his or her lifetime and name a successor trustee to assume responsibility for carrying out the terms of the trust.

Revolving credit, which is a feature of credit cards and home equity loans, allows you to borrow money on a continuing basis without having to reapply. The credit is described as revolving because as you repay an amount you've borrowed, you can borrow it again. As with all forms of credit, you pay interest on your outstanding balance, though the repayment terms vary by the type of revolving credit.

Risk is the potential for losing some or all of the money you invest, having a smaller return than you expected, or losing buying power. Risk results from multiple factors, including the investments you choose, when you invest, how long you own the investments, and the behavior of the financial markets.

Roll over means moving investment assets from an employer's retirement plan to an IRA, from one IRA to another, or from one employer's plan to another's plan.

Roth IRA is an individual retirement account (IRA) to which you make after-tax contributions and from which you may withdraw tax-free earnings any time after you turn 59½, provided your account has been open at least five years. Since Roth IRAs have no required withdrawals during your lifetime, you can continue to accumulate tax-free earnings as long as you like. Eligibility to contribute to a Roth IRA is determined by your MAGI. You may convert a traditional tax-deferred IRA or 401(k) to a Roth IRA though tax will be due on earnings in the accounts you transfer and on the contributions if they were tax-deferred.

Roth TSP, 401(k), 403(b) or 457 is an account in your employer's retirement savings plan to which you make after-tax rather than tax-deferred contributions. A Roth TSP has the same contribution limits, distribution requirements, and investment options as the tax-deferred TSP offered by the employer. But RMDs from your Roth TSP after you turn 72 are tax-free as are voluntary withdrawals after you have left your job if you are at least 59½ and your account has been open five or more years.

Rule of 72 is a way to estimate the number of years it will take to double your principal using a fixed annual rate of return. You can also use the rule to approximate how long it will take for your living expenses to double using a fixed annual inflation rate. In either case, you divide 72 by the rate you have chosen.

Savings account is a deposit account in a bank or credit union that pays interest on your balance, typically at a lower interest rate than you earn on other products, such as certificates of deposit (CDs). You can deposit and withdraw from savings accounts, but you can't transfer money from the account directly to other people or organizations. Bank savings accounts are insured by the Federal Deposit Insurance Corporation (FDIC) and credit union accounts by the National Credit Union Share Insurance Fund (NCUSIF).

Savings bonds are issued by the US government as either Series EE or Series I bonds. You purchase Series EE at face value and earn a fixed rate of interest for a 30-year term. The bonds are guaranteed to double in value in 20 years. You buy Series I bonds at face value and earn a real rate of return that's guaranteed to exceed the rate of inflation during the bond's term.

Share is a unit of ownership in a corporation or mutual fund, or an interest in a general or limited partnership. Though the word is sometimes used interchangeably with the word stock, you actually own shares of stock. The shares you own make you a shareholder and eligible for the benefits of ownership.

Spending plan, or budget, is a method for allocating your income to cover your expenses while saving for the future. The goal of developing a plan is to spend less than you earn, reduce your reliance on credit, and create a positive cash flow.

Standard deviation represents the extent to which the return on an investment or investment portfolio tends to deviate above and below its expected, or average, rate of return. It's used as an indication of the risk and potential return of the investment.

Stock represents ownership, or equity, in a corporation that has raised money from investors by selling the right to a portion of the corporation's earnings if it pays dividends and the right to vote on certain corporate issues.

Subprime loans are made to borrowers who would not ordinarily qualify for credit if customary underwriting standards were applied. To offset the increased risk that these borrowers might default, lenders charge higher interest rates—typically three percentage points higher—than they offer creditworthy borrowers, and may assess additional fees. Subprime lending practices can be abusive or predatory, trapping unsophisticated borrowers in a cycle of debt while providing initially large profits for the lender.

Tax-advantaged describes investment accounts in which earnings, and sometimes contributions and withdrawals, are either tax-deferred or tax-exempt. Examples include certain retirement, education, and health savings accounts.

Tax bracket is a range of income within specific minimum and maximum amounts that is taxed at a specific rate. In the United States there are seven brackets, and the income that falls into each higher bracket is taxed at a higher rate, ranging from 10% to 37%. If your income falls into three brackets, for example, you owe tax at three different rates.

The income in each bracket varies by filing status, so a single taxpayer and a married couple filing a joint return with the same taxable income are likely to owe different amounts of tax.

Tax credit is an amount you can subtract from the income tax you would otherwise owe. Some credits simply reduce the tax you owe. Others are refundable, which means if the credit is larger than the tax you owe, some or all of the remaining credit will be paid to you as if you were receiving a tax refund.

Tax-deferred means that no income tax is due on investment earnings in an account, and sometimes on contributions to the account, until money is withdrawn from the account. The tax on withdrawals is figured at the same rate as your ordinary income.

Tax-deferred annuity is an insurance company product you purchase to accumulate savings for retirement. An annuity provides either a fixed or variable rate of return based on the terms of the contract. Some retirement savings plans include tax-deferred annuities in their menus of investment options.

Tax-exempt, sometimes called tax-free, means that earnings are free of federal income tax. Many municipal bonds (MUNIs) are tax-exempt, as are Roth IRA and Roth TSP withdrawals, certain hazardous duty and combat pay, and some allowances.

Term is a set period of time that's a factor in different financial and insurance products. For example, the term of a fixed-income investment, such as a bond, is the time between the date it is offered for sale and its maturity date. The lifespan of a certificate of deposit (CD) is described as its term, as is the time between when you take a loan and it comes due and must be repaid. It is also the period for which certain life insurance policies are in effect.

Term insurance is a life insurance policy that provides a guaranteed death benefit during a set period, such as five, ten, or 20 years, provided you continue to pay the premiums that are due. At the end of the term, the coverage ends unless you renew the policy. The policy may be level term, where the premium remains the same every year, or graduated term, where the premium increases each year.

Thrift Savings Plan (TSP) is a tax-deferred retirement savings program for federal employees, including military personnel. Each service member enrolled in the Blended Retirement System (BRS) automatically has a TSP account that is funded jointly by deductions from a member's base pay and contributions from the Department of Defense (DoD). Service members in the Legacy retirement plan, which has not enrolled new participants since December 31, 2017, have the option of opening and contributing to a TSP account. The DoD does not match those contributions.

Time value of money is the potential of money to grow in value over time thanks to compounding. The effect of compounding means money that's available to invest in the present is considered more valuable than the same amount invested in the future. In contrast, an uninvested dollar is worth more in the present than it will be in the future because over time its value is eroded by inflation.

Title is a legal document that proves the ownership of real estate, an automobile, or other vehicle. In most cases, if you take a mortgage loan to buy a home, the lender will require you to arrange for title insurance to protect its interest until the full amount of the loan is repaid and you receive the title.

Total return is the gain or loss on an equity or fixed income investment during a fixed period, typically a year. When it is expressed as a percentage, total return is figured by dividing the increase or decrease in the current price of the investment, plus any dividends or interest earned, by the original purchase price. The resulting return may be either positive or negative.

Underlying investments are the portfolio holdings of a pooled investment product, such as a mutual fund, exchange traded fund (ETF), or a separate account. The manager of an actively managed fund selects underlying investments to meet its financial objective. In an index fund, the underlying investments are the same as those in the index the fund tracks.

Transfer occurs when the plan administrator or custodian of an existing tax-deferred account moves the assets in the account to the administrator or custodian of a new tax-deferred account. In a transfer, the assets remain tax-deferred and nothing is withheld to pay taxes. However, sales charges may apply if the assets in the existing account are sold and their value is moved to the new account.

Trust is a legal entity you establish either while you're alive or in your will and to which you transfer assets. You name the beneficiary or beneficiaries of those assets and a trustee to follow the instructions you provide in the trust document for distributing the assets.

Universal life insurance is a type of permanent insurance that offers flexible premiums and a flexible death benefit. Your account earns at least the guaranteed rate of interest, and may earn more if the market rates are higher. You can pay premiums from your cash account and borrow against it, and you can increase the amount of your death benefit. You also get a portion of the cash value back, minus fees and expenses, if you end the policy. Premiums for universal life tend to be higher than for whole, or straight, life policies.

Variable life insurance is a type of permanent insurance in which you allocate your premium payment among separate account funds, also known as investment funds or subaccounts, offered by the insurer. In many cases, the value of your policy depends on how well the investments you've chosen are performing. Variable life is both more complex and more expensive than whole, or straight, life policies but may provide a tax shelter for potential earnings.

Vesting means you are eligible to receive income from your employer's defined benefit or defined contribution plan after completing the required years of service. Vesting periods vary among different types of plans and with different employers. In the military, the vesting period for qualifying for retired pay is 20 years.

Volatility indicates how much and how quickly the value, or price, of an investment may change. The more frequently the value changes, and the greater the range of change, the more volatile the investment is. Highly volatile investments tend to pose greater investment risks but may also provide an above average return.

Whole life insurance is a type of permanent insurance that provides a guaranteed death benefit and fixed premiums. It's sometimes known as straight life insurance or cash value insurance. A portion of the premium pays for the insurance and the rest accumulates tax-deferred in a cash value account. You may be able to borrow against the cash value, but any amount that you haven't repaid when you die reduces the death benefit. If you end the policy or allow it to lapse by not paying your premiums, you receive the cash surrender value, which is the cash value minus fees, expenses, and any outstanding loans.

Will is a legal document that describes how you want your assets to be distributed after your death. It also names an executor, or the person or people who will carry out your wishes, and a guardian for your minor children, if any. You can leave your assets directly to your heirs, or you can use your will to establish one or more testamentary trusts to receive the assets and distribute them at some point in the future.

Withholding is the amount that your employer subtracts from your pay for a variety of taxes and benefits, including federal income taxes, state taxes (where they apply), Social Security and Medicare, and allotments you've designated, such as contributions to your TSP account and specific charities. Contributions to traditional tax-deferred savings plans are deducted from your pretax income, which reduces the income your employer reports to the IRS and lowers your tax bill.

Yield is the income you receive from an investment, expressed as a percentage of either what you invested or its current value.

Resources

Note that web addresses may change over time. If a URL that's provided here or elsewhere in the book no longer works, do a web search for the term or topic to find the current one.

INSTALLATION-BASED RESOURCES

FAMILY READINESS GROUPS
Air Force Key Spouse Program (KSP) www.afpc.af.mil
Army: Soldier and Family Readiness Groups (SFRG)
www.armyfrg.org/skins/frg/home.aspx
Coast Guard Ombudsman www.uscg.mil/Family/
Marine Corps Unit, Personal and Family Readiness Program (UPFRP)
www.usmc-mccs.org/services/family/unit-personal-and-family-readiness/
Navy Ombudsmen
www.cnic.navy.mil/ffr/family_readiness/fleet_and_family_support_program/work-and-family-life/ombudsman_program.html

FAMILY SUPPORT CENTERS
Air Force: Air Force Family Support Program
 afas.org/air-force-family-support-programs/
Army: Soldier, Family and Spouse Services
www.goarmy.com/benefits/soldier-and-family-services.html
Coast Guard: Sea Legs-Family Support
www.dcms.uscg.mil/Our-Organization/Assistant-Commandant-for-Human-Resources-CG-1/
Health-Safety-and-Work-Life-CG-11/Office-of-Work-Life-CG-111/Sea-Legs/Family-Support/
Marine Corps: Marine Corps Community Services Marine & Family Programs
www.mccsmcrd.com/marine-family-programs
Navy: Fleet and Family Support Center
www.cnic.navy.mil/ffr/family_readiness/fleet_and_family_support_program.html

FINANCIAL MANAGEMENT PROGRAMS
Air Force: Personal Financial Readiness Program
www.afpc.af.mil/Benefits-and-Entitlements/Financial-Readiness/
Army: Financial Readiness Program (FRP) and Consumer Advocacy Services
myarmybenefits.us.army.mil/Benefit-Library/Federal-Benefits/Financial-Readiness
Coast Guard: Personal Financial Management Program (PFMP)
www.dcms.uscg.mil/Our-Organization/Assistant-Commandant-for-Human-Resources-CG-1/
Health-Safety-and-Work-Life-CG-11/Office-of-Work-Life-CG-111/Personal-Financial-Management-Program-PFMP/
Marine Corps: Personal Financial Management Program (PFMP)
usmc-mccs.org/services/career/personal-financial-management/
Navy: Personal Financial Management (PFM) program
www.public.navy.mil/bupers-npc/support/21st_Century_Sailor/readiness/Pages/Personal-Financial-Management.aspx

LEGAL SERVICES OFFICES

Air Force: Air Force JAG Corps www.afjag.af.mil
Army: US Army Legal Services Agency www.jagcnet.army.mil/Sites/JAGC.nsf
Coast Guard: Coast Guard Legal Assistance www.uscg.mil/Resources/Legal
Marine Corps: Marine Corps Legal Support
www.hqmc.marines.mil/sja/Branches/Legal-Assistance-Branch-JLA/
Navy: US Navy JAG Corps www.jag.navy.mil

MILITARY RELIEF ORGANIZATIONS

Air Force Aid Society (AFAS) www.afas.org
Army Emergency Relief (AER) www.aerhq.org
Coast Guard Mutual Assistance www.cgmahq.org
Navy-Marine Corps Relief Society (NMCRS) www.nmcrs.org

DEPARTMENT OF DEFENSE OFFICES AND RESOURCES

DEFENSE ENROLLMENT ELIGIBILITY REPORTING SYSTEM (DEERS)

milconnect.dmdc.osd.mil (updating)
www.military.com (benefits)
800-538-9552

DEFENSE FINANCE AND ACCOUNTING SERVICE

www.dfas.mil
800-321-1080

LONG-TERM CASUALTY MANAGEMENT

Air Force: Families Together
www.afpc.af.mil/Benefits-and-Entitlements/Air-Force-Families-Forever/
866-299-0596
Army: Survivor Outreach Services
www.armymwr.com/programs-and-services/personal-assistance/survivor-outreach/
sos-home
855-707-2769
Coast Guard's Long Term Assistance Program
www.dcms.uscg.mil/PSD/fs/Casualty-Matters/
202-795-6637
Marine Corps: Long Term Assistance Program
www.hqmc.marines.mil/Agencies/Casualty-MFPC/Longterm/
866-210-3421
Navy: Long Term Assistance Program
www.public.navy.mil/bupers-npc/support/casualty/ltap/Pages/default2.aspx
901-874-4294

MILITARY ONESOURCE

www.militaryonesource.mil
800-342-9647

MYPAY

mypay.dfas.mil
888-332-7411

SERVICE BRANCH TRANSITION RESOURCES

Air Force: www.afpc.af.mil/Separation/Transition-Assistance-Program/
Army: www.sfl-tap.army.mil/
Coast Guard: www.dcms.uscg.mil/Our-Organization/Assistant-Commandant-for-Human-Resources-CG-1/Health-Safety-and-Work-Life-CG-11/Office-of-Work-Life-CG-111/Transition-Assistance-Program/
Marines: usmc-mccs.org/services/career/transition-readiness/
Navy: www.public.navy.mil/BUPERS-NPC/CAREER/TRANSITION/Pages/TAP.aspx

SGLI INSURANCE BENEFITS

www.benefits.va.gov/insurance/sgli.asp
800-419-1473 (main)
877-832-4943 (fax for claims)

SURVIVOR BENEFITS

Air Force: myarmybenefits.us.army.mil/prebuilt/usaf/Casualty/login.aspx
800-433-0048
Army: myarmybenefits.us.army.mil/custom/casualty
877-827-2471 (report)
888-721-2769 (casualty/survivor benefits)
Coast Guard: myarmybenefits.us.army.mil/prebuilt/uscg/Casualty/login.aspx
703-872-6647 (casualty)
877-827-2471 (survivor benefits)
Marine Corps: myarmybenefits.us.army.mil/prebuilt/usmc
877-827-2471
Navy: myarmybenefits.us.army.mil/prebuilt/usn
800-368-3203

SURVIVOR BENEFIT PROGRAM

militarypay.defense.gov/Benefits/SurvivorBenefitProgram/Overview.aspx
www.dfas.mil/retiredmilitary/survivors/manage.html

TRANSITION ASSISTANCE PROGRAM (TAP)

www.dodtap.mil
www.benefits.va.gov/tap/tap-index.asp

TRICARE

www.tricare.mil
800-444-5445 (east region)
877-988-9378 (west region)

DEPARTMENT OF VETERANS AFFAIRS

va.gov
800-827-1000

OTHER GOVERNMENT RESOUCES

BENEFITS.GOV
www.benefits.gov

NATIONAL RESOURCE DIRECTORY
www.nrd.gov

ONGUARDONLINE
www.onguardonline.gov

SOCIAL SECURITY ADMINISTRATION
ssa.gov
800-772-1213 (general)
877-726-4727 (Expedited Claims Unit)

THRIFT SAVINGS PLAN
www.tsp.gov
877-968-3778

OTHER RESOURCES

AMERICAN RED CROSS
Armed Forces Emergency Services
www.redcross.org
877-272-7337

ASSOCIATION OF MILITARY BANKS OF AMERICA
www.ambahq.org

CONSUMER FINANCIAL PROTECTION BUREAU
www.consumerfinance.gov/servicemembers

DEFENSE CREDIT UNION COUNCIL
www.dcuc.org

MILITARY SAVES
www.militarysaves.org

NATIONAL GUARD FAMILY PROGRAM
https://www.militaryonesource.mil/national-guard/joint-services-support-program

NATIONAL MILITARY FAMILY ASSOCIATION
www.militaryfamily.org
703-931-6632

SAVE AND INVEST
saveandinvest.org

SPECIALLY ADAPTED HOUSING, DEPARTMENT OF VETERANS AFFAIRS
SAHINFO.VBACO@va.gov

Index

ABLE account   99

Adjusted gross income (AGI)   86-87

Allotments   49, 140
    Discretionary   49
    Non-discretionary   49

Allowances   45-46, 51, 58-59, 80-81
    Tax-exempt   46
    Basic allowance for
    housing (BAH)   47, 58, 81, 115
    Basic allowance for
    subsistence (BAS)   47, 51, 58, 115
    COLAs   58-59
    Family separation allowance   59
    Overseas housing allowance
    (OHA)   47, 59, 81

American Red Cross   61, 82

Annual percentage rate (APR)   21-23, 25, 29, 41, 123

Annual percentage yield (APY)   19, 41

Assets   6-7, 32

Automated teller machine (ATM)   12-14, 16, 21, 25

Automated clearinghouse (ACH)   15

Base pay   46, 50, 52

Benchmark   20, 40, 141

Bill payment   9, 12,14, 21, 23, 75, 84-85

Blended Retirement System (BRS)   11, 49, 56, 60, 70-71, 129
    Automatic enrollment   43
    Matching contributions   10-11, 43, 56, 70-71

Cash advances   21

Cash equivalents   37, 39

Cash flow   8, 10, 74

Certificate of deposit (CD)   10, 18-19, 39-4

Checking accounts   9, 14-15, 49, 84-8

Childcare   85, 98-9
    ChildCare Aware   9
    Child Development Centers   8
    Family Child Care   9
    Military childcare   9
    School-age Care Programs   9
    Special needs children   9
    Closing costs   72, 12

Combat Zone Tax Exclusions
(CZTE)   47, 56-5

Compounding   19, 43-44, 14

Consumer Financial Protection Bureau   15, 73, 100, 12

Continued Health Care Benefit Program
(CHCBP)   95, 109, 11

Cost of living adjustment (COLA) 46-4, 58-59, 70, 125, 129, 13

Credentialing   69, 81, 11
    COOL programs   (
    Military Occupational Code
    (MOC) Crosswalk   114-11
    Spouse licensure   8

Credit   20-3
    Credit limit   20, 2
    Creditworthiness   3
    Installment credit   2
    Lines of credit   20, 2
    Loans   2
    Revolving credit   2

Credit cards   20-27, 75, 81, 8
    Choosing   22-2
    Fees   20-22, 2
    Grace period   22-2
    Legal protections   26-2
    Problems   26-2

Credit history   30-31, 73, 9

Credit report   20, 30-31, 81, 113
    Free annual reports   30

Credit score   30-31, 143

Death Gratuity   65, 138

Debit cards   16-17, 143
    Legal protections   16
    Overdraft   16
    Prepaid   17
    Risks of   16-17

Debt-to-income-ratio (DTI)   73, 123

Default   21, 28, 72

Defense Enrollment Eligibility Reporting System (DEERS)   76, 82, 94, 105, 118

Defense Financial Accounting Service (DFAS)   12, 48, 87, 109, 117, 129, 136-137

Department of Veterans Affairs (VA)   60, 64-67, 72-73, 112, 114-115, 118-119, 122-123
    eBenefits Premium account   115
    Disability housing grants   123
    Enrolling   112
    Health benefits   118-119
    Home loan guaranty   72-73, 112-113, 122-123, 139
    Veterans Service Officer (VSO)   127

Dependency and Indemnity Compensation (DIC)   65, 138

Dependents' Educational Assistance (DEA)   65

Deployment   55-56, 60, 74, 82-85
    Bill payment plan   84
    Family care plan   82
    Financial plan   82-83
    Record of emergency data   83

Direct deposit   15, 49, 109, 139

Disability   110, 118-119, 123-127
    Appeals   127
    Claims   126-127
    COLAs   125
    Compensation   110, 124-126
    Housing grants   123
    Multiple disabilities   124
    Ratings   118-119, 124-125

Severance pay   125
Special Monthly Compensation (SMC)   125
Tax-exempt benefits 118-119, 124-125

Discounts for military   61

Divorce   108-111
    Health care eligibility   109
    Family support   109
    Legal assistance   108
    Retirement benefits court order (RBCO)   110
    Social security   111
    Survivor benefits plan   110
    10/10 Rule   108-109
    20/20/20 Rule   108-109
    Uniformed Services Spouse Protection Act (USFSPA)   108

Down payment   72, 122-123

Education   66-69, 100-101, 104-105
    Advanced degrees   69
    DEA   65
    Post-9/11 GI bill 66-67, 100, 104-105
    Spouse benefits   100-101, 104-105
    Scholarships   99-101
    Tuition assistance (TA)   68-69

Emergency fund   10-11, 18, 74, 82

Equities   38-39, 45

Estate planning   78-79, 83, 113, 115, 134-135
    Joint tenants (JTWROS)   134-135
    Living will   79
    Memorandum   134
    Probate   134-135
    Trusts   135
    Wills   83, 134-135

Expenses   8-9
    Fixed   9
    Variable   9

Federal Deposit Insurance Corporation (FDIC)   12, 19

Federal Employees Dental and Vision Program (FEDVIP)   97, 118

Finance charge   20-23

Financial management   6-11, 20-21, 75, 84-85

Financial plan, planning   7, 74-75, 83, 113

Fixed income   32-33, 38-39, 45

Hardship Duty Pay (HDP)   54-55, 57

Hazardous Duty Incentive Pay (HDIP)   55, 57

Health insurance   62-63, 92-97, 118-119
  Allowable cost   92-93
  Copayment   62, 92-93
  Coordination of benefits   95
  Cost share   63, 93
  Deductible   62, 92-93, 143
  Dental   62, 96-97
  Formulary   63, 96-97
  Managed care plans   62-63, 92
  Point of service plans   63, 92
  Prescription drugs   63, 96-97
  Vision   97

HEART Act   60-61

Homeowners insurance   90-91

Hostile Fire Pay (HFP)   54-55, 57

Imminent Danger Pay (IDP)   54-55, 57

Individual retirement account (IRA)   33, 42-43, 45, 47, 49, 56, 86, 110, 128, 132, 139
  Beneficiary   76-77
  Roth IRA   33, 45, 56, 128, 139
  Spousal   77

Inflation   7, 32, 133

Interest   18-20, 28, 30
  Adjustable rate   19, 28
  Compound   19
  Fixed rate   19, 28
  Nominal rate   19
  Subprime   30

Investing   11, 32-45, 132-133
  Actively managed   39
  Asset allocation   36-37, 39, 43
  Asset classes   33, 36-39
  Diversification   38-39
  Equities   32-33, 38-39
  Fixed income   32-33, 38
  Passively managed   39
  Performance   40-41

Return   33-36, 38-39, 40-41
Risk   32, 34-36, 38-39, 133
Volatility   35, 38

Job search   116-117

Joint tenants with rights of survivorship (JTWROS)   77, 134-135

Leave   50, 56, 115
  Expiration of term of service (ETS)   50
  Terminal   115

Leave and Earnings Statement (LES)   46, 48-51, 65, 84-85

Legacy High-3 system   49, 70-71, 128-129
  Retired pay base   128

Legal services offices   21, 83, 108

Liabilities   6-7

Life insurance   60, 64-65, 88-89, 120-121, 139
  Accelerated benefits option (ABO)   121
  Beneficiary of   64, 139
  Cash surrender value   89
  Cash value   88-89
  Convertible term   89
  Decreasing term   89, 143
  Face value   64
  Permanent   64, 88-89
  Renewable term   88, 120
  Term   64, 88-89
  Universal life   89
  Variable life   89

Loans   20-21, 28-29, 31, 72-73, 106-107
  Abusive loans   29, 106-107
  Adjustable rate   29, 123
  Fixed rate   123
  Installment   28
  Secured   28
  Term   20, 28-29
  Unsecured   28
  VA home loan   72-73

Medicare   95, 119

Military Aid Societies   6

Military and Family Support Centers (FSCs)   29, 80, 83, 97

Military OneSource   31, 57, 81, 83, 87, 99, 113, 135

Military Spouse Career Advancement
Account (MyCAA)   100-101

Mortgage loans   72-73, 113, 122-123
    Closing costs   72, 122
    Closing disclosure   73, 123
    Down payments   122
    Interest rate   123
    Loan estimate   123
    PITI   123

Mutual funds   37-43, 45
    Equity (stock) funds   45
    Fixed income (bond) funds   45
    Lifecycle funds   42
    Net asset value (NAV)   43
    Target date funds   42

myPay   18, 46-47, 49, 57, 139

National Credit Union Administration
(NCUA)   15

National Credit Union Share Insurance
Fund (NCUSIF)   12, 19

Net worth   6-7, 32, 65

Nonsufficient funds   14

Overdraft protection   15-16

Permanent change of station (PCS) 80-81
    Allowances   80
    Housing   81
    Personally procured move (PPM)   80
    Personal Statement of Military
    Compensation   46-47

Post-9/11 GI bill   60, 66-67, 68,
                         76, 104-105
    Eligibility   66, 104
    Monthly housing allowance (MHA)
                                 67, 105
    Transfer of Entitlement (TOE)104-105
    Yellow Ribbon program   67, 105

Power of attorney (POA)   79, 83, 111
    Durable POA   79
    Durable POA for healthcare   79
    Special POA

Prepaid debit card   17

Principal   19-20, 28

Qualifying Life Event (QLE) 94, 97, 118

Renters insurance   90-91

Required minimum distribution (RMD)
                                 44, 128

Reserve component   60, 65, 70, 72,
        92-95, 117-118, 130-132, 136, 139
    Health plans   94, 118, 131
    National guard 60, 65, 92-95, 130-131
    Reserve retirement   130-131
    Reserves   65, 92-95, 130-131

Resumes   116-117

Retirement income   47, 70-71,
                         128-133, 138
    COLAs   70-71, 129, 131
    Life annuity   132
    Points   130-131
    Reserve component   130-131
    Retired pay   47, 70-71, 128-129, 138
    Social Security   129
    TSP   132-133

Retirement plans, planning   10, 42-45,
                         49, 70-71, 133
    Defined benefit plan   42, 70-71
    Defined contribution plan   42
    Employer plans   42-43
    Matching funds   10-11, 43, 56,
                         70-71, 133
    Retirement pay base   70-71
    Retirement savings plan   70
    Pension   70-71
    Portability   71
    Vesting   45, 71

Saving for college   11, 47, 102-103, 139
    Education savings accounts (ESAs) 11,
                         47, 102-103, 139
    Prepaid plan   103
    529 college savings plan   11, 47,
                         102-103
    Qualified higher education expenses
    (QHEEs)   103

Savings   9-11, 18-19, 49
    Types of accounts   18-19

Savings Deposit Program (SDP)   47,
                         56-57, 85

Scams   85, 106-107

Servicemembers Civil Relief Act
(SCRA)   21, 60, 111, 120, 122

Servicemembers' Group Life Insurance
(SGLI)   64-65, 77, 88, 120-121
    Beneficiary   65, 77
    Family SGLI   88, 120
    Traumatic injury protection
    (TSGLI)   65

Small Business Administration (SBA) 113

Special pays   52-53

Special Survivor Indemnity Allowance 139

Spending plan (budget)   8-10, 75

Spouse Education and Career
Opportunities (SECO)   81, 101

Survivor Benefit Plan (SBP)   110, 129,
                        136-137, 139

Survivors   138-139
    Assistance officer   138
    Death Gratuity   138
    Dependency and Indemnity
    Compensation (DIC)   138
    myPay   139
    SGLI benefit   139
    VA Home loan guaranty   139

Thrift Savings Plan (TSP)   6, 11, 33,
            37-38, 42-45, 47, 51, 56,70,
                77, 83, 86, 110, 132-133
    Beneficiary   77, 83
    Investment choices,   42-43, 45, 133
    Managing investments   132-133
    Matching contributions   10-11, 43,
                        56, 70-71, 133
    Rollover   132-133
    Roth account 33, 44-45, 56, 128, 133
    Traditional tax-deferred   33, 44,
                            132-133
    Withdrawals   132-133

Taxable income   33, 40, 59, 86-87, 129,
                        132-133, 138
    Filing status   86
    Tax brackets   86
    Tax credits   86-87

Tax-deferred   11, 33, 40, 44-43, 56, 86

Tax-exempt   33, 40, 44-45, 47, 56,
            58-59, 86-87, 129, 138-139

Transition Assistance Program
(TAP)   113-115
    Military Occupation Code
    (MOC) Crosswalk   114-115
    TAP curriculum   114-115

Transition Assistance Management
Program (TAMP)   95, 119

TRICARE   62-63, 85, 92-98,
        108-109, 115, 118-119, 131, 139
    Eligibility   94
    Open season enrollment   94, 118
    Primary care manager (PCM)   62, 92
    Prime   62, 92-93, 96-97, 118
    Reserve component   94
    Retired Reserve   118
    Select   92-93, 96-97, 118
    TRICARE dental   96-97
    TRICARE for Life   95, 118, 131
    US family health plan (USFHP)   93,
                    96-97, 118, 131
    Young adult   94, 96

Tax planning   86-87
    Adjusted gross income
    (AGI) Credits   86-87
    Filing status   86
    Tax brackets   86

Uniformed Services Employment and
Reemployment Rights Act (USERRA) 60

Vehicle insurance   90-91

Veterans Group Life Insurance
(VGLI)   120-121

Wills   78-79, 83, 111, 134-135
    Executor   78, 134
    Guardian   78

Withholding   50-51, 87
    IRS Form W-4   51

Women, Infants and Children (WIC) 99

Yield   19, 41

SPECIAL ACKNOWLEDGEMENT TO THE CONTRIBUTING EDITORS

We wish to acknowledge the very special contribution of the West Point project team, who were instrumental in conceiving the guide, framing its organization and content, and helping to ensure its accuracy and value to servicemembers.

The project team, who worked closely with the author from the guide's inception to its final edits, includes current and former faculty in the Economics and Business Management programs at West Point. Team members are all seasoned military leaders with educational backgrounds in military personal finance and unique expertise in teaching financial topics. Their professional and personal experiences in the military have given the work an authenticity and credibility that would not otherwise have been possible.

Major Sam Perlik has served in the Army for 12 years as an Infantry officer and Operations Research and Systems Analysis officer. He is an Assistant Professor of Business Management at West Point. Major Perlik holds an MBA from the MIT Sloan School of Management.

Captain Tom Bazemore has served in the Army for 10 years as an Engineer officer. He is an instructor of Economics at West Point. Captain Bazemore holds an MBA from the Fuqua School of Business at Duke University.

Major Patrick Bell is a former Army officer who served 14 years as a Military Intelligence officer. He is a former Assistant Professor of Economics at West Point. Major Bell holds an MBA from New York University Leonard N. Stern School of Business.

Major Jason Bogardus has served in the Army for 10 years as an Aviation officer. He is an instructor in the Leadership and Business Management programs at West Point. Major Bogardus holds an MBA from the Fuqua School of Business at Duke University.

Major John Borland has served in the Army for 12 years as an Engineer officer. He is a former Assistant Professor of Business Management at West Point. Major Borland holds an MBA from the McCombs School of Business at the University of Texas and a M.S. in Civil Engineering from Missouri University of Science and Technology.

Colonel Spencer Clouatre has served in the Army for 27 years as an Aviation officer and Academy Professor at the United States Military Academy. He is an Assistant Professor and Program Director of Economics at West Point. Colonel Clouatre holds an MBA from the Owen Graduate School of Management at Vanderbilt University and a PhD in Business Administration from the Kenan-Flagler School of Business at the University of North Carolina.

Major Evan Davies, CFP® has served in the Army for 14 years as an Armor officer and Operations Research and Systems Analysis officer. He is a former Assistant Professor of Economics at West Point. Major Davies holds an MBA from Harvard Business School and a M.S. in Personal Financial Planning from the College for Financial Planning.

Major Steve Fennessy, CFP® has served in the Army for 12 years as an Infantry officer. He is a former instructor in the Business Management program at West Point. Major Fennessy holds an MBA from the Owen Graduate School of Management at Vanderbilt University.

Major Kyle Stramara has served in the Army for 11 years as an Aviation officer. He is an instructor of Economics at West Point. Major Stramara holds an MBA from the Tuck School of Business at Dartmouth College.

ABOUT THE AUTHOR

Virginia B Morris, the Editorial Director at Lightbulb Press, is the author of more than thirty books on investing and personal finance. Formerly Professor of English at John Jay College, CUNY, she holds a PhD from Columbia University.

ACKNOWLEDGEMENTS

Anthony H. Blackstone, LTC, USA (Ret.)

Joseph Montanaro, Military Affairs Relationship Director, Military Advocacy, USAA

CAPT Karin Vernazza, USN (Ret) – SPHR

Rebecca Wiggins, Executive Director, AFCPE